Relying on Others

Relying on Others

An Essay in Epistemology

Sanford C. Goldberg

OXFORD
UNIVERSITY PRESS

OXFORD
UNIVERSITY PRESS

Great Clarendon Street, Oxford OX2 6DP

Oxford University Press is a department of the University of Oxford.
It furthers the University's objective of excellence in research, scholarship,
and education by publishing worldwide in

Oxford New York

Auckland Cape Town Dar es Salaam Hong Kong Karachi
Kuala Lumpur Madrid Melbourne Mexico City Nairobi
New Delhi Shanghai Taipei Toronto

With offices in

Argentina Austria Brazil Chile Czech Republic France Greece
Guatemala Hungary Italy Japan Poland Portugal Singapore
South Korea Switzerland Thailand Turkey Ukraine Vietnam

Oxford is a registered trade mark of Oxford University Press
in the UK and in certain other countries

Published in the United States
by Oxford University Press Inc., New York

© Sanford C. Goldberg 2010

The moral rights of the author have been asserted
Database right Oxford University Press (maker)

First published 2010

British Library Cataloguing in Publication Data
Data available

Library of Congress Cataloging in Publication Data
Data available

Typeset by Laserwords Private Limited, Chennai, India
Printed in Great Britain
on acid-free paper by
MPG Books Group, King's Lynn, Norfolk

ISBN 978-0-19-959324-8

10 9 8 7 6 5 4 3 2 1

Contents

Acknowledgments

Let's start with the obvious: we rely heavily on others for most of what we take ourselves to know about the world. Ours is the age of the twenty-four-hour news cycle, and of information that is disseminated with the click of a button, through social networks or across the world, by way of the Internet. We have seen a proliferation of sources that disseminate information in this way, and we have come to enjoy an increasing number of new technologies which make access to these sources a constant part of our daily lives. Nor should we forget the more traditional avenues through which others serve our informational needs: in our daily conversations, through the more traditional media (print, radio, TV), and in educational settings (where we learn from teachers and books). Insofar as we acquire our knowledge through any of these routes, we are *relying on others* in the sense that will be the topic of this book.

I have been thinking about this topic a great deal over the past decade or so. In this time I have come to think that, while contemporary epistemology (theory of knowledge) has begun to acknowledge the *scope* of this reliance—here I note the renewed attention paid to "testimonial knowledge," the knowledge we get through others' say-so—contemporary epistemology has failed to come to terms with the *nature* of this reliance, or of the knowledge that results. I say that "contemporary epistemology" has failed to come to terms with this. Here I have in mind even those epistemological theories that would appear best suited to doing so: so-called 'externalist' theories of knowledge and justification.

As an avenue into this topic, I offer the following (thumbnail and cartoonish!) history of the topic. Modern epistemology began with Descartes who, sitting alone in his dressing-gown by the fire, thought he could ascertain all that he knew and justifiably believed, merely by inspecting the structure and content of his beliefs. Thus was born the ideal of epistemic autonomy: each of us must seek knowledge as an isolated individual, and any reliance on others must be vindicated by using only those materials one has at first hand for oneself. This ideal arguably runs through Hume and several others involved in the Enlightenment project, and, though there have been some sources of resistance along the way (e.g., Thomas Reid), this picture dominated until very recently. But two developments in mid- to late-twentieth-century epistemology challenged this picture, and chipped away at the viability of the ideal of epistemic autonomy. The first was the recognition that the world is more centrally implicated in our knowledge than Cartesian epistemology supposed. In particular, knowledge requires not merely that our beliefs be true, but also that we arrive at the truth in a way that is not overly dependent on *luck* or *good fortune*. Many epistemologists concluded from this that how epistemologically well-off one's beliefs are—whether they amount to knowledge or justified belief—can depend on 'worldly' conditions whose obtaining cannot be discerned in armchair self-inspection. Thus began the so-called 'externalist' revolution in epistemology. But while externalist epistemology repudiated the sort of epistemic autonomy that can be manifested by an individual sitting in her armchair, nevertheless it continued to hew to the ideal of epistemic autonomy in another sense. In particular, it continued to regard *the individual knowledge-seeking subject* as the focal point of epistemology. This brings us to the second development in twentieth-century epistemology. This came in the form of an acknowledgment of the pervasiveness of our epistemic reliance on others, and a corresponding recognition of the meagerness of the materials that a subject has for vindicating that reliance. This insight is owed primarily to those working in the epistemology of testimony from the late 1970s through the early 1990s: A. Coady, M. Welbourne, and (as a critic) E. Fricker. With this recognition in place, the way was thus paved for a thorough repudiation of the ideal of epistemic autonomy: not only does the individual knowledge-seeker depend on the compliance of the world, what is more this dependence includes *an ineliminable dependence on other knowledge-seekers*. Interestingly, few mainstream epistemologists have drawn this lesson: even those who accept the insights of externalist epistemology continue to focus on the individual subject in isolation from other members of her knowledge community. Everyone (externalists included) recognizes, of course, that a subject's knowledge often depends on the antics of *other* knowledge-seeking subjects. But in accounting for this dependence, virtually all theories (externalist included) relegate other knowledge-seeking subjects to the background, and treat them as just so many more pieces of the external world's furniture. Herein lies my book's main ambition: to establish that this is the wrong way for epistemologists generally, and for externalist epistemologists in particular, to react to the news of our pervasive epistemic reliance on others.

While I have been aided in my thoughts on these matters by a great many people over the years, I am especially grateful here to those who have helped me think through the particular issues I discuss in this book. I owe a special debt of gratitude to a few friends, colleagues, and teachers who have given me a great deal to think about from the outset of this project to its completion. In this connection I would like to express my profound thanks to Alvin Goldman, Peter Graham, and my colleagues Jennifer Lackey and Baron Reed. I cannot imagine having written this book without the stimulation I got from the many conversations I have had with them. Several others have given me extensive and very helpful feedback on earlier versions of the manuscript—far more than I deserved—and for this I would like to thank John Burgess, John Greco, Wayne Riggs, the M&E Reading Group of my own philosophy department at Northwestern (whose members read an earlier version of this manuscript in the summer of 2009), a reading group at St Louis University, led by John Greco and Joe Salerno and three anonymous referees for Oxford University Press. This book would be significantly worse off were it not for their feedback, and I am grateful to them for this.

I would also like to express my gratitude to the audiences of various talks at which I have presented some of the material in this book. These include talks at Bowling Green State University (May 2004); the "Epistemology of Liberal Democracy" Conference in Copenhagen, Denmark (November 2008); a conference on Social Epistemology at the University of Stirling, Scotland (August 2007); Grand Valley State University (September 2008); the Waterloo Graduate Student Philosophy Conference (April 2009); the University of Chicago (May 2009); the Bled Epistemology Conference (June 2009); the Summer School Workshop at the University of Cologne, on "Reliabilism and Social Epistemology" (August 2009); Wayne Riggs's Epistemology Seminar at the University of Oklahoma (December 2009), with whom I discussed the first four chapters of an earlier version of this book over Skype; and the University of Michigan at Flint (January 2010).

Further thanks belong to a variety of people from whom I have benefitted through conversations and email exchanges. With apologies to the many people I have surely forgotten to mention, these include Fred Adams, Jonathan Adler, Ken Aizawa, Robert Audi, James Beebe, Jason Bridges, Jessica Brown, Tony Brueckner, Fabrizio Cariani, Al Casullo, Matthew Chrisman, E. J. Coffman, Allan Collins, Juan Comesaña, Marian David, Ryan Doran, Frank Döring, Igor Douven, David Ebrey, Carl Ehrett, David Finkelstein, Miranda Fricker, Richard Fumerton, Mikkel Gerken, Emily Given, Thomas Grundmann, David Henderson, Terry Horgan, Peter Hylton, Jasper Kallestrup, Mark Kaplan, Klemens Kappell, Tim Kenyon, Hilary Kornblith, Jon Kvanvig, Igal Kvart, Chris Lepock, Peter Lipton, Ronald Loeffler, Peter Ludlow, Jack Lyons, Seth Mayer, Alan Millar, Nenad Miscevic, Ryan Muldoon, Matthew Mullins, Brendan Neufeld, Nathan Oaklander, Erik Olsson, Duncan Pritchard, Wlodek Rabinowicz, Dani Rabinowitz, Lance Rips, Joe Salerno, Fred Schmitt, Joe Shieber, Ernie Sosa, Andrew Spear, Finn Spicer, Jan Sprenger, Josef

Stern, Tim Sundell, John Uglietta, Sandy Waxman, Sarah Wright, and Alison Wylie. I would also like to single out Marian David and Mark Kaplan, who helped me arrive at the title of the book after it became overwhelmingly clear to me—from the feedback of just about everyone—that my original title would not fly. (When my oldest son heard that title—"Socializing Reliability"—he remarked, "Sounds like some sleepy book you'd find in the doctor's office, Dad. I know your work is boring, but do you really want to advertise that fact?")

I would also like to thank Peter Momtchiloff at Oxford University Press, whose support, help, advice, and patience in seeing this project through to completion, was exemplary. I thank Oxford University Press for giving me permission to use large portions of my paper, "If That Were True I Would Have Heard about it by Now," which also appears in A. Goldman and D. Whitcomb, eds, *Social Epistemology: An Anthology* (forthcoming with Oxford University Press); this material appears in Chapter 6 of this book. I would also like to thank all the staff at Oxford University Press, including Sarah Parker and Louise Sprake, and Helen Gray, the copy-editor, for their tremendous professionalism and helpfulness throughout the publication process.

Finally, I want to thank my wife, Judy, and my three children, Gideon, Ethan, and Nadia. I would not have been able to write this book were it not for their love and support throughout. Even though this love and support did sometimes come in the form of cheeky remarks and skeptical queries about the point of philosophy, these, I am fully confident, were always calculated to have maximum impact on my flagging spirits, knowing as my family does that I could not fail to respond.

I dedicate this book, in loving memory, to my grandmother Essie Kossman (a philosopher in the deepest sense of the term), and to my teacher Sidney Morgenbesser (philosophy is so much worse off, and philosophizing less fun, without him). May their memories be as blessings.

Introduction

This book emerges out of my confidence in one core idea: the fact that we rely on others for so much of what we know about the world should prompt a reconsideration of the individualistic orientation of traditional epistemology. In this book I pursue this sort of reconsideration from the perspective of Process Reliabilism, since it is here that I find my epistemological home.

In some respects, the choice of reliabilism as the theory within which to pursue this sort of project may seem a curious one. For one thing, reliabilism itself was part of the "externalist" revolution in epistemology, so it can seem strange to think that such a position is committed to any objectionable sort of epistemic individualism. For another, the theorist most responsible for the development of reliabilism, Alvin Goldman (who remains its most influential spokesperson), has been at the forefront of the recent focus on "social epistemology," and it can seem strange to suppose that the brainchild of someone so positioned should be susceptible to objections deriving from the need to appreciate the social sources of knowledge. At the same time, most versions of Process Reliabilism, including Goldman's own, remain highly individualistic in orientation. One sees this orientation in the way reliabilists have thought about the individuation of belief-forming processes. The explicit assumption has been that the belief-forming processes relevant to the epistemic assessment of a given belief all take place within the mind/brain of the believing subject herself.

I call this assumption 'Process Individualism,' and I use 'Orthodox Reliabilism' as a label for any version of Process Reliabilism
that endorses this individualistic assumption. One of my main
aims in this book is to release reliabilist epistemology from the
grip of orthodoxy. My contention is that reliabilists accept Process
Individualism only at the cost of a distorted epistemic assessment
of at least some of the beliefs we form through epistemic reliance
on others. My key case is testimony. I will be arguing that a
proper reliabilist assessment of testimonial beliefs will require an
assessment of the reliability of cognitive processes that take place *in
the mind/brain(s) of the subject's informant(s)*. But testimony is not the
only type of example of a belief formed through epistemic reliance
on others. After developing my account of testimonial belief I will
round out my discussion by presenting another example of a sort
of belief formed through epistemic reliance on others.

As I say, my main ambition in this book is to advance the
prospects for a reliabilist epistemology that rejects the individualistic
orientation of tradition. While I am confident of the timeliness and
importance of this project, I have significantly *less* confidence in the
particular proposals I make in my attempt to realize this project. In
light of this, it is perhaps best to think of this book as bringing forth
a new set of problems for reliabilist epistemology, deriving from
the need to rethink the nature of our epistemic reliance on others.
My hope is that there is value in highlighting these problems even
if the particular solutions I propose are rejected in whole cloth.

I

The broad outline of the book is as follows.

In Chapter 1, I introduce Process Reliabilism and the various
distinctions familiar within reliabilist epistemology—reliabilism
about knowledge vs reliabilism about justification, global vs local
reliability—before bringing this theoretical orientation to bear
on testimonial knowledge. My main ambition in the chapter is
to employ Process Reliabilism in an argument that takes aim at

the doctrine of Knowledge Individualism, according to which all of the epistemic conditions on knowledge pertain to (states of mind and/or cognitive processes in) the knowing subject herself. This doctrine, I argue, is falsified by ordinary testimony cases: given the sort of epistemic reliance involved, whether a subject S knows through testimony depends on the reliability of cognitive processes 'in' S's interlocutor—in particular, those processes responsible for the production of the testimony S has consumed.

The falsity of Knowledge Individualism need not come as a great surprise. In fact, such a result can and should be endorsed even by Orthodox Reliabilists. In Chapter 2, I argue that the Orthodox Reliabilist can and should endorse the testimonial case against Knowledge Individualism, but there is a cost associated with doing so. Such a theorist is committed to a certain (very traditional) conception of the epistemic significance of testimony. According to this traditional conception, the testimonies a subject S observes (and the factors that go into the production of these testimonies) are simply features of S's local (external) environment. As such, these features can conspire in any particular case to undermine S's claim to know, in a manner akin to a Gettier factor; but this is the extent of their epistemic significance. In particular, these "local environmental" features have no bearing on other epistemic statuses. These other statuses—paradigmatically, doxastic justification—are to be determined by bracketing all of the details of S's merely local environment,[1] and restricting our attention to what is going on in S's own mind/brain.

This traditional conception of the epistemic significance of testimony is very popular among epistemologists generally: it offers what is perhaps the clearest illustration of the individualistic orientation of traditional epistemology. But, popular or not, this conception is decidedly more controversial than most

---

[1] In determinations of reliability, allowance is made for ordinary "background" environmental conditions. What is ignored (for purposes of assessing a belief's doxastic justification) are *local* variations in the environment. More on this in Chapter 2.

epistemologists suppose. Chapters 3–5 aim to show that this conception is fundamentally mistaken.

Chapter 3 presents an initial consideration that bears against the traditional conception of testimony's epistemic significance. Here I argue that the process of testimonial belief-formation is a belief-dependent one: it takes as its input the testimonies that one observes, and yields as its output the testimonial belief in question. If I am correct about this, then it is wrong to think of a particular testimony and its properties (including its reliability properties) as merely "local features" of the hearer's environment. This result, I contend, is a manifestation of the limitations of the individualistic conception of testimony's epistemic significance.

The main contention of Chapter 3—that testimonial belief-formation is a belief-dependent process whose input is the testimony itself—has an important corollary: this process is best seen, not as a process that takes place wholly within the mind/brain of the subject, but rather as "extending" to include those processes implicated in the production of the testimony. Given this "extendedness hypothesis," as I will call it, we would expect that the reliability of a piece of testimony can affect (not just the knowledgeableness, but also) the doxastic justification of beliefs based on that testimony. In Chapter 4, I argue that Process Reliabilists have independent reasons to endorse this expectation. Here I focus on Goldman's (1979, 1986) reliabilist account of the epistemology of *memorial* belief. A reliabilist assessment of the doxastic justification enjoyed by a memorial belief, Goldman argues, must assess an "extended" process that includes not only the process of recollection itself but also those processes implicated in the original formation of the belief. I argue that the rationale for regarding the process of memorial belief-sustainment as "extended" in this fashion has to do with the sort of epistemic reliance that is exhibited by the subject in memory cases. In particular, the remembering subject exhibits epistemic reliance on herself (her "past self") as an information source. From this, I extract the following general principle: in a reliabilist assessment of a belief's doxastic justification, the extent of the processing to be assessed reflects the extent of the subject's epistemic reliance in forming and sustaining the belief in question. Applying this general principle to the case of testimony, we get the following result: a reliabilist assessment of (the doxastic justification enjoyed by a testimonial belief must assess an "extended" process that includes not only the processes of comprehension and credibility-monitoring taking place 'in' the hearer, but also the processes implicated in the production of the testimony (which take place 'in' the hearer's interlocutor). Seen in this light, the "extendedness hypothesis" is a special case of a general principle that reliabilists already endorse.

The picture that emerges from Chapters 1–4 is one that challenges the individualistic orientation of traditional epistemology. My claim is that the nature of our epistemic reliance in testimony cases is such that these cases are best seen as involving an interpersonally extended belief-forming process. Reliabilist orthodoxy, with its commitment to Process Individualism, must be rejected. Still, I am under no illusions regarding the power of my positive arguments to release the grip of the individualistic orientation within reliabilist epistemology. Various objections to my arguments remain to be addressed. I devote Chapter 5 to addressing what I consider to be the most salient of these; I argue that none of them withstands scrutiny.

Testimony is perhaps the paradigmatic example of our epistemic reliance on others, but it is not the only one. In Chapter 6, I consider another. Here my focus is on a type of belief which, though pervasive, has not received very much attention in the epistemology literature. The type of belief in question is one formed through a subject's epistemic reliance on her community for what I call *coverage*—as when one forms a belief in p on the grounds that if ~p were true one would have heard about it by now. (I call this the truth-to-testimony conditional.) I argue that this sort of belief is best understood, not in terms of the "extendedness model," but rather as a belief acquired through an inference involving the truth-to-testimony conditional as a premise. Such an account makes clear that social practices and institutions should be counted among the "background conditions" against which we form our beliefs.

Finally, in Chapter 7, I round out my discussion of our epistemic reliance on others. The claim here will be that reliabilist epistemology holds out the prospects for a social epistemology rooted in the traditional idea of individual subjects as knowers.

2

The book's main contention, then, is that, such is our epistemic reliance on others, that the reliability of at least some of our beliefs is affected by irreducibly social factors. There is one significant implication of this contention that I would like to highlight. In particular, those who endorse Process Reliabilism (whether about justification or knowledge) should also endorse the interest and legitimacy of what we might call "the project of social epistemology": the project of characterizing the epistemic significance of our social arrangements and institutions.

I take this result to be significant for various reasons.

First and foremost, it presents an implicit challenge to a good part of the contemporary epistemological scene. While Process Reliabilism continues to enjoy great popularity in epistemology circles, the project of social epistemology has not yet met with the same enthusiasm. If the main line of argument in this book is correct, the case for the importance of a substantial "social" dimension to epistemology is virtually as strong as is the case for Process Reliabilism itself.

Second, our result suggests a parallel between the taxonomy of positions in epistemology, and the taxonomy of positions in the philosophy of mind and language. Just as we can distinguish *individualistic* from *anti-individualistic* versions of externalism in the philosophy of mind and language (with the former being associated with Donald Davidson, and the latter with Tyler Burge), so too we can distinguish individualistic from anti-individualistic versions of externalism in epistemology. This sort of taxonomy is not yet familiar in epistemology. However, if my argument is sound then this taxonomy is as useful here as it is in the philosophy of mind and language.[2] What is more, a similar kind of argument can be used to establish anti-individualistic results in both domains. Anti-individualism about the mental is typically established using 'twin' cases: we produce two subjects who are internal "duplicates" of one another and who inhabit environments that are type-identical as far as their non-social features go, and then show that these twins can nevertheless differ in the attitudes they instantiate, as a function of differences in the social features of their respective environments. Throughout this book I will be using a similar sort of thought experiment to derive results for reliabilist epistemology: I will be arguing that the reliability properties of twins' beliefs can vary as a function of differences in the social features in their respective environments, even as we hold fixed all features intrinsic to the twins as well as all of the non-social features of their respective environments.

Third, and relatedly, in highlighting this result I aim to establish that standard versions of 'externalist' epistemology do not go far enough. While they serve as a helpful corrective against the old-school tendency to think of the epistemic subject as fully autonomous—as one who can reflectively certify the epistemic credentials of all that she knows or justifiably believes—standard externalisms often fail to do justice to any 'social' elements in epistemic assessment. In this respect, most standard externalisms remain too individualistic: they hold that, while factors beyond the reflective access of the subject herself are sometimes relevant to the epistemic assessment of her beliefs, these factors never include *the cognitive states and processes of other subjects*. It is not that there are no cases highlighting a social dimension to epistemic assessment: arguably, Gil Harman's well-known newspaper case (Harman

---

[2] See Goldberg (2007a), where I develop this theme at great length. (I mention this theme only in passing here.)

1973), which was offered as a kind of Gettier-example against traditional accounts of knowledge, illustrates a social dimension to knowledge. My claim, rather, is that, with few exceptions (one thinks here, of course, of some of Goldman's recent work), social elements have not been the focus of an extended epistemic treatment. And, to the best of my knowledge, even when they are discussed, social elements have yet to be raised in connection with epistemic justification. This last point is certainly true of Harman's newspaper example, which was meant to illustrate the possibility of a social factor among the factors that can defeat knowledge. But the point is true even of Goldman's work: while he discusses social elements in connection with his interest in knowledge as true belief, Goldman has had little to say to date about the relevance of social elements to epistemic justification, reliabilistically construed.

I should add (what may be obvious in any case) that the thesis I am defending embodies an ideological connection between the reliabilist and the social epistemology orientations defended by Goldman himself. Here it is interesting to note that, while Goldman has defended the interest and legitimacy of the project of social epistemology, reliability considerations play little or no *explicit* role in his defense(s). To be sure, reliability is never far from the surface of his treatment of social epistemology. His discussion has (as he calls it) a 'veritistic' orientation: he asks how social arrangements can be made, and social institutions can be organized, so as to maximize the production of true belief. This defense is novel and interesting, and it is not unrelated to issues of reliabilism. Indeed, one might phrase his interest as structured by a desire to enhance the reliability-effects of our social arrangements. At the same time, a more explicit connection between reliabilism and social epistemology is wanted. This is what I aim to provide here. My discussion aims: (i) to assuage any remaining concerns people might have regarding the legitimacy of the project of social epistemology; (ii) to develop a reliabilist program for how at least some such research might proceed; and (iii) to make clear that the epistemic relevance of the social goes beyond the status of knowledge itself. In this way, the project of social epistemology will be revealed to be perfectly continuous with the project of reliabilist epistemology: it results from the application of reliabilist criteria to situations in which belief-fixation involves epistemic reliance on others.

1

Testimony and Individualist Epistemology

The aim of this book is to examine the nature of our epistemic reliance on others. I pursue this out of a sense of conviction that a proper account of this reliance will undermine several individualistic assumptions in epistemology generally, and reliabilist epistemology in particular. This initial chapter focuses on the strongest of these individualistic assumptions: Knowledge Individualism (KI). According to KI, none of the epistemic factors on which knowledge supervenes are social factors. I appeal to testimony cases to argue that KI is false. Although the argument I present here should be relatively uncontroversial, it does raise an important, but heretofore largely neglected, topic within reliabilist treatments of testimonial belief: the relevance of a testimony's reliability to the reliability of beliefs formed through accepting that testimony. That is the topic of the three subsequent chapters.

I

Throughout this book I will be arguing that the nature of our epistemic reliance on others undermines several individualistic assumptions in epistemology. It should come as no surprise that a project aimed at examining the anti-individualistic implications of our epistemic reliance on others should begin by taking an extended look at testimonial belief. After all, testimony occupies a central place in what Audi (1997) has termed "the fabric of knowledge and justification." And, as Fred Schmitt has noted, testimony is "the most fundamental test of epistemological individualism":

> If individualism concerning testimony is defensible, then epistemology will remain in an important sense individualistic. And if it is not defensible, epistemology will have to be profoundly social, whatever may happen on other topics.   (Schmitt 1994: 4)

This first chapter presents my initial case for thinking that a thorough-going individualism concerning testimonial knowledge is not defensible.

While the initial focus on testimony is unsurprising in a book aiming to question the individualistic orientation of epistemology, the use of reliabilism as the theory in which to pursue this topic can seem curious.[1] On this score, the points I mentioned in the introduction of this book are worth highlighting again. For one thing, the development of reliabilism itself has been part and parcel of the move to question the assumptions of "internalist" epistemology. It can seem strange, then, that a theory that has done so much to extend our epistemological focus (beyond those features that are reflectively accessible to the epistemic subject herself) should be guilty of a commitment to any objectionable sort of epistemic individualism. Another point is that Alvin Goldman, who more than anyone else is responsible for the development and continued popularity of reliabilism, has also been at the forefront of the recent development of "social epistemology." It can seem strange as well to suppose that his brainchild should be susceptible to objections deriving from the need to appreciate the social sources of knowledge. Yet, as we will see below, most versions of reliabilism, including Goldman's own, remain highly individualistic in orientation.

A word regarding the sort of reliabilism I am using here, and my understanding of reliability, is in order. I intend to employ a

---

[1] I note that Schmitt's own position on testimony is anti-individualistic but not reliabilist in nature; see Schmitt (2006).

vanilla version of Process Reliabilism, according to which what makes for doxastic justification and knowledge has to do with the reliability of the type of process (or method) through which a belief is formed and sustained. On such a view, any talk of a belief being reliable is shorthand for a claim about the reliability of the type of process or method through which that belief was formed and sustained. What is more, in subsequent chapters I will be drawing heavily on the distinction between the *global* and *local* reliability of a process or method.[2] The difference between global and local reliability pertains to the class of circumstances in which the process or method is evaluated. A process or method is *globally* reliable if and only if it produces (or would produce) a preponderance of truth over falsity, as used across the variety of circumstances in which it is standardly employed.[3] A process or method is locally reliable in a given context C if and only if it produces (or would produce) a preponderance of truth over falsity in circumstances that are relevantly like C.

---

[2] A distinction in this neighborhood is made in Goldman (1986) and McGinn (1984). However, the version I favor is most indebted to Henderson and Horgan (2007). (This said, I should be clear that I eschew the third reliability property Henderson and Horgan introduce in that paper: *transglobal reliability*.)

[3] As formulated, this is the most generic (and non-specific) way to formulate the notion of global reliability. More specific versions result once we specify the world(s) at which the assessment takes place. There are various options here. We might say that a process P is globally reliable in a world w if and only if *at w* it produces (or would produce) a preponderance of truth over falsity across the range of circumstances in which it is (or would be) standardly employed (in w); call this *world-indexed global reliability*. Or we might prefer a notion on which P is globally reliable in a world w if and only if *at the actual world*, @, it produces (or would produce) a preponderance of truth over falsity across the range of circumstances in which it is (or would be) standardly employed (in @); call this *actual-world global reliability*. Or we might favor regarding P as globally reliable in w so long as it produces a preponderance of truth over falsity in those worlds whose most general features conform to how the subject takes those features to be; something like this is what Goldman (1986) called *normal-worlds (global) reliability*. A fourth option would be to test for global reliability (in any given world) at the world in which the process itself evolved; this might be called *evolved-world global reliability*. And there may be other interesting notions of global reliability as well. These differences will not be relevant to my points here. Since I want my argument to be as general as possible—of interest to all Process Reliabilists, no matter their views on the proper reference class for assessments of global reliability—I will ignore these differences, focusing instead on my generic (non-specific) formulation.

The main objective of this chapter is to present an argument on behalf of the following thesis regarding Epistemic Reliance in Testimony cases:

> ERT   Some epistemic properties of testimonial belief depend on the reliability of cognitive processes implicated in the production of the testimony.

More specifically, I aim in this chapter to establish ERT with respect to the epistemic property of *knowledge*.[4] My claim will be that whether a given subject has acquired testimonial knowledge will typically turn on whether the testimony she consumed was itself reliable, which (given Process Reliabilism) will turn on whether the cognitive processes that produced the testimony—processes in the mind/brain of the subject's informant—were themselves reliable. In such cases, the hearer acquires knowledge only if certain cognitive processes *in her informant* were reliable.

I begin my discussion, in Section 2, by presenting cases involving two hearers who are doppelgängers, where one acquires testimonial knowledge but the other acquires a merely true testimonial belief, and where this difference is traceable to a difference in the reliability of the respective testimonies each consumes. I use these cases to illustrate this chapter's main contention: whether a hearer has acquired knowledge through testimony depends on a reliabilist assessment of the cognitive processes responsible for the production of the testimony she has consumed. Although the cases I describe point in this direction, a full defense of this contention involves an explicit defense of two key claims. The first is that the difference in the epistemic status of the hearers' respective testimonial beliefs is to be traced to the reliability of the testimonies each has consumed (Section 3). The second is that Process Reliabilists should understand 'reliable' in 'reliable testimony' as they understand 'reliable' in 'reliable belief', that is, as reflecting the reliability of

---

[4] In the three chapters to follow I aim to establish ERT with respect to doxastic justification.

the implicated cognitive process-types (Section 4). Making out the case for these claims will involve taking some familiar reliabilist ideas and pushing them in new directions. But the resulting claims, I will be arguing, are independently plausible.

2

In this section I present the initial case for this chapter's core contention. The claim in question pertains to Epistemic Reliance in cases of Testimonial Knowledge:

> ERTK   Whether a testimonial belief amounts to testimonial knowledge depends on the reliability of cognitive processes implicated in the production of the testimony.

The basic idea behind ERTK is plain. Whether a testimonial belief counts as *knowledge* depends on the reliability of the testimony on which it was based, which in turn depends on the reliability of the cognitive processes implicated in the production of the testimony.[5] I begin this section by illustrating ERTK itself with a pair of scenarios meant to make its thesis plausible; in the sections immediately following I go on to defend the two claims connecting this illustration with ERTK itself.

I begin with the illustrating pair of scenarios. Consider first this scenario, which we will call the 'good' scenario.

GOOD Wilma has known Fred for a long time; she knows that he is a highly reliable speaker. So when Fred tells her that Barney has been at the stonecutters' conference all day, Wilma believes him. (Fred appeared to her as sincere and competent as he normally does, and she found nothing remiss with the testimony.) In point of fact, Fred spoke from knowledge.

---

[5] To forestall a possible objection, I should be clear at the outset that neither ERTK nor the two claims I will be defending implies the so-called transmission thesis, to the effect that testimony can only transmit pre-existing knowledge. I think this transmission thesis is false (for reasons found in papers cited below). But its falsity is compatible with ERTK, and with the two claims I am making. My claim here is only that the supervenience base for testimonial knowledge includes facts pertaining to the reliability of the testimony. This supervenience claim can hold even in cases in which the speaker failed to know, or reliably believe, whereof she spoke. I develop this point below.

Now imagine a variant on this scenario, which we will call the 'bad' scenario.

BAD Wilma has known Fred for a long time; she knows that he is a highly reliable speaker. So when Fred tells her that Barney has been at the stonecutters' conference all day, Wilma believes him. (Fred appeared to her as sincere and competent as he normally does, and she found nothing remiss with the testimony.) However, in this case, Fred did not speak from knowledge. Instead, he was just making up a story about Barney, having had ulterior motives in getting Wilma to believe this story. (Fred has never done this before; it is out of his normally reliable character to do such a thing.) Even so, Fred's speech contribution struck Wilma here, as in the good scenario, as sincere and competent; and she was not epistemically remiss in reaching this verdict. (Indeed, Fred has never before tried to mislead her, or anyone else; and his performance here was perceptually indistinguishable from his performance in the good scenario.) As luck would have it, though, Barney was in fact at the conference all day (though Fred, of course, did not know this).

Now I submit that Wilma's testimonial belief in GOOD, to the effect that Barney has been at the stonecutters' conference all day, constitutes knowledge; whereas her testimonial belief in BAD to that same effect does not constitute knowledge.

It will be helpful to have a characterization of the sort of case I just described which abstracts away from the irrelevant details. To this end, I offer the following schematic characterization, employing distinct speaker–hearer pairs in the two cases. Let T_1 and T_2 be two pieces of testimony with the following features: T_1 is produced by speaker S_1, whereas T_2 is produced by speaker S_2; both have the same (true) content (where the content in question is *that p*); both are exactly alike with respect to all of the features that hearers would use to assess their credibility (so S_1 and S_2 appear equally competent and sincere in their assertion); but in fact T_1 is more reliable—indeed, much more reliable—than T_2. T_1 is produced by someone who observed first hand what is reported, whereas T_2 is produced by someone aiming to deceive the hearer and who went to great lengths to cover up his deceptive intent.

Finally, let H and H* be two hearers who are doppelgängers, as alike in both the physical composition of their bodies and in their belief corpus as any two distinct individuals can be. H confronts T1 (the reliable piece of testimony produced by S1), whereas H* confronts T2 (the unreliable one produced by S2). Both H and H* are equally highly reliable in distinguishing reliable from unreliable testimony, in the sense that a preponderance of those pieces of testimony that they regard as reliable is in fact reliable. (In the highly unlikely event that H had encountered T2 rather than T1, she, too, would have regarded it, falsely, as reliable.) H accepts T1, whereas H* accepts T2. The verdict is that H comes to know that p through the testimony she has consumed, whereas H* comes merely to believe truly that p through the testimony *she* has consumed.

We can now ask: in virtue of what is it that H knows, but H* merely truly believes? Since these discrepant verdicts obtain despite H's and H*'s status as doppelgängers (type-identical from the skin-in), the source is not to be found in any features internal to the believers. Nor is it to be found in that part of the world that excludes H's and H*'s respective testifiers. After all, both H and H* believe that p, and [p] is true. In addition, we can imagine that both H and H* are in communities the vast majority of whose testimonies are both true and reliable; there is no relevant difference in the features of their surrounding environment. So, if we are to account for the difference at the level of knowledge between H's and H*'s respective testimonial beliefs, this difference is to be accounted for in terms of the difference in the reliability of the respective testimonies H and H* consumed. This should be uncontroversial.

To establish ERTK, however, we need to move beyond this uncontroversial point asserting the dependence of testimonial knowledge on the reliability of the testimony. What is needed is a claim to the following effect: whether a subject knows through testimony depends on the reliability of *cognitive processing in the mind/brain of the subject's informant*. How to get from what is uncontroversial, to what is needed?

We can bridge the gap by appeal to the reliabilist's own understanding of reliability-talk. As I noted in Section 1, for reliabilists, talk of reliability is to be understood in terms of talk of the reliability of some type of process or method. To be sure, in most cases we speak of the reliability of a type of process (or method) in connection with the processes of *belief*-formation and -sustainment. Thus 'reliable belief' is shorthand for 'belief acquired through a reliable type of process or method.' But it would seem that, insofar as we want to speak about the reliability, not of belief, but of *testimony*, the same point should hold: 'reliable testimony' should be regarded as shorthand for 'testimony produced through a reliable type of (cognitive) process.' And if this is correct, then insofar as the acquisition of testimonial knowledge depends on the reliability features of the testimony consumed, it *ipso facto* depends on reliability features of the cognitive processing in the mind/brain of one's informant. ERTK would then be established.

This 'bridging' argument, as we might call it, hinges on two claims. The first is that:

(BA1)   In order to account for the epistemic difference in any pair of cases conforming to the schematic situations of H and H*, we need to cite facts regarding the reliability of the testimony each hearer consumes.

The second is that:

(BA2)   A Process Reliabilist is committed to understanding 'reliable testimony' on the model of how she understands 'reliable belief,' namely, in terms of the reliability of the process or method that yields the output in question.

In the two sections that follow I defend both of these claims.

3

(BA1) seems obviously true. But there is at least one challenge to this claim that should be addressed (I don't know of any others). The challenge in question is suggested by the 'comprehension' account of testimonial knowledge offered by Peter Graham (2000a). Graham's account is of interest in this connection since its characterization of testimonial knowledge makes no appeal to the reliability of the particular piece of testimony consumed. And, although Graham's account of testimonial knowledge is not itself a Process Reliabilist account, we might nonetheless wonder whether a Process Reliabilist might endorse it as a basis from which to reject (BA1). (In pursuing this issue, I do not mean to suggest that Graham himself would endorse what follows; only that someone may think to appeal to Graham's account in an attempt to resist (BA1), and with it the 'bridging argument' for ERTK.)

Graham's 'comprehension' account takes the form of a necessary condition, (IN), and a sufficient condition, (IS), on testimonial knowledge. He formulates these as follows (I quote Graham himself, but the italics are mine):

(IN)   H comes to know that P by accepting that p only if H's basis for believing that P—H's *internal, cognitive* state of taking S to have stated that P—carries the information that P.

(IS)   If H's basis for believing that P—H's *internal, cognitive* state of taking S to have stated that P—carries the information that P and H justifiably accepts that P then H comes to know that P. (Graham 2000a: 365)

(On Graham's gloss, a state φ "carries the information that p" in a given set of circumstances when φ's obtaining is a "guarantee in the circumstances that p" (2000a: 366).)[6] According to this account, one acquires testimonial knowledge just in case (i) one's "internal, cognitive" state of comprehension carries the information that p, and (ii) one's acceptance of p was justified. On the further assumptions, first, that the sort of knowledge in play here is testimonial knowledge, and, second, that whether one justifiably accepts that p does not depend on any facts about the reliability of

---

[6] Following Dretske, Graham appeals to a relevant alternative analysis of knowledge in order to understand what it is for a state to "guarantee *in the circumstances* that p." These details need not concern us here.

the testimony one is consuming, we would have an argument that (BA1) is false.

Unfortunately for those who hope to avoid (BA1) in this fashion, matters are not quite so simple. For, while Graham speaks of the "basis" of testimonial knowledge as the hearer's own "internal, cognitive" state of comprehension, and while this can encourage the idea that the conditions on testimonial knowledge do not require us to extend our focus beyond this state, it turns out that this impression is faulty. In particular, there is an intimate connection between the information-carrying status of the hearer's "internal, cognitive" state of comprehension, on the one hand, and the reliability of the testimony itself, on the other hand.

The point I wish to make here is made by Graham himself, in his example of the reformed boy who cried "Wolf!" (Graham 2000b). In the original version of the story (often attributed to Aesop), the boy (who is responsible for a flock of sheep) regularly cries "Wolf!" merely to attract attention to himself, with the result that when there really is a wolf threatening the flock, no one believes his warning. In Graham's version of the story, we are to imagine that the boy has a sudden change of heart: on seeing a real wolf, he is so scared that he changes his ways. Graham describes the scenario as follows:

He is so scared that his psychology takes a turn for the better. He now says that there is a wolf *because* he sees one. He realizes the gravity of the present situation, and he even realizes how terrible his previous deeds were. Before he was, in a way, a broken alarm. He would go off when no danger was present. But now that he detects danger, his report of the threat to the village is a reliable one. The fright is sufficient to fix the alarm. *In these circumstances* his statement indicates the presence of a wolf. And so it is not so unreasonable to say that [a] stranger [who knows nothing about the boy's past dispositions], when accepting the boy's report, comes to know that a wolf is threatening the flock.   (Graham 2000b: 141)

Graham goes on to acknowledge that there are yet other versions of the revised story on which the stranger does *not* acquire knowledge of the presence of a wolf from the boy. Thus, Graham writes:

Suppose the boy still cares little for honesty, but it is not the attention he is after, but rather the sheer delight in making reports about important matters in a completely random way, that leads him to tell the stranger that a wolf is present. That is, seeing the wolf prompts him to make a report about the presence or absence of a wolf, but the reason why he says a wolf is present and not absent is because he flipped a coin. He says there is a wolf not because he believes on the basis of excellent evidence that a wolf is present, but because the coin turned up heads. He may be a reliable *believer*, but he is not a reliable *reporter*. Here the stranger does not come to know about the wolf. He is in no better shape than he would be in if the boy had asked him if he thought a wolf were present and he made up his mind by flipping the coin himself.   (141−2)

What determines whether the stranger is in a position to acquire knowledge (regarding the presence of a wolf) from the boy? Here is Graham on the matter:

What matters is *whether, on this occasion, the boy would not say that there is a wolf unless there is a wolf*. So even though the boy has made more false reports about wolves than true ones, one can still learn about whether there is a wolf threatening the flock from the boy once he has seen one before his very eyes. *What matters, in short, is the disposition underlying the boy's report and whether it will underwrite the truth of the subjunctive.* It is this mistake, thinking of the relevant reliability in statistical terms, that [might lead one to think] that what matters is whether the speaker knows that P, not whether the speaker's report carries the information that P. [It would be] wrong to think that the stranger can come to know even when the reporter is relevantly unreliable, even when the speaker's report does not *indicate* that P. When it is clear that the stranger comes to know it is because the boy is *now* a reliable reporter.   (142; italics added)

Graham's reasoning here seems to be this. Whether a hearer comes to acquire testimonial knowledge that p through having accepted a speaker's testimony that p depends on whether the hearer's "internal, cognitive" state of comprehension 'carries the information' that p. *But whether a hearer's "internal, cognitive" state of comprehension 'carries the information' that p depends on whether the testimony he consumed 'carried the information' that p*—that is, depends on whether the testimony was reliable (or, in Graham's own words, whether the speaker was a "reliable reporter"). It would thus seem that one should not look to Graham's 'comprehension view' as a way to resist (BA1).

With this case in mind, we can diagnose any impression to the contrary as follows. Condition (IN) requires that the hearer's "internal, cognitive" state carry the information that p. This encourages the idea that whether a hearer satisfies this condition can be determined just by checking her "internal, cognitive" state—i.e., without having any concern for the reliability of the testimony she has consumed. But the variants on the case of the boy who cried "Wolf!" make clear that this is not so: whether the stranger acquires knowledge from the boy—and so, by extension, whether her state of comprehension "carries the information that p"—depends on facts about the reliability of the testimony. So, while it is true that on Graham's view it is the "internal, cognitive" state of comprehension in the stranger that does the epistemic work in determining whether she has attained knowledge, this can be misleading. After all, what determines whether this state carries the information that p is not a fact about this state taken in isolation from the particular piece of testimony she has consumed. It is precisely for this reason that Graham answers the question "Did the stranger acquire knowledge from the boy's cry?" by saying that this depends on *"whether, on this occasion, the boy would not say that there is a wolf unless there is a wolf."* And thus we see that, even on Graham's view, the supervenience base of testimonial knowledge includes facts regarding the reliability of the testimony consumed.[7] Graham's comprehension view does not support the rejection of (BA1).

[7] There is one other case that is worth discussing in this context. (The case, which was suggested to me by Peter Graham (in conversation), is fantastical; I mention it nevertheless as it poses a problem for both (BA1) and ERTK.) Imagine a world involving an individual of whom the following story is true: it regularly happens that he finds himself in a state in which it is as if he was told that p, where, on this basis, he forms the belief that p—only

4

Of course, it is one thing to say that whether a hearer acquires testimonial knowledge turns on the reliability of the testimony; it is another to say that it turns on the reliability of *the relevant cognitive processes in the mind/brain of the speaker*. Making the stronger claim requires defending (BA2), the second of the two assumptions made by my 'bridging argument' above. According to this assumption, a Process Reliabilist should understand 'reliable' in 'reliable testimony' as she understands 'reliable' in 'reliable belief,' namely, in terms of the reliability of the type of process or method that yields the output in question.

I want to begin, however, with two objections that might be leveled against (BA2). After arguing (in Sections 4.1 and 4.2) that these objection can both be met, I will go on (in Section 4.3) to offer positive arguments on behalf of (BA2).

4.1

An initial reason for being skeptical of (BA2) is this. As developed by Goldman and others, Process Reliabilism speaks only of *belief*-forming processes, those processes that eventuate in the formation of belief. It makes no mention of processes that eventuate in, for example, testimonies. One might doubt whether it even makes

the whole thing was a hallucination (he observed no testimony). But in every one of these cases, the hallucination "carries the information" that p: the individual in question does not suffer from this hallucination in any situation in which [p] is false. Furthermore (we are still to imagine) this is a robust (counterfactual-supporting) regularity. Then, by the lights of the information-carrying account of knowledge, in these cases he knows that p. Now imagine that this individual is highly reliable in ordinary circumstances in discriminating reliable from unreliable testimonies. And imagine that he draws on this capacity as he assesses his state of comprehension that p. In that case, it seems as though, by the lights of Process Reliabilism, he satisfies the antecedent of (IS), and so the knowledge in question is testimonial knowledge. But there is no testimony in this case, so we have a case involving testimonial knowledge whose status as such does not depend on the existence, let alone the reliability, of any particular piece of testimony! The case thus falsifies (BA1) and ERTK. In reaction, I submit that if the 'comprehension' account sanctions this as a case of testimonial knowledge, then so much the worse for that account as an account of *testimonial* knowledge properly so-called.

sense to speak of reliable cognitive processes in connection with the production of testimony. So, even if it is granted that a reliabilist assessment of the knowledgeableness (or not) of testimonial belief will need to determine whether the testimony consumed was reliable, it can still be doubted whether such an assessment will involve an assessment of the reliability of cognitive process-types in the speaker.[8]

In response, I submit that proffered testimony should be seen as the *output of a cognitive process that is assessable along the dimension of reliability.*

The initial case for this is straightforward. First, testimony should be seen as the output of a cognitive process. This point should be obvious. The production of testimony, as a case of the production of speech, is a cognitive affair if anything is: it is the result of cognitive (information-processing) processes. Second, the cognitive process in question is assessable along the dimension of reliability. In order to be so assessable, a cognitive process must be such as to produce outputs that are truth-value-bearing. This is because the reliability of a process is understood in terms of its success in producing a preponderance of truths across the contexts in which it standardly operates. But testimony fits the bill here, since pieces of testimony *are* truth-value-bearing. Thus we can speak of the process involved in the production of testimony as reliable just in case that process-type would produce a preponderance of *true testimonies.*

Of course, testimonies are not beliefs. But this does not seem to present an insurmountable difficulty for (BA2). On the contrary, it would seem that testimony is in good company here: there are other cases of outputs that are not themselves beliefs but which the reliabilist is committed to regarding as assessable in terms of their reliability (and the reliability of the processes responsible for their production). Consider perceptual impressions, construed

⁸ I thank an anonymous referee from Oxford University Press for putting the matter this way.

as involving a perceptual representation of how things stand. A subject's perceptual impressions are not beliefs, though they can serve as the ground for beliefs. It is for this reason that there is a point to assessing their reliability (e.g., the reliability of the processes that produce them). Take the case of a perceptual belief that p, formed through taking the perceptual appearances at face value. It would seem that such a belief is reliable—and hence, by the lights of Process Reliabilism, doxastically justified—only if the perceptual impression itself was the result of a reliable process (where this process involves the transduction of sensory inputs into perceptual representations).[9] But then the reliabilist is committed to taking an interest in the reliability of perceptual impressions. And since perceptual impressions are not beliefs, this would show that reliabilists already have a motive for assessing the reliability of (the processes that generate) a non-belief state. Nor is this the only example of the phenomenon; there are other examples of contentful mental states that are not beliefs yet which the process reliabilist will want to assess for reliability: consider memory impressions (the state of seeming to recall that p), or perhaps intuitions (although this case is more controversial).

To be sure, there remains this difference: a perceptual state (also: a memory impression; an intuition) is a cognitive state, whereas a piece of testimony is not. To my mind, this is a reason to reject the claim that only cognitive states are the outputs of cognitive processes; it is *not* a reason to reject the claim that testimony is the output of cognitive process.

4.2

But this brings us to a second objection that might be leveled against (BA2). Some recent accounts of testimonial knowledge distinguish the reliability of testimony from the reliability of belief; and at least one of these holds that a speaker can offer reliable testimony

---

[9] Not all reliabilist accounts of perceptual belief advert to perceptual states in this way. See Lyons (2008).

without being a reliable believer in the content in question. This distinction, and the possibility of this sort of case, might seem to cast doubt on whether reliable testimony should be understood in terms of the reliability of the relevant cognitive process-types.

Two recent accounts that distinguish between the reliability of testimony and the reliability of belief are Graham's and Lackey's. As we already saw, Graham (2000b: 141–2) distinguishes between being a reliable *believer* and a reliable *reporter*, making clear that it is only the reliability of the report that is relevant. This can make it seem as if 'reliable testimony' should not be construed in terms of the reliability of the relevant belief-forming processes. Lackey's account also distinguishes between a speaker's being a reliable testifier and her being a reliable believer. Like Graham's account, Lackey's "statement view" holds that it is the reliability of a speaker's statement, rather than that of the speaker's belief, that does the epistemic work in putting a hearer in a position to acquire testimonial knowledge. Lackey formulates this view as follows ('SVT' for 'Statement View of Testimony'):

> (SVT)   For every speaker, A, and hearer, B, B knows[10] (believes with justification/warrant) that p on the basis of A's testimony that p only if (1) A's statement that p is reliable or otherwise truth-conducive, (2) B comes to believe that p on the basis of the content of A's statement that p, and (3) B has no undefeated defeaters for believing that p. (Lackey 2008: 75)

What is more, Lackey offers several examples in which a speaker offers reliable testimony where she lacks the corresponding belief.[11] Cases of this sort can make it seem that the reliability of testimony should not be understood in terms of the reliability of cognitive processing—contrary to (BA2).

---

[10] Of course, for testimonial knowledge, a condition will need to be added to the SVT requiring the truth of B's belief that p. [SG: This footnote is in the original text of Lackey (2008).]

[11] These are her CREATIONIST TEACHER and CONSISTENT LIAR cases. I will discuss the latter of these at some length, below.

In response, I submit that the considerations that motivate the accounts of both Graham and Lackey are consistent with (BA2). In particular, the cases that motivate their accounts merely require us to distinguish reliability in the formation of *belief* from reliability in the production of *testimony*. What Graham and Lackey establish is that these two can come apart: Graham's variant on the boy who cried "Wolf!" shows that one can be a reliable believer, and so form a belief through a reliable process, while failing to be a reliable testifier, and so fail to produce testimony through a reliable process; whereas Lackey's cases establish the reverse, that one can be a reliable testifier, and so produce testimony through a reliable process, while failing to be a reliable believer, and so fail to form one's belief on the matter in question through a reliable process.

Indeed, both Graham's and Lackey's own accounts of their own cases require construing the reliability of testimony in this fashion. We already saw this with respect to Graham's discussion: whether the boy's cry of "Wolf!" was reliable was seen by Graham himself to turn on "the disposition underlying the boy's report" (Graham 2000b: 94). Graham's talk of "the disposition" here highlights what he sees as the connection between the psychological process by which the testimony is generated, on the one hand, and the testimony's status as reliable, on the other: the testimony is reliable on Graham's account only if it wouldn't have been offered if false, and it counts as satisfying this condition only if grounded in the proper psychological disposition. As Graham's cases thus require, and so offer no basis for resisting, (BA2)'s construal of reliable testimony as testimony produced by a reliable psychological process, I will focus on Lackey's cases. I submit that, by the light of her own account of these cases, Lackey's cases involving reliable testimony in the absence of reliable belief must be analyzed as cases in which the testimony is reliable precisely because it was produced by a reliable cognitive process. The case I will consider is the one she labels 'CONSISTENT LIAR.' (Similar points could be made in the CREATIONIST TEACHER case, another scenario she offers to illustrate the possibility of reliable testimony in the absence of reliable belief.)

CONSISTENT LIAR concerns Bertha, who suffered a head injury as a teenager. As a result of this injury, she became prone to telling lies "especially about her perceptual experiences involving wild animals" (53). Her parents bring her in to see a neurosurgeon, who decides that an operation is needed. In the course of the operation, the neurosurgeon realizes that he cannot rid Bertha of the lesion that is responsible for her tendency to lie. Consequently he decides instead to create a second lesion whose anticipated effect is:

that [Bertha's] pattern of lying would be extremely consistent and would combine in a very direct way with a pattern of consistent perceptual unreliability. . . . As a result of [the success of] this procedure, Bertha is now . . . a radically unreliable, yet highly consistent, believer with respect to her perceptual experiences about wild animals. . . . At the same time, however, Bertha is also a radically insincere, yet highly consistent, testifier of this information. For instance, nearly every time she sees a deer and believes that it is a horse, she insincerely reports to others that she saw a deer; nearly every time she sees a giraffe and believes that it is an elephant, she insincerely reports to others that she saw a giraffe, and so on.   (Lackey 2008: 53–4)

Lackey notes that since Bertha's testimony is mainly true, people who know nothing of her lesion "do not have any reason for doubting Bertha's reliability as a source of information." The result, according to Lackey, is that it is possible for both strangers and those who know Bertha's speech patterns well to acquire knowledge of the presence of a particular wild animal through Bertha's testimony. This sort of case thus illustrates Lackey's key contention: it is not the epistemic status of a speaker's *belief* that is relevant to the epistemic status of beliefs based on that speaker's testimony; it is rather the reliability of the speaker's *testimony* that is relevant. As Lackey puts it, "even though Bertha is a radically *unreliable believer* with respect to her animal sightings, she is nonetheless an extremely *reliable testifier* of this information" (55).[12]

---

[12] Compare Graham (2000b: 141–2), in one version of the case of the modified boy who cried "Wolf!" Of this version, Graham writes that the boy "may be a reliable *believer*, but he is not a reliable *reporter*."

As Lackey herself notes, in order to count as reliable, Bertha's truth-telling must be counterfactually robust: she is a reliable testifier regarding wild animals because she *is likely* to speak truly *whenever* she speaks of wild animals in her visual field. But this counterfactual robustness of her testimony is not a brute fact about Bertha's testimony. On the contrary, it is grounded in aspects of Bertha's post-operative psychology. Lackey's descriptions on this score, suffused as they are with descriptions of Bertha's cognitive states and the actions that are the results of these cognitive states, are clear on this point: "nearly every time Bertha *sees* a deer, she *believes* that it is a horse yet *reports* to others that she saw a deer" (55). Indeed, Lackey is quite clear that the production of testimony is itself a cognitive activity. She insists on this very point in her effort to distinguish Bertha from "non-agential mechanisms." Thus Bertha is described by Lackey as:

> an *agent* with *intentional states* that *affect* the statements that she offers to others. In this sense, Bertha is importantly different from non-agential mechanisms, such as thermometers and odometers, that may reliably convey information but *not through anything reasonably regarded as testimony*. (55; italics added)

Thus Lackey herself holds that what renders Bertha's testimony reliable includes the cognitive processing implicated in the production of that testimony.

Still, it might seem that, while Lackey's case of Bertha does not call into question the involvement of cognitive processing in the production of reliable testimony, it does call into question whether that cognitive processing needs to be *reliable* (if the testimony is to be reliable). After all, while Bertha's beliefs do inform her testifying, she is an *un*reliable believer; and, while her intentions are indeed implicated in the production of testimony, the reliability of her testimony is not owed to any attempt on her part to speak reliably. (On the contrary, she is aiming to lie.)

But I contend that even in this case the reliability of the testimony should be understood in terms of the reliability of the cognitive process implicated in its production. To be sure, the reliability of the processes in question is something that is brought about by the neurosurgeon's lesion. But the fact that the reliability of Bertha's testimony is brought about by a non-standard neurosurgical intervention is no reason to conclude that (BA2) is false.

To bring this out, let us develop Bertha's story a bit. Suppose that some time after the initial surgery the neurosurgeon discovers there is a way to lesion Bertha's brain yet again so that she no longer has any tendency to lie. (Call this the "third" lesion.) Of course, the neurosurgeon realizes that if Bertha continues to exhibit a "pattern of consistent perceptual unreliability," then the fact that she will no longer have the tendency to lie will ensure that her testimonies from (would-be) wild-animal sightings will be unreliable. But the neuroscientist also knows yet another lesion he can make—the "fourth" lesion—which will cancel out the relevant perceptual effects of the second lesion, resulting in a situation in which Bertha's wild-animal-sighting beliefs will return, once again, to being reliable. The strategy, then, is to make these two additional lesions, one to get her to stop having the tendency to lie, the other to return her perceptual system to its initial reliability. So the surgeon calls Bertha back to the hospital, operates, and—lo and behold!—the operation is a success: Bertha's perceptual beliefs about wild animals are now almost always true, and she no longer has any tendency to lie (so her wild-animal testimonies are reliable too).

Notice that these results—in particular, the result that her perceptual wild-animal beliefs are almost always true—are also the causal effects of brain lesions made by the neurosurgeon. Yet here there should be no tendency to infer, from the fact that lesions three and four play a large causal role in bringing about this effect, to the claim that Bertha no longer forms beliefs through a reliable cognitive process. On the contrary, belief-formation (like speech production) is a cognitive process if ever there were one; and even after the second operation, whatever ratio of true to false beliefs there is in the belief-outputs of these processes should be ascribed to the reliability of the processes themselves. It is true that after the second operation these processes work as they do in large part because of the effects of the various brain lesions that the neurosurgeon introduced. But this point, though correct, is irrelevant to the issue at hand: belief-formation remains a cognitive matter, and reliability in belief-formation remains reliability in the cognitive processes involved.

I submit that the case as Lackey describes it is no different. In that case, the mere fact that Bertha's reliable testimony is the causal effect of a lesion does not establish that this testimony is *not* the result of a reliable cognitive process. It is worth underscoring that the effects of the lesion on her speech patterns operate *in the context of her background beliefs*: it is only because she believes as she does that she testifies as she does. In fact, the first neurosurgery (the one described by Lackey) is successful only because this connection holds. If Bertha's beliefs had no systematic effect on her testimonies, then the neurosurgeon could not have ensured that Bertha's "pattern of lying would be extremely consistent and would combine in a very direct way with a pattern of consistent perceptual unreliability." So it remains true that insofar as the production of testimony is itself a cognitive affair, reliable testimony is the result of a reliable cognitive process. The fact that this cognitive process itself works as it does in part because of the effects of the brain lesion that the neurosurgeon introduced is true but irrelevant.

In short, what the case of Bertha calls into question is not the link between the reliability of a piece of testimony and the reliability of the cognitive processes implicated in its production, but rather the link between testimony and belief—precisely as Lackey herself advertises. The case of Bertha (in Lackey's original version) illustrates that we should distinguish the cognitive processes that produce testimony from those that produce belief: testimony, and even reliable testimony, can be produced in the absence of belief (and so in the absence of reliable belief).

4.3

So far I have considered two objections to (BA2), and found both of them wanting. I now want to offer positive reasons in support of (BA2).

I have already argued for (BA1), the claim that the acquisition of testimonial knowledge depends on the reliability of the testimony. In effect, this means that a theory of testimonial knowledge must acknowledge the role of reliable testimony in the production of testimonial knowledge. With this in mind, the Process Reliabilist has two options: either she can regard reliability properties of the testimony as brute (not explicable in terms of other, presumably more basic properties), or else she must explain what it is for testimony to be reliable in some other way. The former option should be deeply unattractive to the Process Reliabilist; while the latter option will force her to endorse (BA2).

Take the first option, on which the reliability of testimony is seen as a brute fact about the testimony. Any theory that endorses this option fails to satisfy an aim that has been associated with Process Reliabilism from the very outset. Part of the reliabilist project has always been to understand reliability in naturalistic terms. This aim is satisfied when 'reliability' is understood in terms of the ratio of true to false outputs of cognitive processes (as assessed across a variety of more or less restrictive set of circumstance-types). It would be unhappy indeed if this project could not be carried out because Process Reliabilism needs an irreducible notion of 'reliable' as it figures in 'reliable testimony.'

Consider then the second option, which involves characterizing what it is for testimony to be reliable in terms of other, presumably more basic, properties. I submit that this cannot be done without appealing to the reliability of the cognitive process producing the testimony—that is, it cannot be done without endorsing (BA2).

A first attempt to characterize the reliability of testimony without appealing to the reliability of the cognitive processes that produce them employs the language that Graham (2000a) uses. On this proposal, a piece of testimony that p is reliable in the relevant sense when it "carries the information" that p: the fact that the testimony has been given "guarantees in the circumstances" that p (Graham 2000a: 366). This 'information-carrying' construal is designed to capture a modal characteristic of reliable testimony: reliable testimony is testimony that wouldn't have been proffered if it had been false. This characterization is fine as far as it goes, but it doesn't go far enough. For we saw above that whether a piece of testimony has this modal characteristic depends in its turn on the process through which the testimony was produced. This was the lesson of Graham's reflections on the variations of the boy who cried "Wolf!"

Graham's insight on this score can be brought out by looking at another case. The case I offer here is a kind of inverse of Graham's case of the reformed boy who cried "Wolf!," modeled loosely on one I presented in Goldberg (2007b).

SAMMY is a rabid Yankees fan who follows the team obsessively in the daily sports pages. Sammy hates it when the Yankees lose. Whenever they do, he is given to form his belief about the outcome of the game on the basis of wishful thinking: in these cases he comes to believe that they won, despite whatever evidence he might have that they lost (including reading in the paper that they lost). However, when the Yankees do win (which is very often!), he reads about it in the paper and forms his belief that they won through accepting the reliable report found there. One morning, a stranger, hoping to find out the winner of last night's game (and knowing nothing of Sammy's habits), asks Sammy who won last night's game. Sammy reports that the Yankees did.

Is Sammy's testimony reliable or not? Here it would seem that the answer turns on the process through which the testimony was formed. In particular, the testimony was reliable if based on his comprehension and acceptance of the report in the morning paper's sports section; unreliable if the result of an episode of wishful thinking. What is more, it is only by variation in these sorts of psychological features that we see variation in the reliability properties of the testimony. (I submit that this is why Graham went to some length to describe the relevant changes in the boy's psychology in each of the versions of the case he wanted to consider.) Thus it would seem that the reliability of the testimony supervenes on the reliability of the cognitive processes implicated in the production of the testimony.

Might one resist this conclusion by saying that Sammy's testimony is reliable so long as he wouldn't have offered it if false? No: such an analysis yields unhappy results in the case at hand. To see this, note that Sammy would have testified to a Yankees win even if they had lost (since in that case he would have employed wishful thinking to come to believe, falsely, that they had won). So, by the lights of the proposed analysis, Sammy's testimony will count as unreliable, period—whether or not it was based on his having read of the result in the (reliable) morning sports section. But this verdict—that Sammy's testimony is unreliable, even in the scenario in which it was the product of his having read the result in the (reliable) morning sports section—is unhappy.

Several considerations support my contention asserting the unhappiness of this verdict. For one thing, such a verdict flies in the face of standard Process Reliabilist assessment. Suppose that it is Sammy's belief, rather than his testimony, that is at issue: what we want to know is whether his belief that the Yankees won, formed (as it was in this case) on the basis of his having read the results in the morning paper, was formed in a reliable way. On this matter, the fact that he would have believed that they won even if they had lost would not settle whether his belief was reliably formed. On the contrary, to settle that, we would want to know how he came to form the belief, i.e., through what process-type: forming a belief through reading the morning sports' section is a reliable way to form beliefs about the outcome of last night's game, whereas wishful thinking is not. But it would seem that *precisely the same thing should be said regarding his testimony*: it is reliable if based on his having gotten the news from the morning paper; unreliable if it is the result of his wishful thinking. These verdicts, I submit, are intuitive in their own right. But they are further supported by thinking about whether an ordinary hearer who knows nothing of Sammy's dispositions[13] could come to know that the Yankees won last night through accepting Sammy's say-so that they did, in a case in which the Yankees did win and Sammy's testimony was based on his having read of this result in the morning paper. I think that the answer is affirmative—after all, in all relevant respects this case is like Graham's case of the reformed boy who cried "Wolf!"

But if this verdict stands, then the testimony in question must be seen as reliable, and so once again we see that 'reliable testimony' is best construed as a matter of testimony produced by a reliable cognitive process-type—precisely as (BA2) has it.

I have argued that the Process Reliabilist has no plausible way to avoid construing the reliability of testimony in terms of the reliability of the cognitive process that produced it. But I think there is a second reason that can be offered on behalf of (BA2). (BA2)'s construal of reliable testimony yields a simple and natural explanation of a generalization that any epistemologist should want to be able to explain. The generalization is this: it is typically the case that reliable testimony involves the linguistic expression of reliable belief. (Typically, but not always; see above.) This generalization is easily explained given (BA2) and a plausible assumption to the effect that (in typical cases) the cognitive processes implicated in the production of testimony involve the cognitive processes implicated in the production and sustainment of the belief that is linguistically expressed in the testimony. But if (BA2) is false, then it is hard to see what explains this generalization. For, insofar as we try to understand 'reliable testimony' without appeal to reliable cognitive processes, we make a mystery out of the (imperfect but nevertheless substantial) covariation between reliable testimony and reliable belief: why then should it be true that the vast majority of cases of reliable testimony involve the expression of reliable belief? Those who reject (BA2) will have to resort to one or another

---

[13] Of course, it is another matter entirely if the hearer knows of Sammy's dispositions, and has no way to tell whether Sammy's testimony is reliable in this case or not. But see below.

auxiliary hypothesis to explain the generalization. Given that we have already seen how to provide the explanation without any such hypothesis, any complication of this sort seems needless.

In the end, the truth of (BA2) should not be all that surprising. After all, construing 'reliable testimony' as testimony produced by a reliable cognitive process is precisely what enables us to differentiate reliable testimony that p from cases involving a 'natural' sign that p. Consider in this light the difference between testifying to one's having the measles, vs having a rash indicative of the measles. The proffering of reliable testimony to the effect that one has the measles is a cognitive achievement, in a way that developing a rash symptomatic of measles is not. A natural explanation of the difference is that the proffering of reliable testimony that p typically involves the very same cognitive processes that are employed in acquiring and sustaining the belief that p. In this respect our proposal (to construe reliable testimony as testimony produced by a reliable cognitive process) vindicates the intuitive idea that the production of reliable testimony is itself a cognitive achievement. If we deny the connection between the reliability of testimony and the reliability of the cognitive processes implicated in its production, we surrender the most natural explanation of that achievement.

I conclude, then, the reliabilist has strong motives to endorse (BA2), the second of my two assumptions in the 'bridging argument' for ERTK. Add to this (BA1)—that the epistemic differences between the subjects in GOOD and BAD are a matter of the reliability of the testimony consumed—and we reach the conclusion of ERTK itself. Relying on others for the acquisition of testimonial knowledge involves depending on the reliability-making features of cognitive processing that took place in their mind/brains.

2

Orthodox Reliabilism and the Epistemic Significance of Testimony

Chapter 1 was the first of five chapters I will be devoting to the nature of epistemic reliance in testimonial belief-fixation. I concluded by highlighting the reliability of the cognitive processes implicated in the production of the testimony. My thesis was ERTK: whether a hearer's testimonial belief amounts to testimonial knowledge depends on the reliability of cognitive processing taking place in the mind/brain of her source. Such a conclusion entails the falsity of the doctrine of Knowledge Individualism.

In this chapter, I explore how these results bear on *another* individualistic doctrine—one that is explicitly endorsed by prominent reliabilists. According to this doctrine, which I will label "Process Individualism," the cognitive processes implicated in the formation or sustainment of a subject's beliefs all take place within *that subject's* own mind/brain. (I will use "Orthodox Reliabilism" to designate the combination of Process Reliabilism and Process Individualism.) My thesis is that the Orthodox Reliabilist can and should embrace ERTK, but that the combination of these views requires a commitment to a very traditional conception of testimony's epistemic significance, according to which particular testimonies and their properties (including their reliability properties) are to be regarded as features of the hearer's local environment. On such a view, testimony that is apparently reliable but *de facto* unreliable (in the manner of T2 from the previous chapter) can constitute a Gettier condition, and so can undermine a subject's claim to knowledge; but this exhausts the epistemic significance of the testimony.

Chapters 3 and 4 are devoted to arguing *against* this traditional conception of testimony's epistemic significance. However, it will be helpful to appreciate why the Orthodox Reliabilist is committed to this conception, and what form this conception takes within the Orthodox Reliabilist framework. That is the aim of this chapter.

Since the pressure on the Orthodox Reliabilist to endorse this conception comes from ERTK itself, I begin, in Section 1, by noting that most epistemologists will regard ERTK itself as a humdrum claim—one which reflects an already widely acknowledged point about the role of local factors in ascriptions of knowledge. In Section 2, I argue that such a reaction to ERTK is mandatory for any proponent of Orthodox Reliabilism. Finally, in Section 3, I suggest how the Orthodox Reliabilist will employ the distinction between *global* and *local* reliability, in order to capture the traditional conception's idea that testimony and its reliability properties are features of the subject's local environment. The result, I argue, is that the Orthodox Reliabilist is committed to the Local Reliability Hypothesis (LRH), according to which facts about the reliability of a piece of testimony, by themselves, can affect only the local reliability, not the global reliability, of beliefs based on that testimony.[1]

This chapter concludes, then, by discussing how the Orthodox Reliabilist will employ the distinction between global and local reliability in her factorization of the reliability of testimony-based

---

[1] LRH does not imply that a testimonial belief based on unreliable testimony is always merely locally unreliable. What it implies, rather, is this: insofar as a testimonial belief is globally unreliable, this is not in virtue of the unreliability of the testimony. (By the lights of Orthodox Reliabilism, the degree of global reliability of a testimonial belief is always a matter of the degree of reliability of the process-type by which the testimonial belief was formed—a process-type that is presumed to be individualistic, and hence having nothing to do with the reliability of the testimony.)

belief. This topic, which will be the focus of the next two chapters, can seem somewhat esoteric. Not only does it presuppose the significance of a distinction—that between local and global reliability—that is not without its own problems (see Gendler and Hawthorne 2005), and which in any case is not universally endorsed by Process Reliabilists (see Greco 2010). What is more, the issue regarding how to factor the reliability of testimonial belief would appear at first blush to be a minor "accounting" matter—an in-house dispute among a certain subset of reliabilists, to be sure, but a dispute that does not tell us very much about the nature of our epistemic reliance on others. An underlying aim of this chapter is to show that these appearances are misleading. It is for this reason that I stress that the Local Reliability Hypothesis is the Orthodox Reliabilist's version of a very traditional conception of the epistemic significance of testimony—a conception that is prevalent among epistemologists generally (not just among reliabilists). The main conclusion of this chapter—that Orthodox Reliabilism is committed to LRH—is meant to pave the way for the subsequent two chapters, where I will be targeting the Local Reliability Hypothesis, in an indirect attempt to weaken the traditional conception's grip on our epistemological imagination.

I

Chapter 1 concluded that the acquisition of testimonial knowledge depends on facts regarding cognitive processing in the mind/brain of one's source. In particular, my claim was that:

> ERTK   Whether a testimonial belief amounts to testimonial knowledge depends on the reliability of cognitive processes implicated in the production of the testimony.

In one respect ERTK can seem strange: how can it be that whether *one* person has acquired knowledge depends on whether cognitive processing in *another* person's mind/brain was reliable? But in another sense ERTK is not strange in the least: whether one person has acquired knowledge can depend in part on whether another's testimony was reliable, which in turn depends on whether the cognitive processing implicated in the production of that testimony was reliable.

In fact, it can seem that ERTK is a special case of an already very familiar point having to do with the role of local features in ascriptions of knowledge. To see this, consider a doppelgänger scenario involving the familiar 'stopped clock' case. Let S and S* be doppelgängers, each of whom is presently observing a different clock: S is observing clock C1, while S* is observing clock C2. Both clock faces read 2 o'clock, so both S and S* come to believe that it is 2 o'clock. In fact it is 2 o'clock; but it turns out that, while C1 was functioning properly, C2 has been stopped at 2 o'clock for weeks. The following verdict then seems apt: S's true belief that it is 2 o'clock amounts to knowledge, while S*'s does not. We would thus appear to have a clock-related analogue to ERTK: whether a belief formed through trusting a clock amounts to knowledge depends on the reliability of the clock at the time in question. And, since the stopped clock case of S and S* appears to mirror the testimonial case of H and H* from Chapter 1, it would appear further that there is nothing particularly special about testimony: like stopped clock cases, cases involving unreliable testimony merely illustrate a general point, already widely acknowledged, regarding the potential role of local features in undermining ascriptions of knowledge.

Before examining why epistemologists might analyze these cases in this way, it is worth acknowledging that the analogy between unreliable testimony and a stopped clock is not perfect. There is, after all, one obvious difference between getting testimony from a person and reading a clock face. In the former case the stimulus (= the testimony) is itself the 'output' of a cognitive process, whereas in the latter case the stimulus (= the arrangement of the hands on the clock's face) is not. Consider in this light the following argument, which might be used to call into question the legitimacy of the analogy:

In the case where the stopped clock happens to give the correct time at the moment S* observes it, the proper verdict is clear: S*'s true belief is justified, but fails to amount to knowledge. Here, the bearing of the scenario on knowledge is clear: the fact that the clock was not properly functioning makes the truth of S*'s belief too much a matter of luck to count as knowledge. And the irrelevance of the scenario to justification is also clear: facts regarding the functioning of the clock are irrelevant to the issue of justification, since these facts are 'external' to to the process through which the belief is formed, to the grounds on which the belief is based, and so forth—and so these facts are 'external' to whatever it is that we assess when we assess the justification of S*'s belief. But—moving over to the case where H* forms a belief through accepting T2 (an unreliable piece of testimony which happens to be true)—it is not clear that we should support a verdict of 'true and justified but not knowledge' regarding H*'s testimonial belief. The bearing of the scenario on knowledge is clear: the fact that the testimony was unreliable makes the truth of H*'s belief too much a matter of luck to count as knowledge. What is *not* clear is the irrelevance of the scenario to justification: it is not clear that facts regarding the production of a piece of testimony are 'external' to the process through which the belief is formed, to the grounds on which the belief is based, and so forth. And if the facts regarding the production of testimony are *not* suitably 'external' in the relevant sense, then the analogy between stopped clocks and unreliable testimony is untenable.

The crucial question, then, is whether facts about the reliability of a piece of testimony are suitably 'external' to the process by which, or the basis on which, testimonial beliefs are formed.

At this point, the defender of the analogy between stopped clocks and unreliable testimonies can defend the viability of the analogy by appeal to a very traditional conception of the epistemic significance of testimony. According to this conception, a piece of testimony and its features (including its reliability features) are no different from any other external feature(s) of a subject's local environment. From this vantage point the analogy between stopped clocks and unreliable testimonies remains as strong as can be: facts regarding the production (and so the reliability) of the testimony, like facts regarding the proper functioning of a clock, *are* relevantly 'external' to the materials that make for the doxastic justification of corresponding (testimony- or clock-based) beliefs. The epistemic significance of such features (the functioning of the clock, the reliability of the testimony) is that of a potential Gettier condition: such features might conspire in a given case to undermine the subject's claim to know, but this is the extent of their epistemic significance.

To see why one might propose to treat testimony and its properties (including its reliability properties) in this way, we do well to review why it is natural to treat *non-testimonial* Gettier cases in this way. Why are the familiar examples of Gettier-type luck—stopped clock cases, Gettier's own case of NoGot and Havit, and so forth—standardly taken to show something about knowledge *and knowledge alone*? Although the standard treatment is perhaps not as clearly articulated and defended as one might like, something like the following picture appears to be in play.

Knowledge requires compliance with the relevant portion of the world: assessing whether a belief amounts to knowledge involves assessing whether the truth of the belief is a matter of luck (given how or on what basis the belief was formed). But doxastic justification is primarily a matter of how or on what basis the belief was formed, and in assessing this we can bracket the highly contingent antics of the "external" world: these antics are irrelevant to how or on what basis the belief was formed.[2]

To be clear, this picture does *not* tell us that, for purposes of assessing a belief's doxastic justification, we can bracket the "external" world

---

[2] To say that we can ignore such features is compatible with saying that we cannot ignore *other* "external" features of the environment, such as those invariant, or in any case more or less enduring, features of our environment—e.g., those features that ensure that our perceptual processes regularly deliver true representations of our surroundings. (One thinks here of the various assumptions about object permanence, the rigidity of object boundaries, illumination from above, etc., that might well be hard-wired into our perceptual system.)

entirely. What the standard treatment of Gettier cases assumes, rather, is that, for the purpose of assessing the doxastic justification of a belief, we can ignore those *highly contingent* features of our *local* environment: the proper functioning of a clock, the actual distribution of Fords among members of the office, the prevalence of fake barns in the local vicinity, and so forth.[3] The idea is that these features are irrelevant to an assessment of the goodness of the subject's grounds, or her belief-forming process, or what-have-you—irrelevant, that is, to the materials that make for doxastic justification.

What I am calling the "traditional" conception of testimony's epistemic significance would treat the reliability-making features of particular testimonies in precisely the same way. That is, the *de facto* reliability of a piece of testimony—whether it is *actually* reliable—is to be regarded as a candidate Gettier condition. It is something that can defeat a subject's claim to know, but it leaves considerations regarding doxastic justification untouched. To be sure, a testimonial belief formed through accepting unreliable testimony can fail to be doxastically justified, as, for example, when the hearer was not sufficiently sensitive to signs of mendacity or incompetence in the speaker. The point is merely that, in those cases, the testimonial belief's status as unjustified reflects an assessment of goings-on *in the mind/brain of the hearer*—and this assessment ignores the *de facto* unreliability of the testimony itself.

To those who think about testimony and its features (including its reliability features) in this way, the analogy between unreliable testimony and a stopped clock remains an excellent one: a testimony's *de facto* reliability, like a clock's *de facto* reliability, are features of the scenario that are relevantly "external" to the way or the grounds on which the belief was formed. It is for this reason that the *de facto* reliability of testimony, like the *de*

---

[3] There is some debate whether fake barn cases ought to be seen as Gettier cases. I return to discuss this issue at greater length in Chapter 4.

facto proper functioning of a clock, can be safely ignored when it comes time to assessing the doxastic justification of beliefs formed through accepting that testimony. This is according to what I am calling the traditional conception of testimony's epistemic significance.

As I say, I think that this conception is broadly popular: it is endorsed by epistemologists of all stripes, no matter what their background ideology is regarding the nature of doxastic justification. To those epistemologists who endorse this conception, ERTK is a humdrum claim that illustrates a familiar point about external factors playing the role of Gettier conditions.

2

How should one think of these matters if one is a Process Reliabilist? I suspect that, like epistemologists generally, most Process Reliabilists will find themselves attracted to the traditional conception of testimony's epistemic significance, and so will regard ERTK in the manner described above. In this section I explain why. To anticipate: it turns out that there is a traditional assumption that Process Reliabilists make, which, once made, renders the traditional conception (and its understanding of ERTK) all but mandatory.

The assumption in question was announced, without much fanfare, in Goldman's (1979) paper "What is Justified Belief?"[4] The key passage is one in which Goldman introduced his pre-theoretical understanding of justified belief. He wrote:

A justified belief is, roughly speaking, one that results from cognitive operations that are, generally speaking, good or successful. But *"cognitive"* operations are most plausibly construed as operations of the cognitive faculties, i.e., "information-processing" equipment *internal to the organism*. (Goldman 1979/2000: 346−7; second italics added)

---

[4] This paper presented one of the seminal arguments for a Process Reliabilist theory of doxastic justification. I will discuss that argument at length in Chapter 4.

For present purposes, it is the second sentence that is the crucial one. In it, Goldman is giving voice to a view that I will label Process Individualism:

> PI   For every subject S, all of the cognitive processes implicated in the formation or sustainment of S's beliefs are cognitive processes that take place within S's own mind/brain.

The doctrine of Process Individualism (PI) embodies the claim that a subject's belief-forming and belief-sustaining processes all take place within her own head; they never extend beyond the boundaries of her head.

It is easy to appreciate why those Process Reliabilists who endorse PI have a strong motive to embrace the traditional conception of the epistemic significance of testimony. In Chapter 1, I argued that the reliability of a piece of testimony is a matter of the reliability of the cognitive processes through which the testimony was produced. These processes take place in the mind/brain of the source speaker, and so are "external" to the 'information-processing equipment' of the hearer. The result is that, by the lights of PI, they are 'external' to the cognitive processes through which the testimonial belief is produced. But, according to Process Reliabilism, doxastic justification is a matter of the reliability of the cognitive processes that are responsible for the production of the belief. It follows that facts about the reliability of testimony, including facts about the reliability of the processes that produced the testimony, are irrelevant to the doxastic justification of the resulting testimonial belief. And herein lies the pressure on the Orthodox Reliabilists to embrace the traditional conception of testimony's epistemic significance: insofar as the Orthodox Reliabilist admits that facts about a testimony's reliability have *some* epistemic significance—and surely this much must be admitted—she must regard that significance as restricted to be that of a feature of the subject's local environment. This is precisely as the traditional conception would have it.

It should be clear, then, that the Process Reliabilist's move to endorse Orthodoxy is a significant one. For what we have just seen is that the reliabilist who endorses PI in effect restricts the epistemic significance she can ascribe to facts regarding the *de facto* reliability of testimony. It is worth underscoring that the Process Reliabilist is by no means *forced* to take on this restrictive view. To see this, suppose that we endorse the point behind Goldman's remark that "A justified belief is, roughly speaking, one that results from cognitive operations that are, generally speaking, good or successful." Even so, we might go on to think that, at least in *testimony* cases, the relevant cognitive operations are *distributed*: while some of those processes take place in the mind/brain of the subject who forms the testimonial belief (i.e., in her comprehension and endorsement of the testimony), some of those processes do not. In particular, there are cognitive processes that take place *in the mind/brain of the speaker* (i.e., in the production of the testimony that was consumed) that are also relevant. A Process Reliabilist who approaches things this way will reject the analogy with the stopped clock case, for the simple reason that the processes involved in the proper functioning of a clock are not themselves cognitive processes. Such a position may or may not be an attractive one; my present point is merely that such a position is *available* to Process Reliabilists. Nothing in the Process Reliabilist position per se forecloses on this option.

Nevertheless, it is clear from Goldman's characterization of the relevant cognitive operations, as " 'information-process equipment' *internal to the organism*," that he himself would reject this option out of hand. What is more, he does so for reasons that are highly programmatic in nature: they reflect views regarding how we ought to think about the processes that are relevant to epistemic assessment. To get a better appreciation for Goldman's reasons on this score, we should expand our focus a bit, and consider the extended passage from which the above quote is taken. In this passage, Goldman is offering what to my mind is the first statement and defense of an individualistic conception of belief-forming processes ever offered by a reliabilist:

Clearly, the causal ancestry of beliefs often includes events *outside the organism*. Are such events to be included among the "inputs" of belief-forming processes? Or should we restrict the extent of belief-forming processes to "*cognitive*" events, i.e., events *within the organism's nervous system*? I shall choose the latter course, though with some hesitation. My general grounds for this decision are roughly as follows. Justifiedness seems to be a function of how a cognizer deals with his environmental input, i.e., with the goodness or badness of the operations that register and transform the stimulation that reaches him. . . . A justified belief is, roughly speaking, one that results from cognitive operations that are, generally speaking, good or successful. But "*cognitive*" operations are most plausibly construed as operations of the cognitive faculties, i.e., "information-processing" equipment *internal* to the organism. (Goldman 1979/2000: 346–7; second italics added)[5]

Here it appears that Goldman's commitment to Process Individualism derives from his more general commitment to excluding *any* causal process that takes place "outside the organism," where this is understood to be any process that is not "within the organism's nervous system." Although matters are not entirely clear, Goldman appears to endorse this restricted focus on the grounds of a programmatic conception of justification, on which "Justifiedness seems to be a function of how a cognizer deals with his environmental input, i.e., with the goodness or badness of the operations that register and transform the stimulation that reaches him."[6]

---

[5] Goldman's use of 'internal' here is unfortunate, since it is not meant in the sense in which people speak of 'internalist' positions in epistemology these days. But his idea is clear enough.

[6] I note in passing the point I made above: in testimony cases, at least, Goldman's programmatic point here is in some tension with his point that "A justified belief is, roughly speaking, one that results from cognitive operations that are, generally speaking, good or successful." After all, in testimony cases one might well regard the cognitive processes that produced the testimony to be among those whose "goodness" ought to be assessed in assessing the goodness of the cognitive processes that produced the testimonial belief. I will return to this point in Chapters 3 and 4, where I will be arguing that Goldman's delimiting

It is worth noting that in the (1979) quote just cited, Goldman endorses PI "with some hesitation." By the time of his ground-breaking (1986), however, Goldman is no longer hesitant in his commitment. Setting up his response to the generality problem, Goldman asks: "But how is it determined, in each specific case, which process type is critical?" His response to this question is instructive:

One thing we do not want to do is invoke factors *external to the cognizer's psychology*. The sorts of processes we're discussing are *purely internal processes*.   (1986: 51; italics added)

Here Goldman's reasoning appears to be that belief-forming processes are to be individuated "internally" (I would say 'individualistically') because (i) they are psychological processes that (ii) are causally operative in producing the belief token.

Goldman is not unique among prominent epistemologists who endorse Process Individualism on broadly programmatic grounds. Another epistemologist to follow Goldman in this regard is William Alston. Speaking of the extended quote from Goldman (1979) cited above, Alston (1995) wrote:

This seems to me just the right thing for a reliabilist to say on this point. If the epistemic status of a belief is a function of the reliability of the process that generates the belief, it is the reliability of the *psychological* process that is crucial.   (1995/2000, 360; italics in original)

And, in a paper in which he is addressing himself to the relevance of "the social" to assessments of reliability, Alston reiterates that:

So long as we are describing and analyzing doxastic mechanisms *we are confined to individual psychology*; we are studying *the internal cognitive structure and processes of individual human beings*. (Alston 1994: 30; italics added)[7]

of the 'cognitive' domain as that domain 'within the organism's nervous system' begs an important question in the current discussion.

  [7] It is noteworthy that Alston's actual quote here is susceptible to two very different readings. On one reading, the claim that "we are confined to individual psychology" amounts to the claim that every belief-forming process is a process the entirety of which

Alston's insistence on PI is all the more striking given that he goes on to acknowledge the "essentially social processes" (48) involved in the sort of cooperative inquiry and transmission of information found in, for example, the scientific enterprise (1994: 45).[8] This gives us a clear indication that Alston, like Goldman, endorses PI on the grounds that belief-forming processes are psychological processes, and that psychological processes are processes that do not extend beyond the (physical) boundaries of individual subjects.

The position being articulated in the quotes by Goldman and Alston advocates a combination of Process Reliabilism and Process Individualism. Although few other Process Reliabilists are as explicit as Goldman and Alston have been with respect to PI, I suspect that the reasons Goldman and Alston have offered are widely endorsed, and that this combination of Process Reliabilism and Process Individualism is widely taken to be "the" Process Reliabilist position. It is for this reason that I use the label "Orthodox Reliabilism" to designate any Process Reliabilist position that endorses PI.

We can now return to the main issue before us, namely, how those Process Reliabilists who are Orthodox Reliabilists will react to ERTK. I submit that such reliabilists will view ERTK in the manner described above, as a special case of the general point that external "local" features of one's environment can be relevant to ascriptions of knowledge, in the manner of a Gettier

takes place *in a single individual subject's mind/brain*. On the other reading, it amounts to the claim that only that which is part of the psychology *of some individual or other* can be part of the reliabilist assessment of a belief-forming process. As I will go on to argue below, the latter reading is compatible with the thesis for which I will be arguing in the latter half of this chapter, and then throughout Chapters 3–5. But it is clear from the context that Alston has the former, stronger, reading in mind.

[8] It is also noteworthy that Alston's 1994 defense of the epistemic relevance of "the social" aims to establish the relevance of social considerations to the case for thinking that *sense perception* is reliable. It is no part of his argument that social considerations themselves are relevant to the reliability of some of our belief-forming and -sustaining processes (except insofar as the reliability of social processes itself is assumed by the case for thinking that sense perception is reliable).

condition. In effect, the commitment to PI *forces* the Orthodox Reliabilist's hand on the matter: she has no choice but to endorse the traditional conception of testimony's epistemic significance. The claim I want to bring out on this score is that, by the lights of Orthodox Reliabilism, two testimony cases that differ only in the *de facto* reliability of the testimony each hearer consumed will be regarded by the Orthodox Reliabilist as exhibiting a merely local environmental difference. To establish this, take any case in which a subject forms a testimonial belief through having accepted a particular piece of testimony. Now construct a variant case involving a hearer who is an intrinsic duplicate of the hearer in the original case, but where the testimony in play, though subjectively indistinguishable to the hearer, differs in its *de facto* reliability from the reliability of the testimony in the original case. We will imagine that this difference in testimonial reliability is the *only* difference between the two cases: in all other respects they are relevantly alike. In particular, the two hearers reside in the same community, and so encounter roughly the same proportion of reliable testimonies, employ the same processes for discerning reliable testimony, and so forth. Then we can say the following: whatever epistemic difference there is between the hearers' testimonial beliefs in such cases cannot be traced to a difference in the doxastic justification of these beliefs. This is because, by hypothesis, the hearers are doppelgängers, and so they employ the same belief-forming process-type; and they live in the same community, and so are in scenarios that share the relevant "background conditions." Process Reliabilism thus requires that they be treated as alike, justification-wise. Given this, it would seem that the *only* relevant difference that can be acknowledged, once one has assumed both Process Reliabilism and Process Individualism, is a relevant difference in the subjects' respective *local* environments. The clearest illustration of this is in a case like that of H and H* from Chapter 1, where one subject knows, and the other doesn't, merely in virtue of differences in the *de facto* reliability of the testimonies each consumed. But the point in question is perfectly general: the Orthodox Reliabilist must regard *any* two cases that differ merely in the *de facto* reliability of the testimonies consumed as differing merely with respect to features of the relevant local environments. This is the basis for my contention that Orthodox Reliabilists must view the epistemic effects of (apparently reliable but actually) unreliable testimony as a special case of the knowledge-undermining effects of "local environmental" factors.

3

I doubt whether any of this will come as a surprise to Process Reliabilists. On the contrary, I suspect that those Process Reliabilists who embrace Orthodoxy will be happy to endorse the idea that a testimony's *de facto* reliability is to be regarded as a feature of the hearer's local environment. In this final section, I want to acknowledge that the resulting Orthodox Reliabilist position is not without its virtues. In particular, the resulting position can exploit the distinction between *local* and *global* reliability, to good effect.

It is easy to appreciate why an Orthodox Reliabilist should want to exploit this distinction. Return to the case of Wilma in GOOD and in BAD from Chapter 1. In both, she accepts testimony from Fred, under conditions in which the testimonies appear exactly the same to her, where the cognitive processes that take place in her mind/brain in the two cases are type-identical. The only difference between the cases resides in the testimonies: Fred's testimony in GOOD was knowledgeable, his testimony in BAD was not (and so was true only as a matter of accident). Regarding cases like these, I submit that all reliabilists—stronger, *all epistemologists*, regardless of their favored theory of knowledge—should want to acknowledge the following point:

(*)   From the point of view of their reliability profiles, Wilma's testimonial belief in BAD compares unfavorably to her testimonial belief in GOOD.

As I say, (*) is a claim that reliabilists of any stripe should want to acknowledge.[9] After all, it is natural to think that unreliability in testimony has *some* effect on the reliability of beliefs formed through accepting that testimony: surely there is *some* sense in which a testimonial belief formed through the acceptance of unreliable testimony should be seen as unreliable, or in any case as less reliable than a corresponding belief formed through the acceptance of a reliable piece of testimony. This is so even if the unreliable testimony had all of the trappings of reliability, and even if the hearer is a cognitively mature consumer of testimony who was epistemically responsible in her acceptance of the testimony in question. It is for this reason that the Orthodox Reliabilist should take an interest in the distinction between local and global reliability: this distinction provides her with precisely what she needs in order to accommodate (*), and (more generally) to represent the effect that unreliable testimony has on the reliability of testimonial belief. After introducing this distinction and characterizing the role that it plays in reliabilist epistemology generally, I will be arguing that it is *only* by endorsing something like this distinction that the Orthodox Reliablist can capture any sense in which unreliable testimony affects the reliability profile of beliefs based on that testimony.

First, some background on the distinction between local and global reliability. The distinction itself was introduced for reasons having nothing to with the testimony cases. Following Goldman's seminal work in epistemology in the 1970s and 1980s,[10] Process Reliabilists were quick to acknowledge that local environmental factors can conspire to render an otherwise reliable belief-forming process less reliable *in a particular context*. The subject in Fake Barn County is perhaps the paradigmatic example of this phenomenon.

---

[9] The idea is that acknowledging (*) is a *desideratum* on any reliabilist account of the epistemology of testimonial belief: a reliabilist account that fails to be able to acknowledge (*) may not be doomed, but such an account would have a strike against it.

[10] Goldman (1976, 1979, 1986). See also McGinn (1984); and, for a more recent version of the distinction between local and global reliability, see Henderson and Horgan (2006 and 2007).

As an ordinary subject who has been exposed to a wide variety of barns and who can recognize them by their visual appearances, such a subject can be said to possess a highly reliable perceptual process of barn-recognition. But this process will be much less reliable when she is traveling through the countryside of Fake Barn County, where virtually every barn-looking structure is a mere facade, a well-constructed "fake barn." In cases like this, a process-type that in more ordinary circumstances is highly reliable would yield a much higher proportion of false belief in local circumstances.

The distinction between global and local reliability was introduced to enable the Process Reliabilist to represent cases like this. The claim is that the mature subject's barn-beliefs in Fake Barn County is formed through a process-type—forming barn-beliefs on the basis of barn-like visual appearances—that is globally reliable but (when employed in Fake Barn County) locally unreliable. The *global* reliability of a process-type is a matter of the preponderance of true belief produced by this process-type across the actual range of situations in which tokens of that process-type are ordinarily used; whereas the *local* reliability of a process-type is a matter of the preponderance of true belief produced by this process-type in environments relevantly like the present one.[11] Beliefs formed in Fake Barn County are globally reliable, since they are formed through a process that would produce a preponderance of true beliefs *in normal contexts*; yet these beliefs are locally *un*reliable since the process in question would not produce a preponderance of true beliefs *in contexts relevantly like the present one*.

Here, then, we have one advantage that accrues to any Process Reliabilist who employs the distinction between global and local reliability: she can handle a certain range of problem cases in a natural way. But there is a second advantage that accrues to the Process Reliabilist who exploits the distinction between global and local reliability, which is that it provides her with a way

---

[11] As noted in Chapter 1, this way of characterizing the difference between local and global reliability has much in common with Henderson and Horgan (2006 and 2007).

to understand epistemic (doxastic) justification in reliabilist terms. Once again, the intuitive point can be made in connection with fake barn cases. The prevalence (or not) of fake barns in the local landscape of an unsuspecting subject does not seem, intuitively, to bear on whether her barn-belief, formed on the basis of the perceptual experience as of a barn, was justified. In particular, facts about the prevalence of fakes in the vicinity are "external" to the considerations pertaining to the process through which the subject's barn-belief was formed, and so are irrelevant to doxastic justification as the Process Reliabilist conceives of this. At the same time, the prevalence of fakes *does* seem to bear on whether this subject's barn-belief counts as knowledge, since it bears on the issue of how lucky it was that the subject's belief was true, given that she formed it as she did (through the process-type in question). This motivates the addition of a 'local reliability' condition on knowledge: if a belief is to amount to knowledge, then in addition to being true and formed and sustained through a globally reliable process, the belief must also be locally reliable—formed and sustained through a process-type that would produce a preponderance of truth in situations relevantly like the one in which the belief was formed.[12]

Return now to how this distinction might be exploited by the Orthodox Reliabilist in her account of the epistemology of testimony. We already saw in Section 2 that, having embraced PI, the Orthodox Reliabilist is forced to endorse the traditional conception of testimony's epistemic significance, and so is forced to regard the reliability of a piece of testimony as a feature of the hearer's local environment. For this reason, the Orthodox Reliabilist cannot regard unreliable testimony as such to have any effect on the sort of reliability that makes for a doxastically justified testimonial belief. Still, it would seem that a testimonial belief formed through accepting unreliable testimony is less well-off, reliabilistically speaking,

---

[12] One interesting issue regards the relation between the local reliability requirement on knowledge, and the anti-Gettier condition on knowledge: does the satisfaction of the former ensure the satisfaction of the latter? I think not, but I do not pursue the matter further here (although it comes up again, briefly, in Chapter 4).

than is the testimonial belief of a doppelgänger which is formed through accepting reliable testimony. ((*) is a special case of this claim.) If the Orthodox Reliabilist wants to acknowledge this, as I said she should, she must distinguish the sort of reliability that makes for the doxastic justification of testimonial belief, from the sort of reliability on which unreliable testimony can affect the reliability of the corresponding testimonial belief. The distinction between local and global reliability recommends itself for precisely this reason: the Orthodox Reliabilist can say that the reliability of testimony is relevant to the *local* reliability, but not to the global reliability, of the resulting testimonial belief.[13] Seen from this perspective, the case of the hearer who accepts true, apparently reliable but actually unreliable testimony is a testimonial version of that familiar phenomenon whereby a globally reliable process yields a true belief which nevertheless fails to amount to knowledge owing to local conditions. A verdict of 'globally reliable but locally unreliable' can seem as apt here, as it is in the case of the unsuspecting subject in Fake Barn County, and as it is in the 'stopped clock' case.

I have little doubt but that this is the standard way to think about the relevance of a testimony's reliability to the reliability of those beliefs that are formed through accepting that testimony. At the same time, I believe that this standard view is the expression of a fundamentally flawed conception of the epistemic significance of testimony. Since this standard view derives from the particular hold that Process Individualism has on our epistemological imagination, it will take some work to dislodge this view. In the two chapters to follow, I attempt just this.

4

In this chapter I have argued that the Orthodox Reliabilist is committed to a very traditional conception of testimony's epistemic

---

[13] Some Orthodox Reliabilists may endorse this because they think that unreliability in testimony has *no* effect on the reliability profile of the testimonial belief.

significance, and that as a result she is committed to the Local Reliability Hypothesis:

> LRH A testimony's degree of reliability affects the *local* reliability, not the global reliability, of the belief formed through accepting that testimony.

This picture is not without its virtues. In particular, the Orthodox Reliabilist can regard ERTK, in the manner suggested by the traditional conception, as a special case of a point about the role of local factors in ascriptions of knowledge; and the Orthodox Reliabilist can use LRH to identify the sense in which a testimonial belief formed through the acceptance of an unreliable piece of testimony is unreliable, while preserving the idea that the facts that determine the reliability of the testimony are "external to," and so (by the lights of Process Individualism) are no part of, the cognitive processing that produced the testimonial belief itself. It is in this way, I suggested, that LRH can be seen to manifest the Orthodox Reliabilist's commitment to the traditional conception of testimony's epistemological significance.

The time has now come for me to begin to push back against the traditional conception. To do so, I will be taking aim at the idea that testimony and its reliability properties are epistemically relevant *only* as a potential Gettier condition. While LRH gives expression to the Orthodox Reliabilist's version of this idea, my claim will be that LRH does not square with the nature of our epistemic reliance in testimony cases. In Chapter 3, I will argue for this on the grounds that testimonial belief-formation is best seen as a belief-dependent process, where testimony is the input into this process. As we will see, the reliability verdicts sanctioned by such a view are different from those required by LRH.

3

Process and Environment in Testimonial Belief-Formation

In Chapter 1, I argued that a hearer's acquisition of testimonial knowledge depends on the reliability of the cognitive processing implicated in the production of the testimony. In Chapter 2, I argued that this conclusion should be uncontroversial even to those Process Reliabilists—"Orthodox" Reliabilists—who are individualists about the extent of belief-forming processes. Such reliabilists will regard testimony and its properties, including its reliability properties, as features of the hearer's local environment: such features can play the role of Gettier conditions, and so can defeat a subject's claim to knowledge, but this exhausts their epistemic significance. This conception of testimony's epistemic significance is a very traditional one, and is endorsed by epistemologists of all stripes. However, in the hands of the Orthodox Reliabilist, it takes the particular form of the Local Reliability Hypothesis (LRH), according to which the reliability of a piece of testimony can affect the *local* reliability, but not the global reliability, of beliefs based on an acceptance of that testimony.

Where Chapter 2 merely aimed to develop the Orthodox Reliabilist's commitment to the traditional conception and to LRH, in this and the following chapter I argue that this commitment is costly, as it entails an implausible account of our epistemic reliance on others in testimony cases. In this chapter, my contention is that the traditional conception itself does not square with what I will be arguing is *the belief-dependent nature* of testimonial belief-formation. More concretely, I argue that the phenomenon of belief-dependence suggests that our epistemic reliance in testimony cases is more profound than the traditional conception allows.

If my contention is correct, Process Reliabilists are well advised to repudiate Process Individualism. After all, I argued in Chapter 2 that it is the commitment to Process Individualism that forces the Process Reliabilist to endorse both the traditional conception and LRH. Freed from any such commitment, the Process Reliabilist can see the cognitive processes implicated in the speaker's production of the testimony, not as aspects of the hearer's "merely local" environment, but rather as part of the very testimonial belief-forming process itself. (In Chapter 4, I argue that Reliabilists have independent reasons to favor such an account.)

I

Forming a belief that Jane has the measles through accepting what she told you is quite different, epistemically speaking, from forming this belief through having observed the measles-like rash on her skin. One difference is obvious: in the former case you are relying on the reliability of Jane's testimony, and so—for this very reason—on the reliability of the cognitive processes implicated in the production of that testimony. In Chapter 2, I argued that Orthodox Reliabilists need not deny this. On the contrary, they can and should accept the claim that testimonial belief-formation involves a hearer's reliance on the reliability of the processes implicated in the production of the testimony. Orthodox Reliabilists *should* accept this claim, since the claim itself would appear to be uncontroversial, and the case for it—at least as formulated as ERTK, a thesis regarding testimonial knowledge—is solid. And Orthodox Reliabilists *can* accept this claim, first, because the claim itself is compatible with the Orthodox Reliabilist's commitment to individualism about belief-forming processes (PI), and, second, because assimilating ERTK would appear to involve nothing more than regarding it as an instance of a familiar and more general claim having to do with the role of local environmental features in ascriptions of knowledge. The resulting picture, I noted, is in keeping with a very traditional conception of testimony's epistemic significance.

In this chapter, I take issue with this whole picture. I will be arguing that the foregoing picture is incompatible with one of the central features of our epistemic reliance on others in testimony cases, having to do with the belief-dependent nature of testimonial belief-formation.[1] Here my central contention will be that testimonial belief-formation is a belief-dependent process whose input is the testimony itself. To establish this will require modifying our understanding of the notion of belief-dependence itself. But if such an understanding can be motivated, the result spells doom for the traditional conception of testimony's epistemic significance—and so spells doom for Orthodox Reliabilism, whose embrace of ERTK depends on that conception. For, in that case, the cognitive process-type implicated in the production of the testimony would be best seen, not as a feature of the hearer's local environment, but rather as *part of the very cognitive process by which that testimonial belief was formed*. This "extendedness hypothesis," as I will call it, is the most far-reaching aspect of our epistemic reliance on others.

Since what I aim to challenge in this chapter is the traditional conception of testimony's epistemic significance, and since I suspect that this conception is deeply ingrained in our epistemological imagination, it is helpful to begin, schematically, by reviewing why a Process Reliabilist might be attracted to the traditional conception, followed by a programmatic statement of an alternative conception. (In the sections following, I will begin my argument in defense of the alternative. It is there that I will be developing

---

[1] As I will go on to explain, I borrow the notion of a 'belief-dependent' process from Goldman (1986).

the claim that testimonial belief-formation is a belief-dependent process.)

At the risk of some repetitiveness, I begin by repeating the passage from Goldman (1979) in which he is setting out (albeit somewhat tentatively) his conception of doxastic justification; it is here that we can appreciate the nature of his commitment both to Process Individualism and to the traditional conception of testimony's epistemic significance. He wrote:

> Justifiedness seems to be a function of how a cognizer deals with his environmental input, i.e., with the goodness or badness of the operations that register and transform the stimulation that reaches him. . . . A justified belief is, roughly speaking, one that results from cognitive operations that are, generally speaking, good or successful. But *"cognitive"* operations are most plausibly construed as operations of the cognitive faculties, i.e., "information-processing" equipment *internal* to the organism. (Goldman 1979/2000: 346–7; second italics added)

As I see matters, Goldman's point in introducing his conception of doxastic justification is to motivate Orthodox Reliabilism.[2] Although I will be examining the details of this argument in Chapter 4, the basic thrust of the argument is clear. Goldman's claim that the theory of justification ought to be looking at the goodness or badness of the cognitive processes that result in belief is meant to motivate a Process Reliabilist approach to doxastic justification; and his claim that the cognitive processes in question are *"internal* to the organism" is meant to motivate an additional commitment to Process Individualism. The result is Orthodoxy.

The phenomenon of testimonial belief introduces a complication into the story—one that apparently was not anticipated by Goldman. In the quote above, Goldman makes two closely related, but not identical, claims: that the theory of justification is interested in assessing "the goodness or badness of the operations that register

---

[2] In Goldman (1979) the view he is defending is one he called "Historical Reliabilism." Historical Reliabilism is the ancestor of the view he later called "Process Reliabilism." But the quote cited above makes clear that, from the very start, Goldman thought of Historical or Process Reliabilism in Orthodox terms, as committed to Process Individualism.

and transform the stimulation that reaches" the "cognizer"; and that justified belief is a matter of the belief being "one that results from cognitive operations that are, generally speaking, good or successful." The difference between these two claims can seem negligible. But the phenomenon of testimonial belief suggests that, on the contrary, these two claims might actually be in some tension with each other. The source of the tension lies in the fact that, where the first claim restricts the relevant cognitive operations to those that "register and transform *the stimulation that reaches [the cognizer]*" (my italics), the second claim introduces no such restriction. In cases not involving testimony—or, more generally, in cases not involving any sort of epistemic reliance on other cognizers—these two claims come to the same thing. After all, if we are interested in the goodness of the cognitive processing that results in belief, it would seem obvious that in cases not involving other cognizers the only relevant cognitive processing is that of the believing subject herself. However, once *other people* enter into the picture, and some of the subject's beliefs are formed in ways that implicate cognitive processes that take place in *their* mind/brains, matters get complicated. For we might then ask what justifies the restriction on the relevant cognitive processes, to include only those that "register and transform *the stimulation that reaches [the cognizer]*." Such an individualistic restriction would appear to stand in need of some justification.

We can bring out the force of this call for justification as follows. Given ERTK, cases of testimonial belief are cases in which there are epistemically relevant cognitive processes *beyond* those that take place in the mind/brain of the believing subject. In particular, there are those cognitive processes that take place *further upstream*, in connection with the production of the testimony. In light of this, it would appear to be a substantial claim to say that the theory of justification should focus exclusively on those cognitive processes that operate on *the stimulation that reaches the cognizer*. Why not think that the upstream cognitive processes are *also* relevant? Such a view, after all, would still be in keeping with the spirit of the view that "A justified belief is, roughly speaking, one that results from cognitive operations that are, generally speaking, good or successful." In short, once we have accepted ERTK, and so have accepted that the Process Reliabilist will need to assess the goodness of cognitive processing implicated in the production of the testimony, it is no longer obvious that, when it comes to a Process Reliabilist assessment *of doxastic justification*, the Process Reliabilist is entitled to ignore the goodness or badness of that "upstream" cognitive processing. An argument needs to be made on this score.

Of course, it is at precisely this point that the Orthodox Reliabilist will insist on the traditional conception of testimony's epistemic significance. The very point of this insistence is to support the claim that facts about testimony and its reliability are facts about the hearer's merely local environment. These facts, like facts regarding the functioning of a relied-upon clock, can defeat a subject's claim to know; but that exhausts their epistemic significance. In particular, they have no relevance to the doxastic justification of the subject's belief.

Or so one will think if one accepts the traditional conception of testimony's epistemic significance. In response, I merely note that this conception is not mandatory. On the contrary, one might reason, in a way that was anticipated in passing in Chapter 2, as follows. Start with the Process Reliabilist's core idea, that assessments of doxastic justification are assessments of the "goodness" of the cognitive processes which result in the formation of a belief; add to this the claim that in cases of testimonial belief-formation these processes include (not only those that take place in the hearer's mind/brain but also) those processes implicated in the production of the observed testimony; and, on this basis, *reject* the idea that the relevant cognitive processes are restricted to those "internal to" the hearer-subject herself. On such a view, our epistemic reliance in testimony cases runs much deeper than the traditional conception allows. In particular, facts about the reliability of a piece of testimony are not to be regarded as facts about the hearer's merely local environment, but instead are to be treated as facts pertaining to *the very process through which the testimonial belief was formed.*

What we have here, then, is a clash of two views regarding the extent of the processes relevant to belief-formation, reflecting two distinct conceptions of testimony's epistemic significance. Both views endorse what above I called the "core idea" of Process Reliabilism: they agree that the assessment of a belief's doxastic justification (whether the belief is testimonial or otherwise) ought to focus on the goodness of the *cognitive* part of the causal transaction between mind and world. Their disagreement is over the *extent* of the cognitive processes that are to be regarded as "the process of belief-formation." This disagreement focuses on testimony cases.

One view, which we might label the 'individualistic' view, and which is endorsed by the Orthodox Reliabilist, holds that only what takes place 'within' the mind/brain of the subject in question can count as part of the process of belief-formation, rightly understood. Lying behind this view is a certain assumption about the boundary between the subject and her "external" environment. The assumption is that the boundaries of the subject are at the same time the boundaries of the processes of belief-formation. Thus, while belief-formation involves a causal transaction between the mind and the world, only that part of the causal transaction that takes place "within the subject" can count as part of the process of belief-formation, rightly understood. Applying this to the testimony case, we get the result that cognitive processes that take place in a mind/brain *other than the subject's own*—in particular, those cognitive processes which take place in the subject's interlocutor, in the course of the production of testimony—fall on the wrong side of the divide. These "upstream" processes are definitely cognitive; and it may well be, as ERTK insists, that the believing subject relies on the reliability of these "upstream" processes; but the fact remains that the cognitive processes implicated in the production of a piece of testimony are "external to" the testimonial belief-forming process itself. As such, the epistemic relevance of such processes is limited to that of any other local feature of the subject's environment. This is the ideology lying behind the characteristic commitments of Orthodox Reliabilism: Process Individualism and the traditional conception of testimony's epistemic significance.

Standing opposed to this individualistic view is another one, which we might describe as an 'anti-individualistic' one. (Though incompatible with Process Individualism, and so with *Orthodox* Reliaiblism, this view is perfectly in keeping with Process Reliabilism itself.) The anti-individualistic view holds that, at least in testimony cases, the relevant cognitive processes—those that must be in the focus of an assessment of a testimonial belief's doxastic justification—include not only those that take place in the subject's own mind/brain, but also those "upstream" processes that were implicated in the production of the testimony. A proponent of the anti-individualistic view might say that the crucial dividing line is *not* that between the subject and her "external" environment, but rather that between the *cognitive* part of the mind–world causal transaction, and the non-cognitive, or brutely causal part of that transaction. In cases not involving other cognizers, it is plausible to think that these two dividing lines are in tandem: in such cases, the cognitive part of the mind–world transaction takes place "within" the subject, whereas that part of the mind–world transaction which takes place in the subject's "external" environment is entirely non-cognitive or brutely causal. But in cases involving testimonial belief-formation, these two dividing lines don't line up so nicely (even to a first approximation). In such cases, there is a part of the belief-forming process which is "external" to the believing subject, yet which is cognitive for all that: this is the part involving the cognitive processes implicated in the production of the testimony. On the anti-individualistic view, the testimonial belief-forming process "extends" to include these processes implicated in the production of the testimony.

Now I do not claim (yet!) to have shown that the anti-individualistic view is plausible, still less that it is to be preferred to the individualistic view. My present point is only that it is an option available to Process Reliabilists. The fact that such an option is available is itself significant: it shows that the Orthodox Reliabilist's appeal to the traditional conception of testimony's epistemic significance is not the end of the story. To decide between these two views, what is needed is a deeper reflection on the nature of our epistemic reliance in testimony cases.

2

The quotes by Goldman and Alston (cited above, and in Chapter 2) give several reasons for favoring the individualistic view. Salient among these are considerations pertaining to the causal nature of belief-formation and to individualism about psychological processes. I believe that none of these reasons is decisive, and will argue as much in Chapter 5. (I postpone my discussion until then since I will be relying on materials I will have introduced below, or in Chapter 4.) In what remains of this chapter, however, I want to offer an initial reason to favor the anti-individualistic view. I will be arguing that the anti-individualistic view is to be preferred, on the grounds that testimonial belief-formation is a belief-dependent process whose input is the testimony itself. Before I am in a position to say why the belief-dependent nature of testimonial belief-formation favors the anti-individualistic view, however, I first need to introduce the notion of a belief-dependent process (below), and develop the hypothesis that testimonial belief-formation involves such a process (Section 3). After doing so, I will examine the costs that must be borne by those who would deny this (Section 4).

The distinction between belief-*dependent* and belief-*independent* processes is owed to Goldman.[3] The former are belief-producing processes (like perception) whose inputs are not themselves beliefs. With respect to beliefs formed through such processes, the reliabilist's epistemic assessment turns on nothing beyond the (global,

---

[3] Although the language of 'belief-dependent' and 'belief-independent processes' was first introduced in Goldman (1986), it is clear that he employed the distinction at least as early as his (1979). See Chapter 4 for a discussion.

local, etc.) reliability of the process itself—a rough index on the extent to which the process produces a preponderance of truth in the relevant class of circumstances. Goldman introduced the category of belief-*dependent* processes because he noted that not all beliefs should be assessed merely by assessing the reliability of the processes through which they were formed (or sustained).

The point is perhaps most obvious in the case of (deductive) inferential belief. Take a subject in whom the process of drawing deductive inferences is as good as it can be: the subject accepts as deductively valid only those inferences that are deductively valid. Even so, if in a given case the materials she uses for her premises are beliefs acquired through wishful thinking, her belief in the conclusion of the (deductively valid) inference she accepts, which she formed on the basis of that inference, will not be reliably formed—and this is despite the unmatched excellence of her powers of deductive reasoning. It is with cases of this sort in mind that Goldman proposed that the reliability of beliefs formed though a belief-dependent process—a process that takes as its inputs other beliefs—must be ascertained in a way that reflects the belief-dependent nature of the process. He proposed that the reliability of a belief produced through a belief-dependent process is a matter not only of the *conditional* reliability of the process itself (roughly, how well it does in cases in which its inputs are themselves true beliefs), but also of the reliability of the inputs (as determined by the reliability of the process-type(s) responsible for the production and sustainment of the input-beliefs).

Although it is perhaps not as obvious, a similar point can be made with respect to memorial belief. Suppose that my memory system is very reliable in the following sense: I suffer from neither *forgetfulness*—all previously acquired beliefs can be recalled—nor *memory confabulation*—only previously acquired beliefs are recalled (my memory doesn't just make things up). But suppose as well that I suffer from regular bouts of wishful thinking, so that many of the beliefs I recall are themselves the result of this very unreliable process. In that case, in any situation in which my memory preserves what in fact was a belief acquired through wishful thinking, such a memorial belief should not count as reliable—and this is despite the fact that my memory is "reliable" in the sense just noted. Once again, this result can be accommodated in a natural way in terms of the idea that memory is a belief-dependent process.

Goldman's distinction between belief-dependent and belief-independent processes is a distinction that every Process Reliabilist should (and presumably will) endorse. I want to suggest, however, that the nature and significance of this distinction has not been fully appreciated. As I understand this distinction, it highlights the epistemic significance of a subject's reliance (in belief-fixation or -sustainment) on a representation-deploying information source. To be sure, the cases that Goldman had in mind—inference and memory—are cases in which the representation-deploying information source on whom one is relying is *oneself* (one's "earlier" self). But the significance of the notion of belief-dependent process outstrips these cases. In particular, there is some reason to think that cases of testimonial belief can be seen as an *inter*personal instance of a belief-dependent process.

Return to the processes involved in the cases of inference-based belief and memorial belief. In the case of a valid inference from premises all of which were provided by wishful thinking, all reliabilists should agree that the process of forming a belief in the conclusion of such an inference results in a belief that is unreliably formed. What is more, there should be no temptation to regard this as a case in which the unreliability in belief-formation here is a merely *local* unreliability. Although the point is perhaps obvious, it is worth making it perfectly explicit. The beliefs that provide the content of the premises employed in the course of reasoning do not constitute some sort of local "environmental" condition. Precisely not: those beliefs constitute the input into the process of deductive reasoning, and for this very reason the processes that produced those beliefs count as 'part of' the very process through which the inference-based belief is acquired.

We can put what is essentially the same point in a slightly different way. Insofar as we want to assess the doxastic justification enjoyed by an inference-based belief, such an assessment must include an assessment of the reliability of the processes that produced the beliefs used as inputs. (Call these processes the *relied-upon* processes.) It is worth underscoring that this assessment of the reliability of the relied-upon processes is not aimed at determining the local reliability of the inferential belief. On the contrary, it is an assessment of the sort of reliability that is relevant to the *doxastic justification* enjoyed by the inferential belief. Even by the lights of Orthodox Reliabilism, the reliability in question is the global reliability of the processes involved in belief-formation and belief-sustainment. Since these processes include the relied-upon processes, the relied-upon processes will be seen by the Process Reliabilist as forming a part of the very process by which the inferential belief is currently formed. And the same point can be made in connection with memorial belief. (Goldman himself endorses this picture of belief-dependent processes; see his discussion of the case of inferential belief in Goldman 1979/2000: 348.)

In sum, it is standard for Process Reliabilism to regard both inference-based belief and memory-sustained belief as 'extended' processes, stretching back to include the processes responsible for the production of the input-beliefs. It is true that, in the case of inference-based belief and memorial belief, the sort of temporal 'extension' that is involved does not extend to include processes that took place beyond the boundaries of the subject herself. But there is no reason in principle why the sorts of extensions that reliabilism endorses in cases of epistemic reliance *can't* do so. Testimony is a case in point. Or so one might think, on the strength of the idea that the process of testimonial belief-formation is a belief-dependent process.

3

But is it correct to assume that the process of testimonial belief-formation is a belief-dependent process? There are several issues that must be addressed before we can accept this hypothesis.

3.1

The first is what I will call the 'input problem.'[4] Insofar as we take Goldman's talk of a "belief-dependent process" literally, the claim that testimonial belief-formation is a belief-dependent process requires that we find relevant belief(s) to serve as inputs into this process. Here we seem to have two choices: either these will be beliefs of the hearer (the recipient of testimony), or else they will be beliefs *of the testifier*. Neither answer is very happy.

3.1.1   Consider first the claim that the inputs into the testimonial belief-forming process are beliefs of the hearer, the recipient of the testimony. An immediate strike against this proposal[5] is that it runs afoul of the natural way to describe our epistemic reliance in testimony cases. It is natural to think that in testimonial belief-formation the hearer *takes the speaker's word* for something, he *accepts her testimony*, he forms his belief *on the basis of her say-so*, and so forth. The proposal on the table cannot accept any of these descriptions at face value. For once we hold that the inputs into the testimonial belief-forming process are beliefs *of the hearer*, then we must reject these natural descriptions in favor of something like the following: testimonial belief-formation is a matter of the hearer coming to believe something, on the basis of believing that some speaker said so, where the hearer's belief that some speaker said so was itself caused by something the hearer believed to be a linguistic signal. Such a description is clearly revisionary.

---

[4] I thank an anonymous referee for raising this issue.
[5] I thank Tim Kenyon (private conversation) for suggesting this way of putting the point.

Let us grant (what may not be the case) that the hearer who forms a testimonial belief does have all of these "subsidiary" beliefs. Even so, I submit that an account of testimonial belief which regards these "subsidiary" beliefs as the inputs into the testimonial belief-forming process is revisionary: it does not get to the heart of the epistemic reliance involved in testimonial belief-formation. To get at that we must see the hearer as actually relying *on the saying itself* — he is relying on the speaker's having reliably gotten things right in her testimony.[6] We go some distance towards acknowledging the interpersonal nature of this reliance, of course, when we acknowledge that whether the hearer comes to *know* depends on facts regarding the reliability of the speaker's testimony. But this does not quite go far enough. For it would seem that the relevant sort of epistemic reliance is in play even in cases in which knowledge is not at issue. For example, when scientists rely on each other's testimony on scientific matters, they are relying on the reliability of their peers' statements. This is so even if they are (as many are) reasonably skeptical about the chances for acquiring scientific knowledge. (All they ask for is reliable belief.) Considerations of this sort lead me to think that the claim, that the inputs into the testimonial belief-forming process are beliefs of the hearer herself, is antecedently implausible.

There is a second reason to be dubious of the claim that the input(s) into the testimonial belief-forming process are beliefs of the hearer herself. This reason emerges when we develop the analogy between testimony and memory a bit further. I take it that the following suggestion about memorial belief is unhappy on its face: in memorial belief, the 'inputs' into the memory system are the subject's beliefs (i) that she has an apparent memory as of p, and (ii) that this apparent memory has all of the trappings of a real memory. I take it that to any reliabilist such a view will be unattractive on its face: it delivers the wrong verdict

---

[6] See, e.g., Goldberg (2007a: Chapter 1), where I develop this point at length.

in any case in which the subject has an apparently very good memory that turns out to preserve a belief that was originally formed, for example, through wishful thinking or some other highly unreliable process. When it comes to assessing the reliability of memorial belief, there is a clear rationale to assess the *entire* process stretching all the way back to the original acquisition of the belief in question; we do not want to assess a mere 'truncated' version of this process that begins only at the point at which the subject has a memory impression (Goldman 1979/2000: 348). But the same thing should hold for testimony. Why should a reliabilist assessment of testimonial belief begin only at the point at which a hearer observes the testimony (i.e., has a 'testimony impression'), when we explicitly don't want a reliabilist assessment of memory belief to begin only at the point of the memory impression? Doesn't this 'truncate' the testimonial belief-fixation process here in a way analogous to the way the process is truncated in the unhappy proposal above regarding memory? Aren't we ignoring the "goodness" (or not) of relevant cognitive processes when we restrict our focus to such a 'truncated' process? As evidence, we can note that the present proposal delivers the wrong verdict in any case in which apparently trustworthy testimony turns out to have been unreliable after all.

The analogy with the case of memory suggests that, at least from the perspective of reliabilist assessment, belief-dependent processes ought to be seen as extending to include all of those cognitive processes that are implicated in the production of its current input. Or, to put matters slightly less tendentiously, the reliabilist assessment of beliefs formed through belief-dependent processes φ is a function of the reliabilist assessment of any other processes responsible for producing φ's inputs. In the case of memorial belief, this means those processes implicated in the original acquisition of the belief in question. In the case of testimonial belief, this appears to point to processes implicated in the production of the testimony. Anything that fails to "reach back" that far will yield wrong verdicts in cases in which that part of the process was itself unreliable.

3.1.2 I just argued that the hearer's *own* beliefs will not do as the inputs into the testimonial belief-forming process; I now want to argue that beliefs *of the testifier* can't serve in this role either. There are at least two reasons for this.

First, there are Lackey cases—those cases (discussed in Lackey 2008 and in Chapter 1) in which the testifier testifies yet fails to have the belief in question. Insofar as these are cases in which the hearer acquires a testimonial belief, these cases undermine the claim that the testifier's belief is the input into the testimonial belief-forming process.

In addition, we typically speak of the ground of testimonial belief as, not the speaker's belief, but rather her *testimony*.[7] To be sure, it may be replied (in the spirit of Owens 2006) that the speaker's testimony is used by the hearer as evidence as to what the speaker believes, in which case we can save the spirit (if not the letter) of the proposal. Still, insofar as there is any input into the process of testimonial belief-formation, strictly speaking it is the speaker's testimony that should be seen as the relevant input. But of course testimony is not belief. This point makes trouble for the claim that the speaker's belief is the input into the testimonial belief-forming process; but it also makes trouble, more generally, for the claim that testimonial belief-formation is a *belief*-dependent process in the first place.

3.2

The foregoing discussion of the 'input problem' leads us to conclude that, insofar as the testimonial belief-forming process has any inputs at all, these inputs are not beliefs at all, but rather are the testimonies that the hearer observes. But in that case it appears we must address another question: in what sense can testimony, which is not a kind of belief, be the input into a *belief*-dependent process? What is needed here is a more liberal understanding of

---

[7] Once again, I thank Tim Kenyon for suggesting the relevance of this point in the present context.

the notion of a belief-dependant process—one that allows, for example, another's testimony to serve as an input.

What would such an understanding involve? Well, the core idea behind a belief-dependent process is that of a process the reliability of whose outputs depends on the reliability of its inputs. This, after all, is the idea behind the GIGO ("Garbage In, Garbage Out") principle that motivates the reliabilist's talk of belief-dependence. This feature (whereby the reliability of the outputs is a function of the reliability of the inputs) is thus the *sine qua non* of any process that is to count as belief-dependent, and so should hold of a process if it is to count as belief-dependent in our more liberal sense.

With this in mind, I propose the following three conditions on any adequate liberalization of our understanding of a belief-dependent process. First, such a process must be a cognitive process the reliability of whose outputs are a function of the reliability of its inputs.[8] This, in turn, requires that the process should have inputs, and that these inputs be assessable in terms of their reliability. And, in order to be strict about what it is for an input to be assessable in terms of its reliability, we will insist that an input satisfies this condition only if it (the input) is itself the output of a cognitive process (process-type) whose reliability can be assessed in *its* turn.

Satisfying these conditions, I submit, amounts to a set of individually necessary and jointly sufficient conditions on a process if it is to count as belief-dependent in our more liberal sense.

These conditions are individually necessary: a process that fails to satisfy any one of them fails to conform to the core idea behind a belief-dependent process. This is obvious in any case in which the reliability of a process's outputs is not a function of the reliability of any of its inputs. But it should also be obvious that a belief-forming process is not belief-dependent in any sense if its "inputs" cannot be assessed for reliability, since in that case the "outputs" of such a process will not be a function of *the reliability* of its inputs. And,

---

[8] Such a function may take more arguments than the reliability of the input, of course. The point I make here is that the reliability of the inputs must be one such argument, where changes in the value that this argument takes can affect the value that the function takes.

insofar as we assume Process Reliabilism, the only items that can be assessed for reliability are those that are themselves the outputs of a cognitive process (process-type) whose reliability determines the reliability of its outputs. (See Chapter 1 for an extended discussion of this point, in connection with testimonial outputs.) Each of these conditions is thus seen to be individually necessary, if a given process is to count as belief-dependent in our more liberal sense.

But these conditions are also jointly sufficient for a process to count as belief-dependent in our more liberal sense. Any cognitive process that satisfies these three conditions will be such that the reliability of its outputs will be a function of the reliability of its inputs, where the reliability of its inputs in turn will be a function of the reliability of the (upstream) cognitive processes responsible for generating those inputs. It is true that a process can satisfy these conditions without having *beliefs* as inputs. Still, the conditions are demanding enough to ensure that any process that satisfies them has *some* reliability-assessable input.

Let us then speak of a process as '*quasi*-belief dependent' when it satisfies these conditions (and so counts as belief-dependent in our more liberal sense). It remains to be seen that the testimonial belief-forming process itself is a quasi-belief-dependent process. This turns on whether the reliability of a testimonial belief is a function of the reliability of the testimony on which it is based, in the way that, for example, the reliability of belief sustained through memory is a function of the reliability of the belief on acquisition. Chapter 4 provides a positive argument on behalf of this claim. In advance of that, however, I want to spend some time raising difficulties for those who would deny the quasi-belief-dependent nature of testimonial belief-formation.

4

In this section I want to examine the costs that must be borne by those who would deny that testimonial belief-formation involves a quasi-belief-dependent process. To deny this is to hold that the (global) reliability of the output of the process of testimonial belief-formation is not dependent on the (global) reliability of any input. Let us describe any process that satisfies this condition as an 'epistemically autonomous' process. I will argue that any view on which testimonial belief-formation is an epistemically autonomous process has unacceptable implications. To this end, I will develop what I regard as the best epistemically autonomous account one might give for the process of testimonial belief-fixation, explore its implications, and then argue that these make the cost of maintaining this account prohibitively high.

The account I will explore is motivated by (psychological and epistemological) similarities between testimonial belief and perceptual belief. Everyone should allow that (in ordinary, everyday cases) both processes are psychologically non-inferential: testimonial belief-formation, like perceptual belief-formation, involves no explicit, conscious drawing of inferences. In addition, there is good reason to think that a reliabilist account will treat both sorts of belief as epistemically non-inferential as well.[9] (By this I mean that a reliabilist assessment of testimonial belief will not regard this as a matter of assessing some inference from, for example, premises asserting that so-and-so said so, and that so-and-so is reliable, etc.) These points, both of which should be accepted by every reliabilist, might tempt one to regard testimonial belief as a species of perceptual belief, and so to regard the process of testimonial belief-fixation as epistemically autonomous. (We might think of the epistemology of testimony as the epistemology of displaced perception, in the spirit of Millikan 1984; see also McDowell 1994/1998.)

How might the reliabilist think of the process of testimonial belief-formation, if she thinks of it as a perceptual (and hence epistemically autonomous) process? The inputs into the process would be certain (acoustic or visual) inputs. These inputs are to be characterized (by the theorist's account of this process) in the manner of any acoustic or visual input: not as utterances or

---

[9] See also Goldberg (2006b) where it is argued that *no* epistemologist (whether reliabilist or not) should regard the epistemology of testimony as inferential.

inscriptions of recognizable sentences, but rather as sounds or marks on a page.[10] An early stage of processing would then involve the transformation of this input into a recognizable form, where it would be represented (by the subject) as a distinctly linguistic signal. This would involve the subject's recovery of the force and propositional content of the observed speech act or inscription, and of any relevant presuppositions or implicatures. A subsequent (or perhaps co-occurring) sort of processing would concern the processes (largely, but perhaps not entirely, subcognitive) involved in credibility monitoring. And in happy cases the upshot of this sequence will be the formation of a belief in (what was represented to be) the content of the say-so.

Now it might be thought that the question of whether the testimonial belief-fixing process is like this is an empirical matter, one that should be decided by the cognitive science of (among other things) language comprehension. And surely no reliabilist should deny that the cognitive science of language comprehension has much to add to our understanding of this process. At the same time, there are some reasons for resisting the claim that the testimonial belief-forming process is an epistemically autonomous one; these can be appreciated in advance of knowing the empirical details.

The main difficulty facing this view is that, in playing up the similarities with perception, the view undermines its ability to acknowledge the important ways in which testimonial belief is more like memorial belief. In fact, there is much to recommend the view that the process of testimonial belief-fixation is the interpersonal analogue of the intrapersonal process of the memorial sustainment of belief. Although this claim will receive

---

[10] The trouble with characterizing the inputs as utterances or inscriptions of recognizable sentences is that, on certain accounts, the existence of an utterance or inscription presupposes the existence of a linguistic subject. For this reason, one might well worry that characterizing the inputs in this fashion would imply that the inputs are something whose status as an input of that sort implies the existence of beliefs, related in a systematic way to the inputs themselves—at which point it is no longer clear whether our account is a belief-independent one.

an extended treatment in Chapter 4, I can give the highlights here. First, both processes aim to be content-preserving, and there are reasons to think that both result in a belief whose epistemic properties depend on the epistemic properties of the 'input.' So, for example, in memory one aims to recall the relevant information (acquired at some earlier time); and a plausible thesis in the epistemology of memory—one to which reliabilists themselves ought to be particularly attracted—is that it is not necessary, in order for one's memory-sustained belief to be doxastically justified, that the subject remember the basis on which she originally formed the belief. Rather, in ordinary cases,[11] it suffices (for the memorial belief to enjoy a reliabilist justification) that the belief was reliable on acquisition, and that one's memory is itself conditionally reliable.[12] The comparison with testimony is obvious. The process here is interpersonal, of course. But otherwise the same general features hold. In forming a testimonial belief one aims to recover the relevant information; and a plausible thesis in the epistemology of testimony is that it is not necessary, in order to for one's testimonial belief to be doxastically justified, that one know the basis on which one's source testified.[13] Rather, in ordinary cases, it suffices (for the testimonial belief to enjoy a reliabilist justification) that the testimony was the result of reliable cognitive processes (operating in one's source), and that the process through which one oneself comprehends the speech act and monitors it for credibility, is itself conditionally reliable. From this perspective it can seem that testimonial belief-fixation is an interpersonal analogue of the intrapersonal case of memorial belief-sustainment.

---

[11] There are extraordinary cases involving wayward causal chains, of course.

[12] But see Chapter 5, Section 1, for a complication.

[13] By "know the basis" here I mean know details about this basis, not just that there is some basis or other. Indeed, if it were necessary, in order for the hearer's testimonial belief to be justified, that the hearer know the basis on which her source originally formed the belief, then it is unclear whether there would ever be a need for testimony in the first place: one's knowledge of the source's grounds would themselves serve to provide support for the belief in question, rendering the testimony itself superfluous.

If this parallel is a good one, we have an argument for repudiating not just the perceptual model of testimonial belief but also the Process Individualism that underwrites that model. The argument here would involve three basic premises: first, the process of testimonial belief-formation (like the process of memorial belief-sustainment) is a quasi-belief-dependent process; second, the testimonies that constitute the inputs into the testimonial belief-forming process are such that their (justification-relevant) reliability depends on processes that took place in the mind/brain of one's interlocutor(s); and, third, a reliabilist assessment of the (justification-relevant) reliability of a belief formed through a quasi-belief-dependent process is a function of the (justification-relevant) reliability of the inputs into this process. From these premises, we could then conclude that a reliabilist assessment of the (justification-relevant) reliability of testimonial beliefs includes a reliabilist assessment of the (justification-relevant) reliability of the processes in the mind/brain of one's interlocutor—those involved in the production of the testimony. If this is so, then it is not the case that a reliabilist assessment of testimonial belief is restricted to assessing " 'information-processing' equipment *internal* to the organism" (Goldman 1979); it is not the case that such assessment focus exclusively on "purely internal processes" which exclude any "factors external to the cognizer's psychology" (Goldman 1986: 51).

To be sure, defending the analogy between memory and testimony requires doing more than I have done here: it remains to be seen what independent considerations can be marshaled on its behalf, and whether the reliability verdicts that the analogy mandates are independently acceptable. I will address these matters in the following chapter. For now, I want merely to characterize the picture we would get if I am correct that the process of testimonial belief-formation is a quasi-belief-dependent one. In that case, we should prefer the anti-individualistic view of this process, described in Section 1, on which the cognitive processes relevant to testimonial belief-formation include the cognitive processes implicated in the production of the testimony. On such a view, these processes are not merely features of the hearer's local environment; they are rather part of the very process by which testimonial beliefs are formed. Some might recoil at this idea of an interpersonally extended belief-forming process. But we have already seen that Process Reliabilists themselves already acknowledge *temporally* 'extended' belief-forming processes: the processes that give rise to memorial and inferential beliefs are already treated in this way. The novelty of testimony cases lies not in the extendedness per se of the process, but rather in the interpersonal nature of that extendedness.

5

Let us now take stock. The main topic of this and the previous chapter has been the relevance of the reliability of a piece of testimony to the reliability of beliefs formed through accepting that testimony. Orthodox Reliabilists—those Process Reliabilists who are individualists about belief-forming processes, and so who hold that all belief-forming processes are processes that take place in the mind/brain of a single subject—have a motive to regard facts about testimonial reliability as at most affecting the *local* reliability of testimonial belief. Although such a view goes hand in hand with a very traditional conception of testimony's epistemic significance, in this chapter I have questioned whether that conception succeeds in capturing the nature of epistemic reliance in testimony cases. My claim here has been that we have some reasons to think that the process of testimonial belief-formation is a (quasi-)belief-dependent one whose input is the testimony itself. If so, the cognitive processes implicated in the production of a piece of testimony are less a part of the hearer's local environment than they are *part of the very process by which testimonial beliefs are formed.*

4

Epistemic Reliance and the Extendedness Hypothesis

Whereas the individualistic orthodoxy within reliabilist epistemology would have us regard testimony and its reliability as merely local features of the subject's environment, such a view (I have been arguing) distorts the sort of epistemic reliance that is involved in testimony cases. My argument on this score has been slowly gravitating toward a radical conclusion: far from being merely local features of the subject's environment, the testimony itself, along with the cognitive processes implicated in the production of that testimony, are more appropriately regarded as *part of the testimonial belief-forming process itself*. Call this the "extendedness hypothesis"; it asserts that testimonial belief-formation is an interpersonally extended process.

In the previous chapter, I laid the groundwork for the extendedness hypothesis. I did so by presenting an initial case for thinking that testimonial belief-fixation is a belief-dependent process, where the "inputs" into this process are the testimonies themselves. If this line of reasoning is correct, then we would expect that a testimony's reliability has a more direct bearing on the reliability, and so the epistemic status, of the subsequent testimonial belief, than what Orthodox Reliabilism allows. In particular, we would expect that a testimony's degree of reliability can affect not just the testimonial belief's status as *knowledge*, but also its status as *doxastically justified*.

The present chapter aims to show that what we would expect is plausible on independent grounds.

My main contention here is that the extendedness hypothesis itself is a special case of a more general point which Process Reliabilists already endorse (for good reasons). The more general point concerns the nature of epistemic reliance, and the connection between epistemic reliance and doxastic justification. In developing this line of argument, I will have occasion to develop the parallel between memory and testimony further, beyond where I left it in Chapter 3. If my present argument is sound, then (not just the knowledgeableness but also) the doxastic justification of a testimonial belief depends on the reliability of the relevant cognitive processes in the hearer's informant.

I

The line of argument from Chapter 3 suggests the following conclusion: insofar as testimonial belief-formation is a quasi-belief-dependent process whose input concerns the testimonies of one's source, this belief-forming process should be seen as an intersubjective one. Such a process involves cognitive processing in the mind/brain of the consumer of testimony, but it also extends back to include cognitive processing in the mind/brain of the producer of testimony as well. My aim in this chapter is to substantiate the case for this "extendedness hypothesis."

It is interesting to note that the extendedness hypothesis itself has received precious little attention in the reliabilist literature. In fact, to the best of my knowledge, there has been no extended treatment of this sort of position, and very few discussions of it of any length in the epistemology literature.[1] The most explicit

---

[1] Interestingly, this basic approach to the epistemology of testimonial belief appears to have been anticipated in the literature on legal testimony: see Friedman (1987), especially the sections on hearsay. Although Friedman does not use the language of 'reliability'—he speaks instead of the likelihood that a given piece of testimony is true—he is explicit in thinking that recovering the relevant likelihoods requires "tracing" the communication links back through the relied-upon source(s) to the fact in question. He also writes that, in

discussions I know of are those of Schmitt (1994, 1999, 2006). But Schmitt's discussions are noteworthy for their brevity: he mentions something like the extendedness hypothesis in passing (in his 1994), he devotes only three pages of critical discussion to the view (in his 1999), and he returns to mention it in passing (in his 2006).[2] It is high time that the position be given more serious consideration.

In this chapter, I present what I regard as the key consideration in defense of the extendedness hypothesis. I aim to show that this hypothesis merely brings to the fore commitments that the Process Reliabilist has, or should have, anyway. I will do so in connection with what I see as the similarities and differences between testimony and memory. The result of this exercise highlights the nature of what I have been calling epistemic reliance, and it makes clear as well that this phenomenon is not restricted to reliance on others. On the contrary, memorial belief offers a glimpse of a subject's epistemic reliance on herself and her own (basic) cognitive resources (those she employed at the time she originally acquired the belief in question).[3] It is helpful to examine the memory case first, if only to make clear that my emphasis on our epistemic reliance *on others* is actually a special case of a more general phenomenon—one that can be seen even when we restrict our attention to the individual subject herself. The chapter's main claim, then, will be that epistemic reliance is the key to understanding the extent of belief-forming processes (whether memorial or testimonial); the extendedness hypothesis is

---

thinking of the likelihood that a given testimonial belief is true, we do better to expand our investigation so that we consider not only how good the believer is at screening testimony for reliability, but also how reliable the testimony she endorsed on this occasion was. For this reason, I regard this sort of view as in the spirit of the proposal I will be offering here.

[2] Philip Kitcher also appears to have considered the view as well, albeit without developing it at any length (see his 1990 and especially his 1994). Also noteworthy is a paper by John Greco (2007), where an explicit appeal is made to an interpersonal characterization of belief-forming processes in (some) testimony cases.

[3] The sort of thing I have in mind by 'epistemic reliance on one's own basic cognitive resources' is in the area of 'self-trust' (Lehrer 1997) and 'intellectual trust in oneself' (Foley 2001). I follow both Lehrer and Foley in regarding this as the intrapersonal analogue of trust in others.

merely a special case of this general phenomenon, reflecting the interpersonal nature of the epistemic reliance in play in testimony cases.

One final point is worth making clear at the outset. The issue before us concerns the individuation of belief-forming processes: it concerns proper individuation of the process of testimonial belief-formation, and in particular whether this individuation should be individualistic or "extended." This topic, of course, touches on a more general issue that confronts reliabilism: the "generality problem" (see Feldman (1985); Conee and Feldman (1998); Feldman and Conee (2002)). The contours of that problem are familiar. A particular belief is formed through a belief-forming process that is a token of indefinitely many distinct process-types, each of which can be ascribed its own degree of reliability. How are we to determine in a principled fashion which of these types is relevant to the epistemic assessment of the belief? Since the aim in this chapter is to establish a conclusion about the individuation of the process-type(s) involved in testimonial belief-formation, the generality problem looms.

At the same time, I do not want to get bogged down in trying to address this problem. For one thing, much has been said in response,[4] and I don't have anything new to add. But, second, and perhaps more importantly, the point I want to establish does not depend on any particular solution to the generality problem. Rather, it follows from a programmatic view about what makes a process relevant to epistemic (reliabilist) assessment in the first place. On this view, a process is relevant to an epistemic assessment of the doxastic justification enjoyed by a subject's belief if and only if it is relevant to the proper epistemic assessment of the justification-relevant reliability with which the belief was formed and sustained. This view is programmatic: it is not meant to be

---

[4] See Goldman (1986); Alston (1995); Heller (1995); Wunderlich (2003); Beebe (2004); Comesaña (2006); Lepplin (2007); some of these are responded to in Conee and Feldman (1998).

informative[5] so much as it is meant to stake out the territory of reliabilism about doxastic justification—something one must hold, on pain of not being a reliabilist about justification. My thesis in this chapter is that cognitive processes that take place outside the skin of the subject herself—in particular, cognitive processes in the mind/brain(s) of her interlocutor(s), responsible for the production of the relevant piece(s) of testimony—are relevant to reliabilist assessments aimed at determining whether a given subject's testimonial belief is doxastically justified. I aim to establish this in a way that does not depend on any particular response to the generality problem.

2

Because this chapter will focus exclusively on doxastic justification, I begin with what I see as one of the core insights of reliabilism regarding justification. The insight has to do with the relevance of diachronic (or "historical") features to epistemic assessments of doxastic justification. The relevant point was articulated by Goldman in his seminal (1979) paper.[6] There he wrote:

The theory of justified belief proposed here . . . is an Historical or Genetic theory. It contrasts with the dominant approach to justified belief, . . . what we may call . . . 'Current Time-Slice' theories. A Current Time-Slice theory makes the justificational status of a belief wholly a function of what is true of the cognizer at the time of belief. An Historical theory makes the justificational status of a belief depend on its prior history. Since my Historical theory emphasizes the reliability of the belief-generating processes, it may be called 'Historical Reliabilism.' (Goldman 1979/2000: 347)

---

[5] At the very least, Process Reliabilists will hold that this claim is perfectly uninformative, since on a belief's reliability *just is* the reliability of the process that produced and sustained it.

[6] Unlike in Chapter 1, where my main focus was knowledge (and so the reliability property examined at length was local reliability), here my focus will be on doxastic justification. Consequently, unless otherwise noted the reliability property in play throughout this chapter will be *global* reliability.

He goes on to contrast his historical reliablism with another 'variant' reliablism that he labels '*Terminal Phase Reliabilism*,' which he introduces as follows:

Suppose S has a set B of beliefs at time t_0, and some of these are unjustified. Between t_0 and t_1 he reasons from the entire set B to the conclusion p, which he then accepts at t_1. The reasoning procedure he uses is a very sound one, i.e., one that is conditionally reliable. There is a sense or respect in which we are tempted to say that S's belief in p at t_1 is 'justified.' At any rate, it is tempting to say that the person is justified in believing p at t. Relative to his antecedent cognitive state, he did as well as could be expected: the transition from his cognitive state at t_0 to his cognitive state at t_1 was entirely sound. Although we may acknowledge this brand of justifiedness—it might be called '*Terminal Phase Reliabilism*'—it is not a kind of justifiedness so closely related to knowing. . . . [In contrast,] my theory of justified belief makes justifiedness come out closely related to knowledge. . . . For a person to know proposition p, it is not enough that the final phase of the process that leads to his belief in p be sound. *It is also necessary that some entire history of the process be sound* (i.e., reliable or conditionally reliable). (Goldman 1979/2000: 348; last italics added)

My guiding idea in this chapter is that the individualistic orientation of Orthodox Reliabilism is in effect guilty of endorsing a kind of Terminal Phase Reliabilism with respect to testimonial belief, and as such it is objectionable in a way that precisely parallels the objection Goldman presents in the quote just cited. In this section, my aim is to bring out the objectionableness of Terminal Phase Reliabilism regarding both inferential and memorial belief; in the following two sections, I argue that these grounds carry over to the Orthodox Reliabilist view, as it applies to testimonial belief.

The key to understanding the objectionableness of Terminal Phase Reliabilism has to do with the way it fails to honor the connection between justification and truth. The sort of epistemic goodness relevant to doxastic justification has to do with those considerations that make it likely that the belief in question is true. Reliabilist epistemology (or at least that of the Process Reliabilist flavor) emerges from the idea that the relevant considerations have to do with the reliability of the processes through which the belief is formed and sustained. But the relevant sort of reliability is the reliability of *all* of those (cognitive) processes that bear on the likelihood of the belief's being true—not just those processes that occur at the time that the belief is formed (and not just the processes in the subject's 'conscious control' at that time).

Although Goldman makes this point about the objectionableness of Terminal Phase Reliabilism in connection with a belief that is acquired through a process of explicit inference, this is not an essential feature of the point he is making. There is a Terminal Phase Reliabilist position one can take regarding memorial beliefs whose objectionableness would be analogous. Terminal Phase Reliabilism regarding memorial belief holds that the doxastic justification of memorial belief is to be determined wholly by the ('terminal') processes involved *at the time of recollection*. It should be clear that no reliabilist should be tempted by this view: it is objectionable in precisely the way that Terminal Phase Reliabilism regarding inferential belief is objectionable.

To see this, consider the processes that are involved at the time of recollection: the processes involved in memory search, retrieval, and assessment of would-be memory traces. Let us suppose that these processes are working perfectly well, in the following sense: all memory searches succeed in retrieving all and only those beliefs that the subject did in fact form previously[7] (i.e., no forgetfulness or memory confabulation). A process of memory that works in the way just described will be perfectly conditionally reliable: in any case in which the input is a memory impression corresponding to a true belief, the output of the process of memory—the memorial belief itself—will be true.[8] Even so, this sort of processing would

---

[7] That is, so long as S has acquired no new information that led her to abandon the relevant belief in the interim. (I will ignore this complication in what follows.)

[8] This assumes that the process is content-preserving, so that the content of the memorial belief = the content of the memory impression = the content of the belief originally acquired.

not, by itself, be sufficient to determine the doxastic justification of any particular memorial belief. This is because whether a particular memorial belief is justified depends, in part, on whether it was justified *on acquisition*. If a recalled belief is one that was unreliably acquired, then this belief was unjustified on acquisition and should continue to count as unjustified even as it is sustained by memory—even if S's memory is working well in the sense characterized above. Indeed, as we saw in the previous chapter, it was for this reason that Goldman distinguished between 'belief-independent' processes (whose inputs are not themselves beliefs) and 'belief-dependent' processes (whose inputs include other beliefs). His claim was that, unlike belief-independent processes, belief-dependent processes are to be assessed (not as reliable or unreliable *tout court* but only) as conditionally reliable—where the ultimate reliability of beliefs formed or sustained in conditionally reliable ways depends further on the reliability of the processes through which the input belief(s) were originally formed.[9]

It is worth underscoring how this point about the justification of memorial belief reflects the reliabilist's conception of justification (in relation to knowledge and truth). Goldman brings out the relevant point as follows:

Justified beliefs, like pieces of knowledge, have appropriate histories; but they may fail to be knowledge either because they are false or because they founder on some other requirement for knowledge of the kind discussed in the post-Gettier knowledge-trade.   (1979/2000: 348)

I take it that Goldman regards his enumeration of the possible ways in which a justified belief might fail to amount to knowledge as exhaustive: such a belief might be false or else "founder on some other requirement for knowledge of the kind discussed in the post-Gettier knowledge-trade." Let us use 'GETTIERED' to designate the state of failing to satisfy one or more of these requirements. (I use all capital letters to highlight that this notion may not be the same

---

[9] See also Chapter 5, Section 1, where I argue that the reliability of a belief acquired through a belief-dependent process depends on still further factors.

notion as that used by epistemologists who speak of a belief's being 'Gettiered.'[10]) With this usage in mind, we can see Goldman as holding that justified belief might fail to amount to knowledge in one of only two ways: it might be false, or otherwise GETTIERED ("founder[ing] on some . . . requirement for knowledge of the kind discussed in the post-Gettier knowledge-trade").

This construal makes sense of the line of argument Goldman is presenting on behalf of Process (or "Historical") Reliabilism in his (1979) article. This argument—henceforth "The Argument"—involves two claims. The first is the programmatic claim, to the effect that epistemic (doxastic) justification is whatever renders true unGETTIERED belief *knowledge*. And the second is the contention that this epistemicizing role is played by reliability in the formation and sustainment of belief. But what sort of reliability plays this role? Here Goldman makes two subsidiary claims. The first, negative, claim is this: the relevant sort of reliability is *not* Terminal Phase Reliability. The second, positive, claim is this: the relevant sort of reliability is "Historical" Reliability. It is worth looking at the arguments for both of these claims.

Goldman's case against Terminal Phase Reliabilism is based on the claim that the property of Terminal Phase Reliability does not play the epistemicizing role. This argument can be made more explicit than Goldman himself makes it. The dialectic is this. Everyone will agree with the 'no knowledge' verdict in the case in question: the subject who acquires a true belief through an inference from a set of premise-beliefs at least one of which is unreliably formed does not thereby acquire knowledge. The question is what explains this. The programmatic point insists that (since the belief is true) there are only two possibilities here: either

[10] GETTIERED beliefs are not only those standardly discussed in connection with Gettier cases (Gettier's own case of Haveit, Evans's case of the sheep on the hill over yonder, etc.), but also those whose status as 'Gettier examples' is itself controversial (barn beliefs formed in Fake Barn County, for example). All of these beliefs "founder on some other requirement for knowledge of the kind discussed in the post-Gettier knowledge-trade." Since my use of 'GETTIERED' is stipulative, I do not here mean to be implying anything substantial about a proper taxonomy of cases involving justified true belief that fail to be knowledge.

the belief was GETTIERED, or else it was unjustified. It is interesting in this regard to note that Goldman's argument against Terminal Phase Reliabilism regarding inferential belief simply *assumes* that the postulation of GETTIERIZING factors is not to the point. That Goldman assumes this, without argument, suggests that he takes the point to be obvious and uncontroversial. I think he is right; but as much hangs on this, and as the Terminal Phase Reliabilist has a strong motive to hold that there *is* a GETTIERIZING factor, it will be helpful to offer an explicit defense of Goldman's assumption on this score. In what follows, I argue that the balance of considerations offers overwhelming support to the claim that the belief in question has not been GETTIERED. (I will be belaboring the point, as I will be arguing below that the same sort of defense can be used to criticize the move to postulate GETTIER factors in testimony cases involving apparently-reliable-but-actually-unreliable testimony.)

First, it is unmotivated to postulate GETTIER factors in the inference case described. It is not generally true that any belief acquired through an inference from an unreliable premise-belief, and so which is not a case of knowledge, fails to be knowledge for "founder[ing] on some . . . requirement for knowledge of the kind discussed in the post-Gettier knowledge-trade." Nor can the postulation of a GETTIER factor be motivated by appeal to the (arguably true) claim that inferences from GETTIERED beliefs are themselves cases of GETTIERED belief: the beliefs used as premises were not GETTIERED, they were unjustified. In fact, it would seem that the only available way to motivate the postulation of a GETTIERIZING factor in the case described would be to hold that the very process of reasoning from unreliably-formed beliefs introduces a GETTIER condition (i.e., *whether or not* any of the premise-beliefs were GETTIERED). While there are some cases in which the very process of reasoning itself might be thought introduce a GETTIERIZING factor, in the sense that the resulting conclusion-belief fails to satisfy some "requirement for knowledge of the kind discussed in the post-Gettier knowledge-trade," these are surely the rare exception rather than the rule. (See Goldberg 2007c, where this point is developed at some length.)

Not only do we lack independent reason to postulate a GETTIER condition in the case before us; what is more, whatever lingering inclination one feels in this direction dissipates once we recognize that the Process Reliabilist already has at hand a simple, independently plausible account of the 'no knowledge' verdict in this case. She can account for the 'no knowledge' verdict *in terms of the unreliability of the whole process used in this case*. By 'the whole process' here I mean not just the process through which the subject draws the inference in question—the 'terminal phase' of the formation of the belief—but also the processes by which the premise-beliefs themselves were formed. To be sure, the Terminal Phase Reliabilist would restrict us from regarding these processes (which took place in the past) as relevant to the reliabilist assessment of the conclusion-belief. But it is precisely this restriction that we are presently calling into question; and in any case the Historical (Process) Reliabilist need not so restrict herself.

There is another point that can be made against the Terminal Phase Reliabilist here. We have already seen that all parties to this dispute—Terminal Phase Reliabilists as well as Process (or Historical) Reliabilists—will have to acknowledge that the inference-based belief (in the case Goldman describes) was unreliably acquired. What is at issue is whether to regard the unreliability of the inference-based belief as a global sort of unreliability, or a merely local sort. The Terminal Phase Reliabilist (who holds the belief to be justified) will have to claim that it is a local sort of unreliability. However, saying this commits her to the following claim: facts about the reliability with which a premise-belief was acquired constitute merely local factors in the process of inference-based belief-formation. This seems wrong-headed in principle.

It would thus seem that the balance of reasons strongly indicates that the inference-based belief in the case Goldman describes was not GETTIERED. So we now have a true unGETTIERED belief that fails to be knowledge. Since the belief in question is Terminal Phase

Reliable, we can conclude that Terminal Phase Reliability is not the sort of reliability that plays the epistemicizing role.

What, then, does play the epistemicizing role? The present conclusion is that the inferentially acquired belief is not GETTIERED. But the belief is true (this much is part of the thought experiment). And all parties agree that it failed to amount to knowledge. Thus, given the programmatic claim, we can reach the further conclusion that the belief in question was not justified. Assuming Process Reliabilism about justification, we reach the still further conclusion that the process of belief-formation in this case—*whatever this process was* (we are leaving this open for now)—was not a reliable one. But how are we to determine the extent of the process? We know that we must look beyond the "terminal phase" of the process: this much follows from our negative results, above. But how far back must we go in order to reach the beginning of the process of belief-formation in inference-based belief? In addressing this we can be guided by the following thought: since it was unreliability in the *acquisition* of the premise-beliefs that led to the unreliability in the process through which the inference-based belief was formed, the process of inference-based belief-formation must stretch back to include those processes that were responsible for the acquisition of the premise-beliefs themselves. And this, of course, is precisely the conclusion that Goldman draws: this is the basis of his case for "Historical" Reliabilism.

For those who are Process Reliabilists, the lesson about doxastic justification is clear: when it comes to the justification of beliefs through inferences, the processes that one ought to assess for reliability include not only those through which the inference itself was drawn, but also those responsible for the production of the beliefs used as premises. Inferentially acquired beliefs serve as a counterexample to Terminal Phase Reliability about justification, since it is not the case that a true unGETTIERED inference-based belief amounts to knowledge when it is Terminal Phase Reliable. Historical (Process) Reliabilism gets it right: "For a person to know proposition *p*, it is not enough that the final phase of the process that leads to his belief in p be sound. *It is also necessary that some entire history of the process be sound*"[11] (Goldman 1979/2000: 348; italics mine). And analogous points can be made in connection with memory-based belief.

3

When it comes to memorial belief and inference-based belief, both sorts of belief count as doxastically justified (by the lights of Goldman's programmatic claim) only if certain cognitive processes are operating reliably. What is more, the processes in question operate *prior to* the moment of the actual formation (or recollection) of the belief itself; and their operations are neither in the explicit control of nor consciously available to the agent. The justification of inference-based belief involves, not just the conditional reliability of the subject's reasoning from premise-beliefs, but also the reliability of the processes that produced (and sustained) each of the premise-beliefs themselves. The justification of memorial belief involves not just the conditional reliability of the process of recollection, but also the reliability of the process whereby the recalled belief was originally formed. Whether she realizes it or not, the subject who aims to acquire justified belief very often depends on the reliability of such processes.

I find it helpful to gloss this by speaking of the subject's *epistemic reliance* on (the reliability of) the processes in question. To a first approximation, we can say that, in forming or sustaining her belief that p, a given subject S epistemically relies on (the reliability of) some cognitive process π (where π itself may be a component in a more encompassing cognitive process) iff (i) S's belief that p was formed and/or sustained through some belief-forming process π^*, (ii) π produced a truth-assessable output r whose content is that q (not necessarily distinct from p), and (iii) the reliability of the belief

---

[11] While it will be noted that Goldman is talking about knowledge here, it is to be remembered that he is using claims about knowledge, together with the programmatic claim, in order to derive conclusions about the nature of doxastic justification.

S formed or sustained through π^* depends on the reliability with which π produced r. We can then employ the notion of epistemic reliance to formulate the core insight of Goldman's Historical Reliabilism, as follows: reliabilist epistemic assessment is assessment of *all* of the processes on which the subject epistemically relies; in these cases the process *extends as far as the subject's epistemic reliance extends*.[12]

Since the notion of epistemic reliance has figured and will continue to figure prominently in this book, it is worth developing the notion a bit. As I am using it here, 'epistemic reliance' is a label for the state of affairs in which reliability in the subject's formation or sustainment of a given belief depends on the reliability with which one or more cognitive processes produced a given output, which output figures as the 'input' into the process which eventuated in her forming or sustaining the belief in question. To say that she is epistemically relying on these cognitive processes is simply to note this sort of dependence. Clearly, such reliance can obtain even if she herself is not aware of this dependence. Compare: I can be said to be relying on the integrity of the structure supporting a bridge when I cross over it in my car, even if I am unaware of my dependence on this structure for success in crossing the bridge. Our reliance on cognitive processes is similar: reliability in belief-formation and -sustainment depends on the reliable operation of certain processes whose reliability is often, and perhaps typically, not in the control of (or reflectively accessible to) the subject herself. Thus, in inference, one epistemically relies on those processes implicated in the (perhaps temporally distant) production of one's premise-beliefs; and in memory one epistemically relies on the operation of those processes implicated in the (temporally distant) formation of the recalled belief.

I am using 'rely' in its ordinary sense, on which to rely on someone or something is to depend on that person or thing in

---

[12] In Chapter 6, I will consider a more diffuse sort of epistemic reliance, and this will prompt us to distinguish the sort of epistemic reliance in play here, in testimony cases, from what is in play there.

some respect or other. I intend the term to connote a certain lack of explicit control in the one doing the relying: to the extent that I am relying on you, I don't have control over you (or else I could simply do what I want done myself, albeit through my control of you). No doubt, the notion of reliance itself can be applied beyond the realm of cognitive processes and agents: I can rely on the regularity of the tides, on the face of my watch or the quarter-hour tolling of the grandfather clock in my living room, and indeed on any variety of natural processes, mechanisms, or instruments whose operation I use in belief-formation. However, if we extrapolate from the "core idea" of Process Reliabilism—the idea that epistemic assessment is a matter of assessing the "goodness" of *the cognitive processes* involved in belief-formation—it appears that reliance on such non-cognitive systems is very different, epistemologically speaking, from reliance on a cognitive system.[13]

The notion of epistemic reliance can be used to diagnose the problem facing Terminal Phase Reliabilism, and to make the case for Historical Reliabilism. Terminal Phase Reliabilism is objectionable since it fails to acknowledge a subject's epistemic reliance on cognitive processes whose relevant operations took place in the subject's own past history (the cases of inference and memory). Here it is worth noting that both memorial belief and beliefs acquired through explicit inference are cases involving what we might call *intra*subjectively extended belief-forming processes: they are processes that extend over time, reaching back to processes that took place in the subject's (sometimes distant) past. As I noted in Chapter 3, the notion of "extended processing" here merely tracks the extent of reliabilist assessment itself: because reliabilist assessment in memory cases requires assessment of the processes through which the now-recalled belief was acquired, we can speak of the process of memorial sustainment as temporally extended. (Goldman glosses this by speaking of "the *entire history* of the

---

[13] This is a vexed matter about which I will have little more to say here (but see Goldberg 2006a, where I discuss this issue at some length).

process" as within the purview of reliabilist assessment.) This is precisely the insight of Historical Reliabilism, which sees the extent of reliabilist assessment as determined by the extent of the subject's own epistemic reliance: since in memory a subject is relying on her own past cognitive processing (that involved in the original acquisition of the belief), reliabilist assessment of memorial belief must include an assessment of those past processes. Insofar as one endorses Goldman's criticism of Terminal Phase Reliabilism, the claim that the process of memory is extended in this sense should be both familiar and uncontroversial.

4

I have been arguing that the extent of a subject's epistemic reliance in a given case of belief-formation or -sustainment delimits the cognitive processes that must be assessed in a reliabilist assessment of the doxastic justification enjoyed by the belief in question.[14] Terminal Phase Reliabilism fails to acknowledge this point. I have been belaboring this because I think that it bears most directly on what a Process Reliabilist should say about the reliability of testimonial belief. In particular, since testimonial belief, like inference-based belief and memorial belief, involves epistemic reliance, the extent of this reliance delimits the cognitive processes whose reliability is relevant to reliabilist epistemic assessment. What makes for the novelty in cases of testimonial belief-formation, then, is not that it involves epistemic reliance, nor that because of this the process itself is properly regarded as involving extended cognitive processing, but rather that the extendedness of the processing is (not merely temporal but also) *inter*personal in nature.

It will be helpful at this point to make explicit the argument I aim to be offering on behalf of the "extendedness hypothesis," the claim that in testimony cases the belief-forming process-type

---

[14] Henceforth, when I speak of 'reliabilist epistemic assessment' in this chapter I mean assessments of (the degree of) doxastic justification enjoyed by the belief in question.

extends to include the cognitive processing implicated in the source speaker's production of the testimony. The argument can be presented as involving two distinct subarguments, one whose conclusion is negative and the other whose conclusion is positive. (I do this to mirror my presentation of Goldman's reasoning in the inferential case.) The argument for the negative conclusion is as follows:

First (Negative) Subargument

(1) Doxastic justification is to be understood as that property that renders true unGETTIERED belief *knowledge*.

(2) The property in question is the (global) reliability of the cognitive process(es) through which a belief is formed and sustained.

(3) (Global) reliability in the cognitive (perceptual, comprehension, and monitoring) processes *internal to the hearer* does not suffice to render true unGETTIERED testimonial belief knowledge.

Therefore:

(4) (Global) reliability in the cognitive processes internal to the hearer does not determine the doxastic justification of testimonial belief.

To this first (negative) argument we then add a second (positive) argument on behalf of the extendedness hypothesis, as follows:

Second (Positive) Subargument

(5) In cases of testimonial belief, the cognitive processes whose (global) reliability is needed to render a true unGETTIERED testimonial belief knowledge include (not only those perceptual, comprehension, and monitoring processes internal to the hearer but also) those processes implicated in the source's production of testimony.

Therefore:

(6) In cases of testimonial belief, doxastic justification is a matter of the (global) reliability of a cognitive process-type that includes (not only those perceptual, comprehension, and monitoring processes internal to the hearer but also) those processes implicated in the source's production of testimony.

Therefore:

(7) The cognitive process-types through which testimonial beliefs are formed include (not only those perceptual, comprehension, and monitoring processes internal to the hearer but also) those processes implicated in the source's production of testimony.

These two arguments contain four premises, (1)–(3) and (5), and three conclusions, (4), (6), and (7), the last of which is the extendedness hypothesis itself. Of the four premises involved, the one most likely to attract critical attention from Orthodox Reliabilists is (3). It is easy to see why. The conjunction of (1)–(3) entails (4), which asserts the falsity of Process Individualism. So Orthodox Reliabilists, who are committed to Process Individualism, must reject one of (1)–(3). But (1), on my reconstruction, is the programmatic claim on whose basis Goldman's case against Terminal Phase Reliabilism, as well as his case in favor of Historical (or Process) Reliabilism, both depend. And (2) itself is just a generic statement of Process Reliabilism itself—something that will be endorsed by any Process Reliabilist (whether Terminal Phase or Historical or what-have-you). That leaves (3): in order to avoid refutation, the Orthodox Reliabilist must challenge it. To be sure, the Orthodox Reliabilist will want to reject (5) as well. But since ∼(5) follows from ∼(3), and since it is not clear that there is some other way to argue for ∼(5)—how else is the Orthodox Reliabilist going to undermine the extendedness hypothesis save by defending the individualistic orientation itself?—a look at the case against (3) is at the same time a look at the case against (5). Finally, I note in passing that (6) follows from (1), (2), and (5), and that (7) is the gloss one can give (6) on the assumption that the cognitive process-type whose reliability determines the justificatory status of a belief just is the cognitive process-type through which the belief was formed and sustained. (In Chapter 5, I will be arguing at length that a Process Reliabilist of any stripe ought to accept this assumption.) The case for the extendedness hypothesis, then, boils down to the case for (3).

5

The idea behind my case for (3) is that a Process Reliabilist who denies (3) will be guilty of a version of Terminal Phase Reliabilism regarding testimonial belief. In particular, it is no more reasonable to restrict the belief-forming process in testimony cases to processes that start at the (terminal) point at which the subject receives the speaker's message, than it is to restrict the process in memory cases to processes that start at the (terminal) point at which the subject has an apparent recollection. Both views are instances of Terminal Phase Reliabilism, and both are objectionable in the way diagnosed above.

How might we show that an Orthodox Reliabilist view about testimonial belief—one that assesses only those processes 'internal' to the hearer—is guilty of a version of Terminal Phase Reliabilism? We can do so by focusing on cases. What is wanted is a case in which we have a true, UNGETTIERED testimonial belief where all of the processes 'internal' to the hearer's mind/brain—the 'terminal phase' processes—are reliable, yet which fails to amount to knowledge. For reasons that will emerge in due time, we do best to take a case in which the testimonial belief is formed through accepting a piece of testimony that has the following property: it expresses (what in the informant is) a true belief formed through a process that, though formed in a way that was not epistemically irresponsible, was not quite reliable enough to count as knowledge (and not for having been GETTIERED). I will call this property the property of being 'not quite good enough.' To get a situation in which the testimony that is accepted is not quite good enough, let us imagine a case in which the testimony expresses a would-be recognition-based belief formed through a momentary glance at what appeared to the subject to be a familiar object, but where the object in question was slightly obscured to the subject, at a bit of a distance from her, under non-ideal lighting conditions. Suppose now that when the informant expressed this belief in the testimony she gave, her testimony had all of the trappings of competence and sincerity. Finally, suppose an ordinary hearer observes this testimony and, having subjected it to the sort of credibility monitoring that standardly operates in the minds of mature consumers of testimony, accepts the testimony. I want to claim that this testimonial belief in the hearer has the following features: it is true, unGETTIERED, and Terminal Phase Reliable (in the sense that all of the relevant processes 'internal' to the mind/brain of the hearer are reliable), yet it fails to amount to knowledge. (As this belief is true by stipulation, I will focus on the other three features.)

It should be patent that the hearer's testimonial belief fails to amount to knowledge. Even those who think that testimony can generate knowledge[15] should reject that this is such a case. The hearer's true testimonial belief is no better related to the truth than was the testimony on which it was based. Since the testimony itself was not quite good enough—it expressed a belief (the informant's) that itself did not amount to knowledge—it would seem patent that the hearer's belief, which was based on that not-quite-good-enough testimony, does not amount to knowledge.[16] The cost of denying this would be considerable. After all, it would be a curious process indeed that turned what in the mind/brain *of the source* was a belief that was not reliable enough to count as knowledge into what in the mind/brain *of the hearer* is a belief whose reliability

---

[15] See, e.g., Lackey (1999); Graham (2000a); and Goldberg (2005, 2007b).

[16] I develop this point at length in Goldberg (2007b).

suffices for knowledge—and this, despite the fact that from an epistemic point of view the hearer was less well placed regarding the truth of the proposition in question than was her source!

It should also be clear that (the story can be developed so that) this testimonial belief is Terminal Phase Reliable. The 'terminal phase' of the process of testimonial belief-formation is that which begins at the point at which the hearer observes the testimony and includes all of the processes through which the hearer apprehends, and ultimately accepts (or rejects), the testimony. These processes include those relevant to the hearer's comprehension of the testimony, and also those relevant to her assessing the testimony for credibility. We can stipulate (as part of the thought experiment) that all of these processes are globally reliable: in a preponderance of cases, our hearer does not comprehend a piece of testimony as having the semantic content [p] unless it does have the semantic content [p]; and in a preponderance of cases, our hearer does not regard a piece of testimony as credible unless it is credible. (This was a rare exception to the rule, which snuck in, no doubt, owing to the fact that the testimony in question had all of the trappings of credibility, and expressed a belief—the source's—which was just below the threshold of reliability needed for doxastic justification and knowledge.) In this case, the testimonial belief is Terminal Phase Reliable.

The only question that remains, then, is whether the hearer's testimonial belief has been GETTIERED—that is, whether this belief "founder[s] on some other requirement for knowledge of the kind discussed in the post-Gettier knowledge-trade." In Chapter 2, I argued that this is precisely what the Orthodox Reliabilist will say about cases like this. (More generally, this is the sort of thing that will be said by anyone, whether Orthodox Reliabilist or not, who accepts what I called the traditional conception of testimony's epistemic significance.) While the Orthodox Reliabilist thus has a clear motive to argue that this is such a case—that a GETTIER condition is present—I want to argue that the prospects for making good on this claim are not good. In particular, the sort of 'flaw' in the process of testimonial belief-formation in the case we are examining is in all relevant respects like the flaw discussed above in connection with the inference and memory cases. With respect to those, I argued that the postulation of a GETTIER factor is without independent support and in any case is unnecessary (making for a more complicated and less natural account than one that is already within the reliabilist's possession).

In bringing this out, it must be borne in mind that by 'GETTIERED' belief I mean a belief that "founder[s] on some . . . requirement for knowledge of the kind discussed in the post-Gettier knowledge-trade." This is a loose characterization. It is intended to cover any case in which the belief has been Gettiered (lower-caps); but it is also intended to cover any case (like that of the fake barns) where the knowledge-undermining factor in question is a matter of the *local unreliability* of the process (whether or not we count such cases as Gettier cases).[17] In order to bolster my claim that the testimonial belief formed through an acceptance of the 'not quite good enough' testimony in this case is *not* a GETTIER case, then, I will be arguing that this belief does not suffer from Gettierization nor does it suffer from a form of merely local unreliability.[18] Admittedly, there may be requirements for knowledge that go beyond anti-Gettier and local reliability requirements; if so, the belief might still be GETTIERED for all my argument has shown. But at the very least the burden would then be on the Orthodox Reliabilist, to identify the relevant requirement on knowledge, and to show how the belief in the 'not quite good enough' testimony fails that requirement.

I begin by underscoring several points I have already made in connection with memorial belief. A belief that is (by the lights of reliabilist epistemology) unjustified on acquisition remains

---

[17] Here I am playing on the potential difference between Gettier cases and GETTIER cases.

[18] 'Merely' local unreliability: I will be arguing that the proper diagnosis of the case is that the belief suffers from a form of global unreliability (and so is not justified). I do not deny that it suffers from local unreliability as well (although its doing so reflects its suffering from global unreliability).

unjustified on recollection even when the process of recollection itself is conditionally reliable. In such a case the recalled belief fails to amount to knowledge; but here there is no temptation to trace this 'no knowledge' verdict either to Gettierization or to a failure of local reliability. There is no temptation to account for this verdict in terms of Gettierization, as (i) the postulation of a Gettierizing factor is *ad hoc* (the belief was not Gettiered on acquisition, and there is no plausible account of how such a factor would be generated in the course of the process of recollection), and (ii) the postulation is unnecessary (the reliablist has a perfectly good account of the 'no knowledge' verdict in terms of the lack of justification-relevant reliability enjoyed by the recalled belief). But neither is there any temptation to account for the 'no knowledge' verdict here in terms of a failure of local reliability. In particular, facts about the reliability of the process through which the belief in question was originally formed are not merely facts about the 'local environment' in which memory is presently working. On the contrary, such facts are facts about *the very process* through which that belief was formed and sustained (see Chapter 3).

Precisely the same point holds for testimonial belief as well: the facts regarding (the reliability of) the processes that produced the inputs into the testimonial belief-forming process should not be regarded as Gettier factors; nor should they be accommodated as mere facts about the 'local environment' in which testimonial belief-fixation takes place.

To begin, the testimonial belief in the 'not quite good enough' testimony is not Gettiered. I want to establish this in two steps: first, by arguing that *the source speaker's* belief—the belief expressed in the testimony—was not itself Gettiered; and, second, by arguing that nothing in the communication chain (eventuating in the hearer's formation of the testimonial belief) provides the basis for postulating a Gettier factor.

Consider first the source speaker's belief, the belief that is expressed in her testimony. That belief was formed through a process whose reliability was 'not quite good enough' to render the belief doxastically justified. It seems patent that this belief was not Gettiered. Whatever its fundamental nature, a Gettier factor is a factor that introduces a certain kind of luck pertaining to the truth of the belief in question: Gettiered beliefs are beliefs whose truth is a matter of luck in this (admittedly not entirely clear) sense. Paradigmatic cases include Nogot and Haveit, as well as the stopped-clock case. In cases of this sort, it is clear that the truth of the subject's belief is preponderantly a matter of luck: given that the subject acquired the belief in the way that she did, she was lucky to have acquired a *true* belief in the present circumstances. This point suffices to make clear that the source speaker's perceptual belief was not Gettiered. That belief failed to be knowledge because, given the conditions under which the observation was made, the source's belief was not quite reliable enough to count as doxastically justified. But to say that it was *not quite reliable enough* is to imply that it did enjoy *some* non-negligible degree of reliability—just not enough to count as doxastically justified. And because the source's perceptual belief did enjoy a non-negligible degree of reliability, the truth of this belief is not predominantly a matter of luck. This is the basis for my first claim, which I take to be uncontroversial: the source subject's perceptual belief—the one she expressed in the testimony—was not itself Gettiered.

Those who would postulate a Gettier factor to explain the 'no knowledge' verdict regarding *the hearer's* belief (acquired through accepting the speaker's testimony), then, must hold that a Gettier-izing factor was generated in the process of communication itself. But once again such a postulation seems *ad hoc*. To be sure, we might well imagine cases in which facts about the testimony con-stitute a Gettierizing factor with respect to the hearer's testimonial belief. Imagine a case in which a liar aims to deceive a hearer, and so testifies that p, where it turns out that (unbeknownst to the would-be liar) [p] is true after all. If a hearer accepts this testimony, and so forms the testimonial belief that p, we might be tempted to say that she has acquired a true belief that has been Gettiered. After all, given that the hearer acquired her belief through accepting this person's testimony, she was lucky that the belief she acquired in this way was true. But even if (for the sake of argument at least[19]) we agree with the postulation of a Gettier condition in *that* case, the present case is different. In the present case, the speaker is sincere and aims at truth; only her testimony, though based on visual contact with the object in question, is 'not quite good enough' to count as knowledgeable. The very same considerations (regarding luck) that we used to show that the *source speaker*'s (perceptual) belief was not Gettiered appear to show that *the hearer*'s testimonial belief was not Gettiered. In particular, the truth of the testimonial belief is not predominantly a matter of luck. What is more, any lingering temptation we have to postulate a Gettier factor in this case dissipates once we realize that the postulation is unnecessary: the reliablist has a perfectly good account of the 'no knowledge' verdict in terms of the lack of justification-relevant reliability enjoyed by the testimonial belief.[20] The postulation of a Gettier condition is both unnecessary and without independent support.

It would seem, then, that if the Orthodox Reliabilist is to vindicate her claim that the testimonial belief has been GETTIERED, she must show that it suffers from a form of (merely) local unreliability. But there are good reasons to think that the testimonial belief (formed through accepting the 'not quite good enough' testimony) does not suffer from a form of merely local reliability. To do so we can fill in more details of the case. First, we will suppose that all testifiers in the local vicinity are highly reliable and would have testified reliably on this and other related topics (had the hearer been with them). And suppose as well that the speaker whose testimony the hearer consumed virtually always testifies in a highly reliable fashion—the present case is the lone exception in

[19] For what it's worth, I don't accept this analysis. But the present argument does not depend on the verdict I would offer.

[20] Such an account depends, of course, on the "extendedness hypothesis," and the Orthodox Reliabilist, committed as she is to Process Individualism, will reject this hypothesis; but it is precisely Process Individualism that I am calling into question here. To appeal to this doctrine at this point in the dialectic would be question-begging.

the speaker's whole life. Then, insofar as we assume that the testimonial belief-forming process is an 'individualistic' one, we get the following result: in most or all of the easily occurring counterfactual circumstances, this process-type will produce a preponderance of truth over falsity. In such a case we can conclude that the testimonial belief does not suffer from merely local unreliability.

In short, it seems that the Orthodox Reliabilist's case against (3) fails. This case requires that the Orthodox Reliabilist regard the belief acquired through accepting the not-quite-good-enough testimony as having been GETTIERED. But such a view is implausible: the belief in question is not Gettiered, and it does not suffer from anything that the Orthodox Reliabilist can recognize as a form of merely local unreliability. I conclude, then, that the Orthodox Reliabilist is without recourse in her attempt to resist (3); and with this I conclude my case for the extendedness hypothesis itself.

6

In this chapter I have argued that the reliability of a piece of testimony has a more direct effect on the reliability of beliefs based on that testimony than is allowed by Orthodox Reliabilism. In particular, we have reasons to think that belief-forming processes involved in testimonial belief are intersubjective in extent. I claim that these reasons derive from a point (about epistemic reliance) to which reliabilists are committed independent of considerations pertaining to testimony. Still, the extendedness hypothesis itself, and with it the ascriptions of doxastic justification that this hypothesis warrants, might continue to seem objectionable, for reasons having nothing to do with the positive case on behalf of this hypothesis. I devote the next chapter to exploring these objections.

5

Objections to Extended Reliability

In the last chapter, I presented an argument from the nature of epistemic reliance in testimony cases to the conclusion that testimonial belief-fixation should be regarded as an interpersonally extended process. My claim was that this 'extendedness hypothesis' is a special case of a point that Process Reliabilists accept anyway, having to do with the extended focus of reliabilist assessment in any case in which a belief is formed or sustained through a process in which the subject exhibits epistemic reliance on a representation-deploying information source. I acknowledge that, despite being backed by such an argument, the extendedness hypothesis can continue to seem decidedly strange. In this chapter, I address several remaining objections that might be made against this hypothesis; I argue that none withstands scrutiny.

I will be addressing six objections in total. The first is the objection from credulity or blind trust (anticipated in Fricker 1994), which accuses the extendedness hypothesis of making false predictions in cases in which a subject accepts out of blind trust what turns out to be a reliable piece of testimony (Section 1). The second is the 'bad company' objection. Here the allegation is that the extendedness hypothesis implies a view in the philosophy of mind known as the 'extended cognition' hypothesis, and that this is a reason to reject the former (Section 2). The third is the objection from the causal nature of belief-formation, which alleges that the extendedness hypothesis fails to square with the point that belief-forming processes consist of that part of the cognitive process that constitutes the casual antecedents in the process of belief-formation (Section 3). The fourth is the objection from epistemic assessment. This objection contends that, unlike what the extendedness hypothesis would lead us to expect, real-life assessments of the doxastic justification of another's testimonial beliefs do not include assessments of the cognitive processing implicated in the production of the testimony (Section 4). The fifth is the objection from control, according to which cognitive processing in the mind/brain of one's informant cannot be part of the process through which a hearer forms her testimonial beliefs since that 'extended' processing is not in the hearer's control (Section 5). And the sixth and final objection is the indistinguishability objection (owed to Schmitt 1999). This objection is based on the claim that the extendedness hypothesis makes false predictions in classes of cases that are subjectively indistinguishable to the hearer (Section 6). I will argue in each case that the objection fails to undermine the extendedness hypothesis; in presenting my responses, I will have occasion to further develop the extendedness hypothesis itself.

I

I begin with the objection from blind trust. Most epistemologists (reliabilist or not) would agree that it is not an epistemically good thing to form testimonial beliefs through blind credulity.[1] Accommodating such a claim need not be a problem for Orthodox Reliabilism. Given its commitment to Process Individualism, Orthodox Reliabilism will construe the process-type involved as

---

[1] This is the basis of Fricker's well-known (1994) criticism of the view known as "anti-reductionism" in the epistemology of testimony. For the connection between anti-reductionism and reliabilist approaches to the epistemology of testimony, see Goldberg (2007a: Chapter 5); and for a response to Fricker's argument, see Goldberg and Henderson (2006), to which Fricker (2006b) is a response in its turn.

something like "credulously accepting testimony." It is reasonable to anticipate that, given the amount of false testimonies offered even in normal conditions, the process-type *credulously accepting testimony* is one that is not globally reliable: it is not the case that a preponderance of beliefs acquired through this process-type, across the range of cases in which this process would be employed, are true. For this reason, beliefs produced through this process-type will not be doxastically justified; blind trust presents no difficulties for the Orthodox Reliabilist.

Matters appear otherwise, however, for the Process Reliabilist who surrenders Process Individualism and accepts the extendedness hypothesis. It is easy to see why. By the lights of the extendedness hypothesis, the process involved in a case in which a blindly credulous person accepts a reliable piece of testimony will include whatever processing was implicated in the production of the testimony, as well as whatever processing was implicated in the credulous hearer's reception of that testimony. But in that case the process from the (G-reliable) production of the testimony to the (credulous) acceptance of that testimony would itself appear to be G-reliable: a preponderance of beliefs formed in this way will be true. (Since the process through which the testimony was produced was itself G-reliable, a preponderance of those testimonies will be true; and so, assuming that the process is content-preserving, a preponderance of beliefs formed through accepting these testimonies will be true, no matter how discriminating the hearer is.) It appears, then, that the extendedness hypothesis is committed to the view that beliefs formed through blind trust are doxastically justified whenever the testimony accepted was reliable. This is not a happy result.[2]

In response, I want to argue that the proponent of the extendedness hypothesis can avoid this result—initial appearances to the contrary notwithstanding. In what follows, I will argue that the

---

[2] In fact, it was with cases like this in mind that I continued to endorse an individualistic reliabilism regarding testimonial belief in my (2007a). See especially the case of Sid and Nancy, discussed at length in Chapter 1 of my (2007a).

objection from blind trust must make one of several assumptions, and that in each case the proponent of the extendedness hypothesis can respond, sometimes by rejecting the assumption in question, sometimes by arguing that the assumption in question fails to yield the unhappy result.

1.1

To begin, let us highlight the *reductio* claim at the heart of this objection. The claim is that the extendedness hypothesis will have the following unhappy result: so long as the testimony consumed is reliable, the credulous subject's testimonial belief is doxastically justified. I formulate this *reductio* claim follows ('BTR' for 'Blind Trust *Reductio*'):

> BTR   For every subject S and testimonial belief B, if S forms B through blind trust in what happens to be a reliable piece of testimony, B is doxastically justified.

What is the basis for the allegation that the extendedness hypothesis implies BTR? Two claims are salient here; these are claims to which the proponent of the extendedness hypothesis is (or should be) committed, and which the objector will exploit in developing the case for her allegation. The first is that a testimonial belief formed through blind trust in a reliable piece of testimony is a belief that is formed through a belief-dependent process whose input in this case is reliable. The second is that the belief-dependent process in play is itself conditionally reliable. The allegation is that BTR can be established given these two claims.

In response I submit that, even if we assume that the extendedness hypothesis is committed to these two claims, the proponent of the hypothesis has the resources to avoid BTR—the objection's allegation to the contrary notwithstanding. So let us ask: how does the objection from blind trust proceed to argue from these two claims to BTR?

The simplest case to be made for BTR from the two claims above would involving making the following assumption:

SUFF   A testimonial belief is doxastically justified so long as (i) the testimony consumed was reliable and (ii) the process operating in the hearer was reliable (conditionally reliable).[3]

If SUFF is true, then BTR follows directly from the two claims above, and the objection would be vindicated. But no reliabilist should accept SUFF. On the contrary, SUFF faces an obvious problem: a testimonial belief might fail to be doxastically justified, despite being the product of a (conditionally) reliable process with a reliable testimonial input, because of the presence of a *relevant defeater*. Below, I will talk more about the role of a 'no relevant defeaters' condition in reliabilist accounts of doxastic justification. For now, I simply note that it has been customary for such accounts to incorporate something like a 'no defeater' condition, and insofar as this move is legitimate, SUFF is objectionable.[4]

In light of this, the objection's proponent might think to establish BTR with the following weakening of SUFF:

SUF2   A testimonial belief is doxastically justified so long as (i) the testimony consumed was reliable; (ii) the process operating in the hearer was reliable (conditionally reliable); and (iii) there are no relevant defeaters.

At this point matters get a little bit tricky. Surely, in *some* cases involving the credulous acceptance of reliable testimony, there is a relevant defeater. (Imagine that the testifier spoke reliably, but any reasonable hearer should have questioned whether the testimony was reliable, since the testimony had all of the usual trappings

---

[3] I formulate condition (ii) as I do, where I speak of reliability and/or conditional reliability, so that SUFF covers both those who think that testimonial belief formation is a belief-independent process, and those who think that it is a belief-dependent process. The former will assess the processes operating in the hearer in terms of their reliability, the latter in terms of their conditional reliability.

[4] In this book, I am assuming that reliabilist epistemology is otherwise acceptable, so I am assuming that this move is legitimate—I will not be exploring it much further, save in a few brief comments below. It goes without saying that if this assumption is wrong—if reliabilism *can't* incorporate something that plays the role of a 'no defeater' condition—then reliabilist epistemology is in much greater trouble than the difficulties I am presenting for Orthodox varieties of Reliabilism.

of unreliability: the speaker couldn't look the hearer in the face, seemed incompetent, etc.) So, insofar as the objection from blind trust depends on SUF2, the claim at the heart of the *reductio*, BTR, will be false, since in that case some beliefs formed through blind credulity in reliable testimony are *not* doxastically justified (even assuming the extendedness hypothesis). Still, a fix is nearby: the objection from blind trust can be reformulated so as to avoid making such a strong claim. On the new formulation, the key allegation would be that the extendedness hypothesis implies the following weaker, but still unhappy, claim ('WBTR' to indicate that it is a Weaker version of BTR):

> WBTR   For *some* subject S and testimonial belief B, if S forms B through blind trust in what happens to be a reliable piece of testimony, B is doxastically justified.

The new allegation is based on the idea that a blindly trusting consumer of testimony satisfies conditions (i)–(iii) of SUF2 in at least *some* cases, and so counts (by the lights of the extendedness hypothesis) as having acquired a doxastically justified belief in those cases.

The objection from blind trust requires that WBTR be an objectionable claim—one such that, if the extendedness hypothesis implies it, it indicates that this is so much the worse for the extendedness hypothesis. But, in order for WBTR to be an objectionable claim, it must be the case that at least some of the subjects who instantiate WBTR are subjects regarding whose testimonial beliefs a verdict of 'doxastically justified' is *not plausible*. This requirement is not trivial. Imagine a community in which all speech is competent and sincere. In that community, the vast preponderance of testimonies can be clearly seen as true and reliable. What is more, imagine that this feature of the community embodies a long-standing tradition in the community: it is no accident that most testimonies are both competent and sincere. Now, a hearer who accepts testimony in this community is most likely to acquire a true belief. This is true even if the hearer is blindly trusting. What is more, given the long-standing tradition of this community as one in which the vast majority of testimonies are both sincere and competent, it would appear that there is no relevant defeater even in cases involving blind trust. I submit that, under these circumstances, it is not implausible for a Process Reliabilist to think that a testimonial belief acquired through blind trust is doxastically justified. So long as the blind trust is restricted to the community itself—here we can imagine a subject who never leaves the community—the process of blindly trusting what others tell her is one that will yield a great preponderance of true belief. In that case, a verdict of 'doxastically justified' would seem perfectly acceptable on reliabilist grounds.[5] If every positive instance of WBTR were like this, WBTR itself would be unobjectionable—in which case it would be no objection to the extendedness hypothesis that it implies WBTR. In this way, we see that if the objection from blind trust, construed as aiming to establish that the extendedness hypothesis implies WBTR, is to succeed, this objection must show that at least some of the 'doxastically justified' verdicts that instantiate WBTR are implausible.

This said, the purport of (the present construal of) the objection from blind trust is clear enough. Let it be granted, as I just argued, that there can be cases in which a verdict of 'doxastically justified' is acceptable even with respect to a testimonial belief that satisfies conditions (i)–(iii) of SUF2. Even so, there are *other* cases involving a testimonial belief that satisfies conditions (i)–(iii) of SUF2 in which such a verdict is *not* acceptable. Imagine a scenario in which the range of testimonies the hearer is likely to encounter in her lifetime (as she goes about her business in the world) is *not* uniformly, or nearly uniformly, high-quality. Let us call such conditions 'non-ideal' conditions. Under non-ideal conditions, blind trust is not an epistemic virtue. Yet, even so,

---

[5] In Goldberg (2008) I used considerations of this sort to argue that very young children, who are highly credulous, might nevertheless acquire beliefs that (by the lights of reliabilist epistemology) count as doxastically justified.

the blindly trusting hearer might 'luck on' to a reliable piece of testimony from time to time. If there is such a case in which there is no relevant defeater, then the proponent of the extendedness hypothesis is committed to holding that SUF2's conditions are all satisfied—in which case the extendedness hypothesis must endorse a verdict of 'doxastically justified.' In this case, under such non-ideal conditions, the verdict seems patently implausible. It is in this sort of case that the objection from blind trust has force.

But even here the proponent of the extendedness hypothesis is not without a response. In particular, such a proponent can deny that SUF2's condition (iii), the 'no relevant defeaters' condition, is *ever* satisfied in any case involving the credulous acceptance of testimony *under non-ideal conditions.*[6] In fact, the proponent of the extendedness hypothesis might offer this as her account of the epistemic vice of credulity ('DA' for 'Defeaters Account'):

> DA   Beliefs formed through blind trust in testimony under prevailing conditions that are non-ideal do not enjoy doxastic justification, since whatever justification such beliefs might otherwise enjoy (i.e., in cases in which the testimony was reliable) is *defeated.*

Insofar as the objection from blind trust employs SUF2, then, it would appear to succeed only if DA is false (or otherwise unavailable to the proponent of the extendedness hypothesis).[7] In what follows, I want to argue that, while matters are not entirely clear, arguably there *is* a relevant defeater in any case involving

---

[6] It must be borne in mind that non-ideal conditions do not describe the merely local features of the hearer's environment, but rather describe the enduring conditions that comprise the relevant "background conditions" on testimonial belief-formation, in the manner described by Kornblith (1994: 97).

[7] It might be thought that the objection from blind trust is helped in this regard by cases involving very young children. On the assumption that very young children are blindly trusting, (DA) implies that very young children cannot have doxastically justified testimonial beliefs. (And if knowledge implies justification, we would get the further result that very young children cannot have testimonial knowledge.) I think that this line of argument can be resisted *precisely by the proponent of the extendedness hypothesis.* See Goldberg (2008) for details.

a testimonial belief formed through blind trust under conditions that are non-ideal. (Since this is only arguably true, however, I will then go on, in Section 1.2, to consider what other options the proponent of the extendedness hypothesis has for addressing the argument from blind trust, should it turn out that DA is ultimately unwarranted.)

One motivation for accepting DA, and so postulating a relevant defeater in any case involving credulously accepted testimony under non-ideal conditions, can be discerned if we consider in more detail how Process Reliabilists typically react to Bonjour's case of the reliable clairvoyant (Bonjour 1985). Bonjour held it against reliabilist theories of justification that they would regard as justified any reliably formed belief, no matter how irrational it was for the subject to have formed that belief. This was supposed to be illustrated by Norman, who forms beliefs through what happens to be a reliable faculty of clairvoyance, where Norman himself has no reasons to regard his clairvoyance as reliable (and many reasons against believing in such a faculty).[8] It has become standard for reliabilists to embrace Bonjour's 'not justified' verdict regarding beliefs formed through such clairvoyance. To accommodate this verdict, reliabilists have modified reliabilism so as to include a 'no relevant defeater' condition.[9] Brought to bear on the case of Norman, such a modified reliabilism yields the claim that the *de facto* reliability of Norman's clairvoyance yields a belief whose (reliability-generated) doxastic justification is nevertheless defeated by relevant reasons to doubt the reliability of clairvoyance. Here I underline (what should be obvious anyway) that this reaction regards the clairvoyance-based belief to be doxastically unjustified,

[8] Bonjour had variations on this theme. In some cases, the subject merely lacked reasons to think that her clairvoyance was reliable. In others, the subject had beliefs to the effect that reliable clairvoyance is unlikely. I am not being careful with these details here, as they are not important to the point I am making.

[9] Goldman (1986) is the first of many attempts to give the 'no defeater' condition a reliabilist-friendly gloss. As I want to remain neutral on the details of how such a condition is incorporated into a reliabilist epistemology, I will continue to speak of the 'no defeater' condition itself, without attending to the details of how such a condition might be incorporated into a thorough-going reliabilist account of justification.

despite being otherwise reliably formed, owing to these reasons defeating whatever justification would otherwise be generated by the reliability of the process itself.

Let us assume that this response is acceptable in the clairvoyance case. (I acknowledge that some critics of reliabilism will dispute this.) It might then occur to proponents of the extendedness hypothesis to make a similar claim in connection with beliefs formed through credulous acceptance of reliable testimony, under conditions that are non-ideal: the credulous subject's acceptance of a piece of reliable testimony yields a belief that (by the lights of the extendedness hypothesis) is otherwise reliably formed but nevertheless doxastically unjustified, owing to a relevant defeater.

Some care must be employed by the proponent of the extendedness hypothesis in developing this sort of reply. By the lights of the extendedness proposal, the process in play is an extended one, characterized roughly as *blindly accepting testimony produced in this way* (where by "this way" we mean to be referring to the very cognitive process-type implicated in the production of the testimony). So the sorts of reasons that will count as relevant defeaters need to be reasons for thinking that *this* process—an extended testimonial process involving testimony produced *in this way*—is unreliable. Is it plausible to think that there are such reasons? If the person in question is really supremely trustworthy, and the process through which she produced the testimony is a highly reliable one, what reasons might there be to doubt that trust in what she says (when she employs processes of this sort)—even *blind* trust in what she says—is a reliable way to form beliefs? Note that it will not do at this point to say that there are reasons not to be blindly trusting *in general*; for, while true, this point does not constitute a reason to doubt the reliability of trusting *this particular person's* testimony (or testimony produced *in this way*; below, this is understood). So, insofar as we think of the process (with the extendedness hypothesis) as one of *blindly trusting testimony produced in this particular way*, we face the challenge of getting the generic injunction against blind trust to bear on the extended process.

The proponent of the extendedness hypothesis might get what is needed by reconsidering the situation of the blindly credulous subject. Such a subject can't tell, and doesn't make any effort to tell, whether the particular person she trusts has produced reliable testimony on this occasion—whether the testimony she has accepted was in fact reliable. That is, she is not in a position to tell whether the (interpersonally extended) process through which she formed her testimonial belief is a G-reliable one. This point alone, of course, does not make for a relevant defeater. If it did, we would have to count a perceptual belief as doxastically unjustified unless the subject were in a position to tell that the perceptual process was a reliable one—not a result any reliabilist should countenance. But the fact that the blindly credulous person is not in a position to vindicate the reliability of the process-type she is employing, together with *other* relevant facts (pertaining to the non-ideal conditions that prevail), generates a relevant defeater. These facts have to do with the distribution of incompetent and insincere testimonies in human society. The reliability of the (extended) process-type involved in the credulous subject's process of forming testimonial belief is, in any given case, dependent on facts pertaining to the reliability of the processes implicated in the production of the testimony she accepted. But, given the facts about human speakers (including the prevalence of incompetent testimony as well as the prevalence of non-epistemic motives for speech), it would appear that the reliability of the testimony she consumed is not something that can simply be taken for granted. (In particular, it is not something that can be taken as a relevant "background condition.") Arguably, under these circumstances, a testimonial belief formed through a process that fails to address these live questions is one that faces a relevant defeater.[10]

---

[10] These questions must be addressed in the process of belief-formation; but this is not to say that *the subject herself* must direct conscious attention to them. They might be adequately addressed by, e.g., a subcognitive process of credibility-monitoring, one that is counterfactually sensitive to indications of unreliability (and hence to the presence of defeaters). See Goldberg and Henderson (2006) for a discussion.

Even with the point just made, I am not completely confident in the soundness of the DA-involving reply to the objection from blind trust. A schematic analogy will help to explain my feelings of unease. Suppose (perhaps counterfactually) that there is a phenomenological experience-type, ρ, that is correlated with two distinct belief-forming process-types, δ_1 and δ_2, where δ_1 but not δ_2 is G-reliable, and where both process-types are used with some regularity. And suppose further that for a typical mature subject in good cognitive health, there are no other ways to distinguish cases involving δ_1 from cases involving δ_2. Now consider the hypothesis that, even in those cases in which the subject forms her belief through (the G-reliable) δ_1, her belief will fail to be doxastically justified, owing to this justification's having been defeated. Is this hypothesis plausible?

Those proponents of the extendedness hypothesis who endorse DA should expect an affirmative answer to this question. After all, as construed by the extendedness hypothesis, the credulous subject who forms a belief through blindly accepting reliable testimony is facing a situation precisely analogous to the situation faced by the subject in the paragraph above: neither one is in a position to distinguish the actual (reliable) process-type involved in the production of her present belief, from another process-type that might easily have been in play but which is unreliable. If the testimony case calls for a relevant defeater, it seems that so, too, should the perception case above—for precisely the same reasons.

I must confess, however, that it is not entirely clear to me that this is the right thing to say in the perception case above. After all, it would appear to be one thing to have grounds for being uncertain of the reliability of the process you are employing, and another to have grounds for being uncertain of *which* process you are employing. In the latter case, it is arguable that you have grounds for being uncertain of the reliability of your process only if it is *this* process rather than *that* one. What is unclear to me on this score is whether, in cases involving distinct yet internally indistinguishable belief-forming processes only some of which are G-reliable, grounds for uncertainty regarding which of these processes one is employing in a given case immediately count as grounds for uncertainty over the reliability of the process one is employing. I am inclined to answer this in the affirmative, but I am not fully confident of this. And so it is not entirely clear to me that the proponent of the extendedness hypothesis can respond to the objection from blind trust by appeal to relevant defeaters and DA.

1.2

Happily, there is another option available. This option involves re-examining the conditions on doxastic justification in cases of beliefs formed through a belief-dependent process. (The same thing goes, *mutatis mutandis*, for beliefs acquired through quasi-belief-dependent processes.) The point itself can be brought out in terms of what I will argue is a crucial but false assumption that is shared by SUFF and SUF2. The assumption in question is this:

SF*   In cases not involving relevant defeaters, a testimonial belief is doxastically justified so long as (i) the testimony consumed was reliable and (ii) the process operating in the hearer was reliable (conditionally reliable).

I want to argue that SF* is false, and that as a result the objection from blind trust can be met even if we agree to bracket the issue of defeaters.

Let me begin, however, by considering why one might think that SF* is true. More specifically, why might a proponent of the objection from blind trust think that, at least for the sake of developing the objection itself, it is appropriate to assume SF*? I take it that the answer is supposed to be something like this: the proponent of the extendedness hypothesis regards testimonial belief-formation as a (quasi-)belief-dependent process, and SF* itself is a special case of a more general principle having to do with the conditions on the doxastic justification of *any* belief acquired through a belief-dependent (or quasi-belief-dependent) process. The more general principle would be this:

> GSF*   In cases not involving relevant defeaters, a belief formed through a belief-dependent process is doxastically justified so long as (i) the input into the process was reliable and (ii) the process itself was conditionally reliable.

But in response I want to argue that GSF* itself is false, for a reason having nothing to do with testimony cases; and that the reasons for this suggest how the objection from blind trust can be met (even after we agree to bracket the issue of defeaters).

To bring out that the falsity of GSF* has nothing to do with testimony cases, I will focus on an example of another sort of belief acquired through a belief-dependent process: memorial belief. Let M1 and M2 be two distinct memory systems that are both equally (highly) conditionally reliable. When their respective inputs are true, M1 and M2 operate in a very similar fashion. But both operate in environments in which a good many of their inputs are false. And in those cases in which they operate on false inputs there is an important difference between M1 and M2: whereas M1 invariably produces an output in all of these cases, M2, by contrast, does not always, or even typically, produce an output in these cases. This is because M2 has a component—call it the F-filter—operating at the earliest stage of its processing, whose job it is (first) to detect those inputs that exhibit the F-property, and (second) to interrupt M2, and so prevent M2 from producing an output, in all and only those cases in which such an input is detected. What is more, the F-property itself is a property that highly correlates with *falsity* in the input. (To make matters concrete, we might suppose that the inputs into M1 and M2 are memory impressions, and that F is the property of *lacking relevant specificity and detail*—something that, actual memory studies suggest, is a relatively reliable indication of a "false memory."[11]) It is because M2 includes the F-filter, whereas

---

[11] See, e.g., Koutstaal et. al. (1999) and Mather et. al. (1997).

M1 does not, that M2 differs from M1 even in cases in which the inputs are true: the F-filter is operative (in M2) in these cases as well. But we will imagine that, in the part of the process that occurs after the F-filter has completed its work, M2 proceeds exactly as M1 does.

Now consider M1 and M2 from the perspective of the truth-ratios of their respective outputs. As noted, M1 and M2 are equally highly conditionally reliable: in cases in which their respective inputs are true, both M1 and M2 produce outputs, with a preponderance of these being true. To make matters vivid, let us say that in the "true input" condition, M1's performance matches M2's performance exactly: 95 percent of their respective outputs in these cases are true. But matters are very different when we look at cases in which the inputs are false. Given a false input, M1 (which has no F-filter) produces a false output 99 percent of the time (the other 1 percent of the time it produces a true output—by luck, as it were). By contrast, M2 produces a false output in the "false input" condition only 5 percent of the time; approximately 94 percent of the time the F-filter works and the process is interrupted before any output is produced, while the other less than 1 percent of the time it produces a true output (again as a matter of luck). When we aggregate the cases of true and false inputs to ask what proportion of the respective processes' outputs is true, it is clear that M2 outperforms M1 by a large margin: M2 outputs far fewer false beliefs, proportionally, than does M1.

How should a Process Reliabilist understand this difference? Everyone can agree that M1 will produce more unjustified beliefs than will M2. The crucial question, as I see it, is whether M1's and M2's respective performance in the *false*-input cases should be seen as affecting the reliability profile of those beliefs that are produced in *true*-input cases. A corresponding question concerns doxastic justification: given a belief-dependent process (like M1) which does quite poorly in cases in which its inputs are false (producing a high percentage of false beliefs in these cases), does this poor performance in false-input cases affect the degree of doxastic justification enjoyed in *true*-input (better: true-and-reliable-input) cases as well?

A proponent of GSF* will have to give a negative answer to this question. Assuming GSF*, any case (not involving relevant defeaters) in which we have (i) reliable inputs and (ii) a conditionally reliable process, the belief-dependently-produced belief counts as doxastically justified. But this, I submit, is implausible: even if we concede (for the sake of argument) that there are no relevant defeaters in these cases, a conditionally reliable belief-dependent system that regularly has a high preponderance of false (or unreliable) inputs does *not* yield doxastically justified belief in those rare cases where it happens to have reliable inputs. Or so I will argue in what follows.

Let us fill in the story regarding M1 and M2 in greater detail. As noted, these processes operate in an environment in which a good many of their inputs—say, 50 percent—are false, so that *true*-input cases occur only 50 percent of the time. (These numbers are not meant to be realistic, of course; I use them to make the point vivid.) Now imagine a series of trial runs each of which involves 1,000 inputs. In these trial runs of 1,000 inputs, M1 will average 520 false outputs and 480 true outputs, whereas M2 will average 50 false outputs, 480 true outputs, and 470 cases of no outputs.[12] Putting our results in terms of percentages, M1's truth-ratio—the percentage of true outputs among its total outputs—is 48 percent, whereas M2's truth-ratio is 90.6 percent. This is a significant difference, and it might be thought to bear on the doxastic justification of *all* of the outputs produced by these processes, not just those produced in the false-input cases.

---

[12] These numbers reflect the performance in true-input cases and false-input cases. In the false-input cases, which occur 50 percent of the time, M1 produces true belief 1 percent of the time, and false belief 99 percent of the time; whereas in the true-input cases, which occur the other 50 percent of the time, M1 produces true belief 95 percent of the time, and false belief the other 5 percent of the time. Although the 50/50 false-input/true-input ratio remains in place for M2, the other numbers differ, and the false-input condition includes a third outcome (no output produced).

What might support this last contention? Anyone attracted by Terminal Phase Reliabilism would endorse this contention. After all, M1 and M2 differ in the "goodness" of the terminal phase of the process—as is seen in the great difference in their respective truth-ratios. But even if we reject Terminal Phase Reliabilism, and so reject that Terminal Phase Reliability is *sufficient* condition for doxastic justification (as Chapter 4, following Goldman 1979, did), we might still think that it is *necessary* for doxastic justification.[13] If so, any process that is not Terminal Phase Reliable is one that does not produce doxastically justified belief.

But why should Process Reliabilists—especially those who reject Terminal Phase Reliabilism, and so who reject that terminal phase reliability is *sufficient* for doxastic justification—think that reliability of the terminal phase of the process is *necessary* to doxastic justification? Actually, Goldman's own programmatic conception of doxastic justification, cited throughout Chapters 3 and 4, provides such a reason. He wrote:

A justified belief is, roughly speaking, one that results from cognitive operations that are, generally speaking, good or successful. But *"cognitive"* operations are most plausibly construed as operations of the cognitive faculties, i.e., "information-processing" equipment internal to the organism. (Goldman 1979/2000: 346–7)

Now I have already argued that Goldman's assimilation of "cognitive" with "information-processing equipment *internal* to the organism" is question-begging against the proponent of the extendedness hypothesis. For this reason, the foregoing quote offers no independent support for Process Individualism. At the same time, Goldman is surely right about one thing: how well such "internal equipment" is working is relevant to whether the belief in question is justified. This point should be endorsed by reliabilists of all stripes. Once we reject Process Individualism, and so reject the assimilation of "cognitive" with "information-processing equipment *internal* to

---

[13] At least it might be thought necessary in those cases in which Terminal Phase Reliability can be computed.

the organism," Goldman's point on this score is best captured by the idea that the proper functioning of internal equipment, while not a *sufficient* condition on doxastic justification, is nevertheless a *necessary* one. With this in mind, we can say: if a (quasi-) belief-dependent process ψ ordinarily operates in circumstances which are such that, in a non-negligible percentage of these ordinary cases the inputs into ψ are false, then it can be regarded as a flaw in ψ—one affecting ψ's "goodness," and so the doxastic justification of ψ's outputs—that ψ does nothing to distinguish between high-quality (true) and low-quality (false) inputs. Such a proposal is motivated by the claim that doxastic justification requires "cognitive operations that are, generally speaking, good or successful." The goodness or success of any belief-dependent process that regularly deals with a high percentage of false (or otherwise unreliable) inputs depends on the process having some way to "weed out" such inputs. The necessity thesis is meant to honor this point, in a way that accommodates the insight that it is the *whole* process that must be assessed for justification-relevant reliability.

Our present point can be illustrated in connection with yet another memory system, M3, with the following features: it is *perfectly* conditionally reliable, in the sense that every true-input case is a true-output case; but the *vast majority* of its inputs are false, and M3 employs no F-filter of the sort described in connection with M2. To make matters vivid, suppose that 99.99 percent of M3's inputs are false, and that in every one of these cases M3's output is false. Do we really want to say that, nevertheless, in that 0.01 percent of the time, when M3's input is true and reliable (and so, given M3's perfect conditional reliability, its output is also true), the result is a G-reliably-sustained belief (and so a belief that enjoys doxastic justification)? On the contrary, it would seem patent that M3 itself produces too high a ratio of false outputs ($\approx$99.99 percent) for its outputs to count as doxastically justified in those extremely rare ("happy") cases in which its input is both true and reliable.

As I say, the 'unjustified' verdict is intuitive in the extremely rare cases in which M3's input is both true and reliable. Here it is helpful to bear in mind that, at the end of the day, what the Process Reliabilist really cares about is the preponderance of truth in the products of cognitive processes. The conditional reliability of a belief-dependent process is valuable because, and insofar as, it contributes to this end. But the conditional reliability of a belief-dependent process contributes to a greater preponderance of true belief-outputs *only in proportion to the prevalence of true inputs in normal circumstances*. This, in turn, suggests that the conditional reliability of a belief-dependent process is not the only dimension along which we can measure how well the belief-dependent process itself conduces to the end of a preponderance of true output-beliefs. For the conditional-reliability measure is a measure of the process's performance in the *true*-input condition; what the case of M3 makes clear is that, insofar as the belief-dependent process has a substantial percentage of false inputs in normal conditions, we can and should also assess how well it performs in the *false*-input condition. It would be too much to ask, of course, that the process transform false inputs into true outputs; I don't know of processes that do this. Rather, the best that can be hoped for is that the process can with some success discriminate true inputs from the false ones, and prevent the generation of a belief-output in those cases in which it discerns a false input. We might call this measure the *filtering effectiveness* of the process.

Let us step back now and ask about M3's performance in normal conditions. Its performance in such conditions is poor: it will produce false belief the vast majority of the time. In one sense, this poor performance is not M3's fault: the fault can be traced to the fact that most of the inputs into M3 are false. But in another sense, this poor performance *is* M3's fault: a process which *regularly* (and *in normal conditions*) receives false inputs and yet does nothing to rectify the situation can be seen as a process with performance issues. Compare: if our perceptual system were not finely attuned to the conditions under which the perceptual appearances are not to be trusted, that system would be much less good, epistemically speaking, than it is. It is precisely because mature perceivers hesitate in forming perceptual beliefs when perceptual conditions are not good, and because such perceivers tend not to form perceptual beliefs when conditions are too risky, that perception is as G-reliable a process as it is. A similar thing can be said with memory: its goodness consists not only in what it does under happy (true-input) conditions, but also what it does to minimize the risk of unreliable belief owing to the prevalence of unhappy (false-input) conditions. It is precisely this, I submit, that is brought out by the case of M3: given the high percentage of falsity in the inputs into the memory system M3 (under conditions standard for the use of processes with this terminal phase), the fact that the terminal phase lacks a sensitive filter should be seen as an epistemic flaw in the system. For precisely this reason, M3's lack of a sensitive filter can be taken to bear on the doxastic justification of *all* of M3's outputs, not just those produced in the false-input conditions.

The foregoing considerations suggest that GSF* is false. Even if we agree for the sake of discussion to bracket issues of defeaters, it is simply not the case that a belief formed through a belief-dependent process is doxastically justified so long as (i) the input into the process was reliable and (ii) the process itself was conditionally reliable. This is precisely what the case of M3 is designed to show: conditions (i) and (ii) are satisfied, yet the output-belief is not doxastically justified. But what else, besides (i) and (ii), is involved in the doxastic justification of belief-dependent beliefs? Here again we should remember that one thing the Process Reliabilist cares about is the preponderance of truth in the products of cognitive processes. In the case in which the cognitive process is a belief-dependent one, this translates into a concern that the belief-dependent process yields a preponderance of truth. And this, in turn, points to what GSF* is missing: namely, a condition meant to ensure *Terminal Phase Reliability* in the outputs of a belief-dependent process. Terminal Phase Reliability may not be sufficient for doxastic justification, but it is necessary.[14]

I submit that testimonial belief should be understood in a parallel fashion, with credibility-monitoring playing the role of the relevant filter.[15] Consider the credulous consumer of testimony. If the extendedness hypothesis is to be trusted, the process-type involved in such cases is something like this: *credulously-accepting-testimony-produced-by-this-process-type*. The terminal phase of the process is that part of the process that takes place "in" the hearer, the recipient of testimony. (This part of the process is regarded by the Process Individualist—wrongly, in my book—as the whole of the process of testimonial belief-formation.) When blind trust is involved, the terminal part of the process will not be Terminal Phase Reliable (at least not in any world in which there is a good deal of false testimony—what above I called 'non-ideal conditions'). We would then get the result that blind trust—which

---

[14] One side issue might be worth noting. As it is, I claim that GSF* is false: conditions (i) and (ii) are not sufficient for doxastic justification in cases of beliefs formed through a belief-dependent process. But are (i) are (ii) *necessary*? This is unclear; the matter is somewhat vexed. Jack Lyons (in conversation) has described a case in which memory appears to *generate* reliability (rather than preserve it). His case is that of "gist" memory. There is good empirical evidence to suppose that we often remember scenes or lists by encoding the "gist" of the scene or list (see, e.g., McClelland 1995). Suppose that such an encoding scheme is part of a conditionally reliable memory system, in the sense that in those cases in which true beliefs are the inputs, a preponderance of the outputs of the "gist"-involving memorial system are true. Even so, it can happen on occasion that this memory system yields a false belief through a "gist"-induced distortion. For example, a subject might claim to remember that the word "doctor" was on a list she was presented with last week, when in fact that list contained only "nurse," "patient," "hospital," "emergency room," "illness," and "health." If her 'memorial' belief, to the effect that "doctor" was on the list, is to be counted as reliable (reliably formed and sustained), this would be proof that memory can be *the source* of reliably formed belief. (See also Lackey (2005) for an argument, independent of reliabilism, for the conclusion that memory can be a generative source; although Lackey's case is one in which memory generated a belief that the person hadn't previously formed, whereas Lyon's case is one in which memory generated not only the belief but also the justification as well.) It would be controversial, however, to suppose that this sort of case is a counterexample to the thesis that reliable inputs are a necessary condition on the reliability of beliefs formed through belief-dependent processes. In the case Lyons describes, the input into the process may well be the "gist"-generated belief, to the effect that the list contained words pertaining to hospitals—and such a belief was both true and reliably formed.

[15] This is an idea that can be found in Audi (1997) and Goldberg and Henderson (2006).

amounts to an insensitive credibility-monitoring filter—can render a testimonial belief doxastically *un*justified even under conditions in which the testimony consumed was reliable and the process itself was conditionally reliable. (We would get such a result in any world involving non-ideal conditions, since any such world will be one in which the testimonial belief-forming process has to deal with a sizable proportion of false inputs in ordinary circumstances.) Since this is precisely to deny WBTR, the weaker version of the *reductio* claim at the heart of the objection from blind trust, that objection is directly met.[16]

The foregoing response to the objection from blind trust bracketed considerations of relevant defeaters. What should be said if we want to complicate the story, so as to have such considerations back in the picture? Here we must reconsider the role of SUF2 in developing the objection from blind trust. Above, I argued that it is not obvious that the proponent of the objection from blind trust can appeal to SUF2 without undermining her main contention. In particular, since SUF2 involves a 'no relevant defeaters' condition, its opens the way for a defender of the extendedness hypothesis to endorse DA, the claim that blind trust generates relevant defeaters, and in this way to avoid implying that blind trust can give rise to doxastically justified testimonial belief. At the same time, I acknowledged that it was not entirely clear that the proponent of the extendedness *can* endorse DA. What we now see is that the issue of relevant defeaters is a bit of a red herring. In particular, there is a deeper point in the vicinity: the formation of beliefs through blind trust is an epistemic vice in any world with a high percentage of false or unreliable testimonies—whatever the status of DA turns out to be. This is a point that any card-carrying reliabilist—and so, by extension, any reliabilist who is a proponent of the extendedness hypothesis—can and should endorse. If DA holds, then the

---

[16] It might be thought that this would leave the objection from credulity intact, albeit only for worlds in which the hearer did not confront a sizable proportion of false testimonies. But above I argued that it is not clear at all that credulity is an epistemic vice in such situations.

proponent of the extendedness hypothesis can regard blind trust as an epistemic vice, at least in part, because the formation of a testimonial belief through blind trust always generates a relevant defeater. But even if DA does not hold, the proponent of the extendedness hypothesis can still regard blind trust as an epistemic vice, albeit on the grounds that beliefs acquired through blind trust *are not Terminal Phase Reliable*, and hence are not doxastically justified—at least, not in any world in which false or otherwise unreliable testimony is common. Whatever the preferred account of the 'not justified' verdict in these sorts of cases may be, the proponent of the extendedness hypothesis can and should say that testimonial beliefs formed through blind trust are not doxastically justified, however reliable the consumed testimony.

2

According to the 'bad company' objection, the extendedness proposal is (or implies) a version of the 'extended mind' hypothesis, and should be rejected for this reason.[17] According to the 'extended mind' (henceforth 'EM') hypothesis, when in the course of problem-solving a thinking subject exploits information-storing or -processing tools in her external environment, in such a way that her reliance on these tools is itself reliable (she regularly makes use of these tools when they are accessible to her), then we should regard this as a case in which there is a single cognitive system that 'extends' to include whatever information-processing is done by the tools in question. (In this way, the computations done by a calculator might themselves be regarded as part of a single 'extended' cognitive system which includes Sam, who regularly relies on this calculator to do arithmetic.) EM has struck many people as false, both for implying the existence of "expanded" cognitive

---

[17] For some of the literature on the hypothesis of 'extended cognition,' see Wilson (1994); Chalmers and Clark (1998); Hurley (1998); Adams and Aizawa (2001, 2005, forthcoming a, forthcoming b, and forthcoming c); Clark (2001, 2003, 2005, 2006, and 2007); Rupert (2004); Sterelny (2004); Dartnall (2005); Menary (2005); and Robbins and Aydede (forthcoming).

systems, and also for having untoward implications for taxonomy in cognitive psychology. In reply, I submit that the extendedness hypothesis is immune to both of these objections. The result is that if the extendedness hypothesis *does* entail EM, it entails a version that is not susceptible to the standard objections to EM.

I want to begin discussion on this topic by underscoring that the extendedness hypothesis defended here is advanced as an epistemological proposal, not a psychological one. Once this is appreciated, we will see that this proposal has no implications regarding the existence of "expanded" cognitive systems, nor does the proposal entail anything regarding a proper taxonomy for cognitive psychology.

A first point on this score is this: there are solid grounds for distinguishing between the notion of 'belief-forming process' as it is in play in reliabilist epistemology, and the one which is in play in cognitive psychology. To be sure, both Process Reliabilists and cognitive psychologists are interested in features of the processes by which beliefs are acquired and sustained. However, their interest in these features differs. Reliabilists are interested in those features that bear on *reliability*, and in particular on reliability in the formation and/or sustainment of belief. Cognitive psychologists, by contrast, are interested in those features that support interesting cognitive-psychological generalizations, and those features that give us insight into the nature and structure of the information-processing systems corresponding to individual psychological agents. It is an open question whether the features that make for reliability in belief-formation and belief-sustainment also support interesting cognitive-psychological generalizations, or give us insight into the nature and structure of the information-processing systems corresponding to individual psychological subjects.[18] But given that psychology is interested in more than reliability—it is also

---

[18] Here it might be worth noting that even within psychology there are differences in the grain of analysis, with social psychologists typically taking interpersonal relations as part of what explains psychological phenomena. With thanks to Lance Rips for suggesting this point (in conversation).

interested in the ease and speed of information-processing and retrieval, the format of mental representations, and the relationships between information-processing and behavior, among other things—it would seem that cognitive psychologists have a clear motive for slicing psychological reality differently than by way of the features that matter to epistemologists. To see this, suppose the existence of what from the epistemologist's perspective is a reliable belief-forming process, but which process nevertheless fails to integrate fully within what the psychologist has characterized as a given system's various channels of information-processing. Then, even if the psychologist agrees that the epistemologist is free to count this as a single "process" from the point of view of an epistemic assessment of reliability, the psychologist may well deny that the 'extended' part of this process is part of anything that she, the psychologist, recognizes as a single psychological system in the first place.

I just noted that the cognitive psychologist need not defer to the epistemologist on the question of what should count as part of a single psychological system. It is also worthwhile noting that the epistemologist need not think that what matters for reliability is exhausted by those features the psychologist identifies as part of a single psychological system, taken in isolation from its wider (social and natural) environment. One obvious example of this involves the use of eyeglasses or hearing aids. The psychologist might well have good reasons to resist regarding these things as "part of" the psychological subject, yet clearly they matter to the epistemologist interested in reliability. To be sure, insofar as cognitive psychology studies what we might call basic belief-forming processes—perception, memory, etc.—these will be highly relevant to issues of reliability. Even so, it is unclear why the epistemologist should suppose that the features of such processes *exhaust* the materials out of which we determine whether the subject's beliefs are reliably formed and/or sustained. On the contrary, it is open to the reliabilist to argue that there are cases in which features *other than* a subject's own basic belief-forming processes are relevant to whether the subject's beliefs are reliably formed and/or sustained. In particular, features of *another* subject's (basic or non-basic) belief-forming processes might be relevant in this way. I have been arguing throughout that testimonial belief is precisely such a case.

But there is a second point to be made on behalf of my claim that the extendedness hypothesis has no untoward implications for taxonomy in cognitive psychology. In particular, the extendedness hypothesis is something that is in keeping with commitments that the Process Reliabilist already has—and there are clear reasons to suppose that those commitments have no implications for taxonomy in cognitive psychology. (Here I return to a theme that will be familiar from the argument of Chapters 3 and 4, so I will be brief.) Consider the standard Process Reliabilist account of memorial belief. As we saw at the end of the last chapter, the standard treatment is to regard the reliability of memorial belief as determined not only by the (conditional) reliability of the process of memory itself, but also by the reliability with which the belief now being recalled was acquired.[19] The process that eventuates in memorial belief is thus 'temporally extended': a proper reliabilist assessment of a memorial belief must include an assessment of the reliability with which that belief was acquired (some time ago). Note that this claim about the temporal extendedness of the process that eventuates in a memorial belief does not have any implications for taxonomy in the cognitive psychology of memory: it does not force the cognitive psychologist who is interested in memory to distinguish the process involved in the sustainment of a memory-of-a-visually-acquired-belief from that involved in the sustainment of a memory-of-an-intuited-belief. Here we see the present point quite clearly: it is one thing to regard something as a single process from the perspective of a reliabilist assessment of the relevant belief, and it is quite another to regard something as

---

[19] And, if the argument from Section 1 is sound, on the Terminal Phase Reliability of the process.

a single process from the perspective of an illuminating taxonomy of our cognitive-psychological nature. The reliabilist should find it natural to say something similar about testimonial belief.

It is now easy to appreciate that the extendedness hypothesis does not imply the existence of "expanded" cognitive systems. My contention is *not* that in testimonial belief-formation there is a single cognitive system whose processes include both the processes implicated in the production of testimony (in the speaker) and those implicated in its comprehension and consumption (by the hearer). My contention is rather that those epistemologists with an interest in assessing the "goodness" of the cognitive processing implicated in the production of testimonial belief must assess both of these processes. Nothing in this contention implies that these are processes of something which itself is a single cognitive system in its own right—one distinct from both the speaker and the hearer. To reach such a conclusion, we would need to introduce a claim about the conditions on having a single cognitive system. The proponent of the extendedness hypothesis remains free to reject such a claim.

Still, there is the question whether the extendedness hypothesis implies some version of EM. On this score, I can imagine that a proponent of EM might defend an affirmative answer to this question. She might do so as follows: "It's one thing to taxonomize processes differently for different purposes, but another thing to individuate processes differently. Our claim is that it's arbitrary to individuate cognitive processes by stopping at the skin, and reliability considerations support this claim."[20] Actually, I would be happy to live with this conclusion, since it is compatible with the main points I have been anxious to make, to the effect that the extendedness hypothesis has no implications for taxonomy in cognitive psychology or for the existence of "expanded" cognitive systems. If, having conceded these points, proponents of EM claim

---

[20] With thanks again to Lance Rips for making this point on behalf of proponents of EM.

support from reliability considerations, that's fine by me. My main concern is to make clear that such a position has no implications for how belief-forming processes are taxonomized in the course of research within cognitive psychology. (Any version of EM that respects this point is not such "bad company" after all.)

3

With the 'bad company' objection thus dismissed, let us turn now to another objection, this one from the causal nature of the process of belief-formation. The core allegation here is that the extendedness hypothesis fails to square with the point that a belief-forming or -sustaining process is a cognitive process that constitutes the *causal antecedents* of belief-formation or -sustainment.

This objection flows from considerations that appear to have played a role in both Goldman's and Alston's endorsement of Process Individualism. Alston put the point as one of needing to individuate belief-forming processes in terms of the "*proximate* causal history" of a belief (the italics are mine; the phrase itself is from Alston 1995/2000: 363). On this view, individualism is supported by the idea that belief-forming processes are constituted (not by distal or 'external' effects on cognition but rather) by the proximate causal history of a belief. Any rejection of Process Individualism, then, must show that the appropriate starting point of the causal history of testimonial belief begins further upstream. To do so it is not enough to point out, as I did in Chapter 4, that testimony is a case of interpersonal epistemic reliance. Rather, what is wanted is to see how processes that take place in another person's mind-brain can be appropriately *causally* relevant to the production of belief in oneself.

Actually, it is not all that hard to see how processes that take place in a speaker's mind-brain can be causally relevant to the production of a hearer's belief. Consider the process a whose origin is the point at which the source S formed her belief, which extends temporally through her sustainment of that belief up until the time that she gives expression to it in her testimony, and then continues as the hearer H observes and understands this speech act, and moves to accept S's testimony. From the perspective of an interest in the causal history of the hearer H's belief, there is no mystery here. Let us use 'a_S' to designate that part of a which involves all and only the relevant cognitive processes in source S. So a_S begins at the point at which S initiated the formation of her belief and ends at the point at which she gives verbal expression to that belief in the testimony she offers in the company of H. How is a_S causally relevant to H's belief? Well, consider that if H hadn't observed S's testimony, H wouldn't have formed the belief he did (or so we can assume). Consider also that the tail end of a_S is directly linked to the formation of H's belief: the event of S's testifying, which occurs at the end of a_S, is part of *the cause* of H's forming the belief he does. Or rather this testimony is the distal cause that initiates the proximate causal history, a_H, of H's belief. Here we should bear in mind that if the *epistemic basing relation* is a causal relation, as many have argued,[21] then, if S's testimony were not the distal cause initiating the proximate causal history of H's belief, it would be false to say that H's belief is based on the testimony. Finally, note that features of a_S must be cited to explain various other counterfactuals true of H's belief, or the process through which H formed this belief.[22] To see this, suppose that S's source belief—the one expressed in her testimony—was formed on the basis of seeing that o is F, and that S had no further source of support (beyond her visual experience) for her belief that o is F. Then the following counterfactuals will be true: if S hadn't seen that o is F, then H wouldn't have come to believe that o is F

---

[21] For a simple but paradigmatic version of a causal account of the basing relation, see Moser (1989: 157). For a more complex analysis that regards the basing relation as involving a causal relation, see Audi (1986/2003). The most popular alternative to causation-involving conceptions of the basing relation is Swain's counterfactualist account (1979, 1981, 1985). Interestingly, this analysis is satisfied by belief based on testimony as well (as I will try to indicate above). For a succinct overview of the literature on the basing relation, see Korscz (2002).

[22] It is for this reason that testimonial belief can be seen to satisfy Swain's counterfactualist account of the basing relation.

(i.e., since S wouldn't have attested to o's being F); and if S had forgotten that o is F (and so was unable to recall the belief at the time when she actually testified), then H wouldn't have come to believe that o is F (since S wouldn't have attested to o's being F). These counterfactuals—and others could be produced—suggest that features of a_S are *causally* relevant to H's forming the belief that o is F. What is more, other counterfactuals suggest that features of a_S contribute to the reliability of H's belief, in precisely the way we would anticipate if a_S is part of the process through which H acquired the belief. For example: if S caught only a fleeting glimpse of o, at a distance, and under bad lighting conditions, then H's belief that o is F will suffer from a corresponding sort of unreliability (i.e., even if H's monitoring of S's testimony did not uncover any grounds for concern); if S's memory is poor on the matter of whether o is F, then H's belief that o is F will suffer from corresponding unreliability; if S is an unreliable speaker, often producing speech whose 'face value' interpretation conflicts with what she means, then H's belief that o is F will suffer from corresponding unreliability; and so forth. In short, there is a strong prima facie case to be made for thinking that features of a_S are causally relevant to H's belief that o is F.

Another worry one might have in connection with the 'causal antecedents' of testimonial belief is this: while another's testimony is causally relevant to one's forming the belief, not everything that is causally relevant to belief-formation is part of the belief-forming process itself. As an analogy, consider my belief that there is a cup in front of me, when in fact there is a cup in front of me. Here, the fact that there is a cup in front of me is causally relevant to my perceptual belief that there is a cup in front of me; yet the causal history that eventuated in the cup's being where it is clearly is not part of the relevant causal history of my belief. In response, I submit that there is an important (and obvious) disanalogy between the two cases. The causal history that eventuated in the cup's being where it is is perfectly irrelevant to the reliability, and hence the epistemic status, of my belief: so long as the cup got there (and I perceive it, etc.), I know that there's a cup in front of me. This is certainly not the case with testimony. There are all sorts of histories that might have led to a speaker's testifying as she did, not all of which are compatible with the hearer's acquiring reliable belief through her acceptance of that testimony. "External" events or features are relevant to the process through which a belief was formed only when these events or features are relevant to the belief's reliability; and if we agree further that the only features that count are those that are part of the *cognitive* process that led to the belief's formation, we are even further restricted. The reliabilist, it would seem, has plenty of resources with which to make principled distinctions here, and so to respond to this face of the problem from the causal nature of belief-formation.

But there is one other related worry one might have in this connection. The worry is that, in cases of extended communication chains, there will be far too much processing going on in the formation of a subject's belief. (It might stretch back over a long period of time, and include cognitive processing in the mind/brains of a good many other subjects.) Even those who don't blanch at the thought of a process extending over quite some time—something all Process Reliabilists have a reason to concede in memory cases (for which see Chapter 4)—might balk at the idea of a process lasting longer than the lifetime of any single participant in the chain.

One immediate response that can be made is this: my talk of "extended processing" is meant merely to indicate the extent of the processing that needs to be assessed from the perspective of determinations of the G-reliability of the belief in question. Thus even if the extendedness hypothesis is committed to *intergenerationally* extended processing, this does not imply any thesis about trans-generational agents; nor, as I argued in my reply to the 'bad company' objection, does this have any implications for proper taxonomy for cognitive psychology.

Still, one might continue to worry that extended chains of communication will make it practically impossible to determine the G-reliability of any testimonial belief that comes at the end of such a chain. Take a testimonial belief that is formed at the tail end of a chain of communication whose origin is in the remote past. Insofar as the G-reliability of such a testimonial belief depends on the reliability of testimonies made in the remote past, it would seem that the inaccessibility of the remote past deprives us of any sound way to reach a verdict regarding the belief's G-reliability.

In response I submit that, at least in most cases, the main determinants of the G-reliability of a testimonial belief are accessible even when the testimonial belief is formed at the tail end of a chain of communication whose origin is in the remote past. To see this, consider the proposal developed in Section 1 above, according to which a testimonial belief is doxastically justified (and so G-reliable) if (i) it was based on reliable testimony, and the "on-board" part of the belief-forming process was both (ii) conditionally reliable and (iii) Terminal Phase Reliable (and there are no relevant defeaters). I submit that the extendedness of a chain of communication poses no problem for ascertaining whether conditions (ii) or (iii) have been satisfied; and, while extended chains can make it difficult to determine whether condition (i) is satisfied, nevertheless in most cases of extended communication a third-party assessor can have a good indication whether (i) is satisfied.

The extendedness of a chain of communication poses no problem for determining whether the "on-board" part of the testimonial belief-forming process was conditionally reliable and/or Terminal Phase Reliable. These determinations require access only to the truth-value of the 'inputs' and the 'outputs' of the "on-board" part of the testimonial belief-forming process. The temporally remote origin of a chain of communication poses no distinctive difficulty for assessing these truth-values. To be sure, if the content of the testimony itself is a proposition regarding the remote past, its truth-value may be hard to ascertain. But the problem here is the generic one of assessing truth-values of claims about the remote past—a problem *whether or not* the chain of communication was extended. (Imagine hearing a lecture today on the temperature in some region of Antarctica some time in the remote past, from a research scientist who reached her conclusions through her recent investigations in which she drilled hundreds of feet into the ice caps, to examine the conditions of the ice there. It may be hard to assess the truth-value of her claims about the temperatures of the remote past, but the difficulty here has nothing to do with the extendedness of the chain of communication: that starts and stops with her.)

This said, the extendedness of a chain of communication might cause difficulties with regard to an assessor's attempt to ascertain whether condition (i), the reliable testimony condition, holds. Suppose that S is a subject who accepts a piece of testimony, t, that is itself at the tail end of chain of communication whose origin is in the remote past. It can seem that assessing t's reliability requires us to assess the reliability of the testimony on which t was based (call this testimony t'), which in turn requires us to assess the reliability of the testimony on which t' was based, and so on, stretching back to the origin. If this is so, then our determination requires us to determine the reliability of most or all of the testimonies that constitute links in this communication chain; and this can seem practically impossible.

Nevertheless, there are reasons for thinking that an assessor can get a good (though by no means infallible) indication of t's reliability without assessing the reliability of all of the testimonies that constitute links in this communication chain. The key point to be made here is this: any piece of testimony is itself a potential object of social scrutiny. The relationship between testimony and social scrutiny places a "reliability check" on long chains of communication. Whereas extended chains might be such that the message has a tendency to 'degrade' over time and across speakers, with a corresponding decrease in the reliability of the transmitted message as one moves further downstream—consider the children's game "Whisper Down the Lane"—this is to some extent counterbalanced by the 'external' check provided by social scrutiny. A message that has seriously degraded is one that is most likely to elicit doubting or even critical comments from a would-be audience. Insofar as this manifestation of doubt or skepticism is effective in getting the speaker herself to doubt whether she has it right, social scrutiny plays the role of a sort of social 'filter' on downstream testimonies in an extended communication chain.

Given this sort of social-scrutiny-realized "reliability check" on messages that pass through extended chains of communication, worries to the effect that the extendedness of a chain of communication undermines our ability to determine the reliability of a piece of testimony appear to be overblown. To see this, consider how facts about the relevant background social conditions—in particular, the knowledgeableness and level of skepticism among community members, the value placed on reliability, and the kinds and prevalence of "reliability-checks" undergone by ordinary testimonies in the community—might give some indication of the reliability of pieces of testimony that are proffered under those background conditions. For example, imagine two communities, an "uncritical" community and a "skeptical" one. In the "uncritical" community, members are generally very credulous and uncritical, and have a good many false beliefs in their world-view. As a result, even those rumors that you or I would consider to be literally incredible spread rapidly throughout this community. In the "skeptical" community, by contrast, members exert withering skepticism regarding any testimonies that strike them as dubious, and they have very high epistemic standards and a good deal of worldly knowledge on which to draw in assessing incoming testimony. As a result, little but the most well-confirmed claims passes through the community. Now suppose that Unhappy is a hearer in the uncritical community, and that Happy is a hearer in the skeptical community. Both receive a piece of testimony, where the testimony in question is the end link of an extended chain of communication. How might we assess these testimonies for reliability? More to the point: how can we do so on the assumption that we cannot assess the reliability of the "upstream" testimonies in the chain?

We can do so by making some inferences from background social conditions. In the "skeptical" community chances are good that, had the last testimony in the chain (the one observed by Happy) been false, testimonies with this content would have been "weeded out" by the skeptical community.[23] So the fact that a testimony with this content was offered in the first place gives some indication that the proposition in question is true.[24] In the "uncritical" community, by contrast, false testimony is prevalent (and there is no tendency for it to be "filtered out" through the process of social scrutiny). So the fact that a testimony with this content was offered in the first place gives very little, if any, indication that the proposition in question is true; on the contrary, the prevalence of false testimonies might lead us to assign a higher probability to the claim that the testimony is false. To be sure, this sort of inference is not foolproof: when reached through this sort of inference, verdicts about the reliability of a piece of testimony are highly fallible. My only claim is that background social conditions give a third-party assessor something to go on as she tries to ascertain whether condition (i), the reliable testimony condition, was satisfied in a given case. There remains a degree of uncertainty in the assessor's verdict on this score, and to that extent there will be a degree of uncertainty in the assessor's corresponding verdict regarding the G-reliability (and the doxastic justification) of the testimonial belief in question. But it seems to me that this is as it should be. Insofar as the reliabilities of the "upstream" testimonies of the relevant communication chain are lost in the shrouds of time, and insofar as no new considerations bear on the likelihood that the most recent testimony in the chain was true, it would appear that we cannot tell whether this testimony, or the beliefs based on it, are G-reliable. If so, then the extendedness of a chain of communication, far from posing any sort of difficulty

---

[23] See Chapter 6 for some related discussion.
[24] The chance that [p] is true, given that a piece of testimony that p was presented in the skeptical community, is relatively high; in any case it is higher than the chance that [p] is true, given that a piece of testimony that p was presented in the *uncritical* community.

that should lead us to reject the extendedness hypothesis, may actually provide us with independent evidence supporting that hypothesis.

4

I now move on to the objection from epistemic assessment. According to this objection, real-life assessments of the doxastic justification of another's testimonial beliefs do not include assessments of the cognitive processing implicated in the production of the testimony—and this flies in the face of what the extendedness hypothesis would lead us to expect. In response I will argue that the alleged fact is no fact at all: insofar as there are such assessments in "real life," such assessments sometimes do involve assessments of the reliability of cognitive processing in the mind/brain(s) of the subject's source(s). What is more, the fact that this is only 'sometimes' true can be explained in a way compatible with the extendedness hypothesis itself.

Let us begin with the claim that epistemic assessments of a subject's testimonial belief sometimes involve assessments of the reliability of cognitive processing in the mind/brain(s) of the subject's source(s). As an initial entry into this topic, consider the following sort of scenario. S asserts that p. H, thinking that [p] is not the sort of thing S could have come to learn first hand, responds by asking: "From whom did you learn that?"[25] This sort of scenario is familiar, and its familiarity makes clear that we sometimes do take an epistemic interest in our interlocutors' sources of information. In light of this, I want to claim that it sometimes happens that the interest an assessor (henceforth "Assessor") takes in a subject's testimonial belief ("Subject") leads Assessor to take an interest in the (global) reliability of the original speaker's testimony ("Original Source").

This claim can be developed by reflecting on the variety of situations in which Asssessor (standing in for any third-party assessor)

25 With thanks to John Burgess for reminding me of these cases.

might be interested in assessing the reliability with which Subject (standing in for any other person) formed and sustained a given belief.[26] These situations vary along several dimensions, including the interests (epistemic and otherwise) of Assessor and/or Subject, the stakes involved in the assessment, and the institutional features (if any) of the context. In a great many contexts, Assessor may well be satisfied to make an assessment of reliability based solely on processes 'internal to' Subject herself. I grant that this may be so even in testimony cases: perhaps Assessor's interests will be satisfied so long as she determines how reliable Subject is at distinguishing trustworthy from untrustworthy testimony. However, in other contexts Assessor will want more than this, and may extend the scope of her interests to include cognitive processes in Source's mind/brain.

We can illustrate this with the following case of Jones. The context is one involving a large group of researchers, not all of whom are personally known to each other, but who nevertheless depend on one another in their relevant areas of expertise on matters notorious for their difficulty. Now imagine that in such a context the issue whether p comes up, and that Jones asserts that p on the basis of having trusted Smith's word on the matter. (Smith is a far-off colleague who is not present at the time of this discussion.) If Smith is unknown to the rest of the group, it would seem that at least some in the group (and perhaps even many or most) would still hesitate before accepting Jones's word for it. For such colleagues, the issue whether Jones's testimony (and his belief) were reliable is seen to turn on how reliable *Smith's* testimony itself was, given that it was Smith's (purportedly expert) testimony that formed the basis for Jones's (belief and his subsequent) testimony. Assuming that the sort of reliability in play here is G-reliability—the sort which is relevant to doxastic justification—this case would suggest that assessments of the G-reliability of testimonial belief sometimes do

---

[26] The argument to follow, as well as the example I use to illustrate the argument's key contention, is based on a suggestion made to me (in conversation) by Erik Olsson.

involve taking an interest in the G-reliability of cognitive processes implicated in the production of the testimony.

We can do more to make clear that the sort of reliability at issue here *is* G-reliability. Suppose that the researchers themselves are under no illusions regarding their own epistemic position within the broad scientific domain in question. All of them are agnostic regarding whether they have any knowledge within the domain; what they are aiming at is objectively well-supported, reasonable belief. Such a scenario is not only conceivable but familiar. Indeed, it would appear to describe the case of a good many scientific research teams involved in the more theoretical parts of their science: they don't claim knowledge; they merely claim epistemically well-supported belief. In such a scenario, the motive behind an assessment of the reliability of *Jones's* belief (which is dependent on that of the relevant expert, Smith) is this: even if Jones himself is globally reliable in distinguishing reliable from unreliable testimony, one might still want to know whether the testimony he relied on *in this particular case* was reliable. After all, one might think, it would be epistemically remiss to accept that p (where [p] is the content of the testimony in this particular case) if the testimony in *this particular case* wasn't reliable; and they hold that, in precisely the same way, *Jones's belief*—the belief expressed in his assertion—is unreliably formed if the testimony on which he relied was unreliable.

The focus on the reliability of the testimony *in this particular case* might tempt some to suppose that what is at issue here is not the *global* reliability of Jones's testimonial belief, but instead the sort of reliability that pertains to a performance in a local context—i.e., local reliability. But—even if we disregard the various considerations I offered in Chapters 3–4 against construing the reliability of testimony as affecting only the local reliability of testimonial belief—this interpretation is faulty. The scientists want to know whether to believe (or better: whether to accept) that p. Jones himself has already settled on the matter: he believes that p, and expresses his belief in testimony to his colleagues. As

Jones makes clear to them, this belief of his is based on Smith's testimony. They are well aware that Jones is good at distinguishing reliable from unreliable testimony. They know that most of the time his discriminations are correct. Still, they think that if this is a case in which his discrimination was *not* correct, then, though he is generally quite good at discriminating reliable testimony, his belief was not reliably formed. The parallel that comes to their mind is this: a subject who is generally very good at spotting lies but who is taken in by a lie on a given occasion, and so who comes to believe the lie, has formed a belief that (they think) was not well-grounded, epistemically speaking—despite the subject's general competence at being able to spot liars.

When might we expect to encounter the phenomenon whereby the assessor's interest in a subject's reliability in belief-formation extends to include an interest in the reliability of the testimony consumed by the subject? I submit that such cases can be expected when the assessment of the subject's belief is informed by a desire to know how well-supported, objectively speaking, the subject's belief is. No doubt, part of what might interest the reliabilist here is how reliable the subject is at distinguishing reliable from unreliable testimony: as I noted in Section 1 above, a subject who is unreliable in this way is a poor consumer of testimony, and the more unreliable one is in this regard the more one is at the mercy of one's environment (see also Goldberg 2008). Getting a sense of how reliable the subject is at distinguishing reliable from unreliable testimony would give us a sense of how likely it was that the testimony she consumed on this occasion was reliable; but (unless our subject were perfectly reliable in this way) it would not tell us whether the testimony she consumed on this occasion *was* reliable (or, more generally, how reliable that testimony was).

Facts about the consumed testimony's reliability matter to how objectively well-supported the subject's belief is. To see this, it might help to think of things from a slightly different, more schematic point of view. Suppose that you are asked to assess how likely it is that a given testimonial belief is true, given the "goodness" of the cognitive processes that produced the belief. And suppose that you are granted access to only one of two sets of facts regarding the "goodness" of the cognitive process: either you can have access to the 'individualistic' facts regarding the hearer, those that determine the global reliability of the processes through which she comprehends testimony and scrutinizes it for credibility; or else you can have access to the 'extended' facts (those regarding the hearer's informant), those that bear on the global reliability of the testimony proffered on this occasion. You can have access to one of these sets, but not both. And, to ensure that you are focusing on doxastic justification rather than knowledge, you are not given any information about the "surrounding" environmental context, and so in neither way will you be able to determine whether the subject under assessment has acquired knowledge.

I submit that, under these circumstances, you ought to choose the facts in the 'extended' set, not those in the 'individualist' set. In fact, it would seem that the facts in the 'individualist' set are valuable only as indicating the likelihood of something that the 'extended' facts themselves would directly establish: namely, the *de facto* reliability of the testimony consumed on this occasion. This supports the idea that, when it comes to the objective well-groundedness of testimonial belief, the facts most directly relevant are those pertaining to the G-reliability of the testimony.[27] Insofar as we want our notion of G-reliability to reflect the objective support enjoyed by a belief, an interest in the G-reliability of testimonial belief ought to extend to include an interest in the G-reliability of the testimony itself. I would even go so far as to say that those reliabilists who reject the proposal to regard the reliability of testimony as relevant to the G-reliability, and hence the doxastic justification, of testimonial belief, do so more out of

---

[27] I do not claim that these are the only relevant facts, of course. If the subject failed to comprehend the testimony, she might well have been in a position in which her belief is false even given true, reliable, testimony. My claim is merely that the *primary* determinant of the G-reliability, and hence doxastic justification, of testimonial belief is the G-reliability of the testimony.

a prior commitment to Process Individualism than they do out of any independently plausible account of the role of testimonial reliability in the justification of testimonial belief.

Still, the foregoing leaves us with a perplexing question: if (as I am arguing) the reliability of testimony is always relevant to the G-reliability of the testimonial belief, why then do many, and perhaps even most, assessors stick to assessing the reliability of *only those processes that take place within the testimony-consuming subject*? I think that the explanation here is a practical one: most of the time the original testifier is nowhere to be seen, and so the assessor makes do with the only facts to which she has access.

We might put matters as follows. One whose belief is testimonial is at one remove from the original grounds for the belief. (These grounds were had by the testifier, assuming that she was the original source of the information in question.) Since the hearer does not have the original grounds in question, she makes the best of what she has available: she assesses the reliability of the testimony itself, as a measure of how likely it was that her informant knew (or warrantedly believed) whereof she was speaking. Now consider how things stand from the perspective of the *assessor* of the testimonial believer. She (the assessor) is at *two* removes from the original grounds of the belief in question: not only does she (the assessor) lack the original grounds in question; what is more she also lacks access to the informant's testimony (and so is not in a position to scrutinize this testimony as the hearer had). Consequently, our assessor makes the best of what *she* has available: she assesses the reliability of those processes 'internal to' the hearer with which the hearer apprehended the testimony. Our assessor scrutinizes these processes with an eye towards seeing how reliable the hearer is, for example, in distinguishing reliable from unreliable testimony. That the assessor restricts her search in this way is not surprising: she doesn't have access to anything more than this, and in any case what she does have access to does give her a sense of how likely it is that the consumer consumed what in fact was a reliable piece of testimony. In short, the assessor is making do with the evidence that she has available. Thus we see that the fact that the assessor doesn't always, or even typically, take an interest in the reliability of the testimony can be explained in a way that is compatible with the extendedness hypothesis.

5

I move now to the penultimate objection I will consider: the objection from responsibility. This objection derives from the suspicion that a subject cannot be held epistemically responsible for cognitive processing that takes place in another subject's mind/brain.

The objection assumes that one's epistemic responsibility extends as far, but *only* as far, as one's own cognitive processes do. Our question is this: given that a subject epistemically relies on (the reliability of) a stretch of cognitive processing, why does it matter, from the perspective of an interest in epistemic responsibility, whether that processing took place in the subject's own mind/brain? One reason that might be offered is that what goes on in another's mind/brain is never reflectively accessible to one. But much of the processing that goes on in *one's own* mind is not reflectively accessible to one, and I doubt that a proponent of this objection will want to say that a subject is not epistemically responsible for the results of such processing. Perhaps it will be said instead that this ownership-motivated notion of responsibility captures important aspects of epistemic agency, as in: one bears epistemic responsibility only for that over which one exercises some control, and one does not exercise any control over cognitive processing in another's mind/brain. But it is far from obvious that there is a relevant sense of 'control' on which one exercises the relevant control over one's own cognitive processes; and if there isn't, then the notion of control will be of no help to anyone who hopes to press this objection.

Several mutually reinforcing points can be made here. First, a subject has little or no control over many processes that should count (on any plausible theory) as part of that subject's own belief-forming processes. These include not only (a good portion of) the processes in perception and memory, but also some of the 'internal' processes involved in the reception of testimony.[28] So one cannot press the control version of the objection from responsibility without jeopardizing the individuation of a good deal of independently plausible and highly intuitive accounts of belief-forming processes. Second, the point that the subject has no control over the processes that took place in the mind/brain of her informant has an analogue in the case of memorial belief. For, at the time of recollection, the subject has no control over the processing that took place at the time of original acquisition. Surely this does not mean that the processing that took place at the time of acquisition is not part of the (temporally extended) process involved in memory sustainment. It is true that the now–temporally remote processing involved in the belief's original acquisition took place in the subject's own mind-brain; but we must remember that even then, at the time of acquisition, a good deal of the processing was out of her control. Finally, it would seem that one has as much control in the situation of observing another's testimony, as one has in a situation in which an apparent memory just 'pops into' one's head (perhaps because elicited by some external simulation). In particular, at the time of the reception of testimony, a subject does have control over whether to accept the testimony (although this control is less than one might think: see the Gilbert references in the previous footnote). This would seem to make testimony a bit like memories that just 'pop' to the surface of consciousness in a way that is out of our conscious control. The remembering subject herself has no control over the 'popping into consciousness,' but she does have control over whether to endorse the apparent memory, and so whether to form (or sustain) the memorial belief. It would seem, then, that the proponent of the objection from responsibility cannot look to spell out that

[28] For the case of perception, see, e.g., Shepard (1987 and 1992); Zeki (1993); and Hubel (1995). For the case of the 'internal' processes involved in testimonial belief-formation, see Gilbert et. al. (1990, 1993); Gilbert (1991, 1992).

objection's key notion of epistemic responsibility in terms of the notion of control.

6

I come, finally, to the last objection I will consider, which is the indistinguishability objection (owed to Schmitt 1999). This objection contends that the extendedness hypothesis makes false predictions in classes of cases of testimonial belief in which the testimonies themselves are subjectively indistinguishable to the hearer. Here is how Schmitt presents matters:

> [B]egin with a paradigmatic case of testimonial justification: a doctor performs a thorough test to determine whether you have strep throat and tells you that it's certain that you do; you then believe that you have strep throat on the basis of the doctor's testimony. Now modify the case in such a way that it merely appears to you that the test is thorough; in reality the doctor is irresponsibly guessing and saying that the result is certain. Alternatively, modify the case even further, so that he is faking its performance. We might even imagine a case in which the doctor appears to be performing the test, but in fact you are just hallucinating the whole thing: there is no test, or even a doctor. On [the "extendedness" hypothesis], your belief in either of these modified cases fails to be justified. But intuitively your belief is (at least in the first modified case and perhaps in the second as well) as justified as in the paradigmatic case.   (Schmitt 1999: 370)

If Schmitt is right about this, then it would seem that the reliability of the testimony one consumed is not relevant to determining whether one's testimonial belief is (justified, and hence) G-reliably formed. And this, of course, would present a striking blow to the extendedness hypothesis. In response, I deny the claim that your belief in the modified cases *is* as justified as in the paradigmatic case.[29] Since Schmitt's 'equally justified' verdict merely reflects the individualistic orientation of Process Individualism, I will direct some of my objections to that orientation.

---

[29] In fairness to Schmitt, I should acknowledge that he himself no longer regards this argument as decisive (personal communication).

I begin by noting a curiosity about Schmitt's presentation here. He considers four cases. We might label these the *good* case (in which the doctor reports to you the verdict on the basis of having performed a reliable test); the *not-so-good* case (in which "it merely appears to you that the test is thorough; in reality the doctor is irresponsibly guessing and saying that the result is certain"); the *even-worse* case (in which the doctor is "faking" the experiment); and the *worst* case (in which you are hallucinating the whole thing). Curiously, Schmitt hedges his epistemic verdict in the hallucination case. Thus his "equally justified" verdicts extend "at least" to the not-so-good case and "perhaps" to the even-worse case; but he says nothing of the worst case. These varying reactions call out for an explanation. Why does Schmitt have these different reactions to these cases? After all, it would seem that to the extent that one is inclined to the 'equally justified' verdict in any two of these cases, one should be equally inclined to accept such a verdict regarding all of them. This is because the only thing backing the 'equally justified' verdict (so far as I can tell) is the fact that all of these scenarios are indistinguishable-to-you. Of course, if the scenarios are all equally indistinguishable from one another, the committed individualist should have exactly the same attitude towards the 'equally-justified' verdict in each case. The fact that Schmitt does not have the same attitude towards all of them, I submit, suggests that he himself feels the pull of a more 'social' reliabilist assessment of doxastic justification.

This point holds in the hallucination case itself, where Schmitt does not so much as register a verdict regarding the justification of the belief in question. Here I note that you (as the subject in question) can't tell the difference between the good case and the hallucination case either. Again, if Schmitt were employing a consistently individualistic version of reliabilism, he would not distinguish the G-reliability of the belief formed in the hallucination case from that of the belief formed in the good case (assuming that you are alike from the skin-in in these cases). But this is truly an unhappy implication. One might think to save Schmitt from this implication, on the grounds that "forming a belief through hallucinated testimony" is not the same belief-forming process-type as (and so need not be seen as having the same G-reliability as) "forming a belief through real testimony." Note, however, that "forming a belief through hallucinated testimony" is not an *individualistically sanctioned* belief-forming process-type: insofar as the hallucinated testimony case is indistinguishable to you from the actual testimony case (and that you are alike from the skin-in in these cases), what differentiates the hallucination case from the testimony case is something in the world, not within you. Of course, Schmitt might grant this, and so grant that there is the same degree of G-reliability in the hallucination case as in each of the other (indistinguishable) cases, and yet still deny that your belief in the hallucination cases is "equally justified," owing to the presence of a defeater. But I submit that this remains an unhappy position. For one thing, the defeater in question would be a *factual* one, not a normative or doxastic one, and factual defeaters (that are not also normative defeaters[30]) are usually taken to bear against knowledge but not against justification. So it looks like the appeal to a defeater does not help warrant Schmitt's verdict, which was that in the hallucinated testimony case the testimonial belief is not *justified*. In addition, there is a second problem with the proposal to defend Schmitt's differential treatment of the hallucination case by appeal to a relevant defeater. Should the reliabilist really allow that the hallucination case results in a belief that *is as G-reliable as* (alternatively: has the same prima facie justification[31] as) that in the good case (albeit not ultima facie justified owing to a relevant defeater)? The 'equally G-reliable' verdict is not a plausible one, and the sense of implausibility remains even if we add that the belief is not justified owing to a relevant defeater.

An additional point that can be made against the Process Individualism that underwrites the hallucination objection is this: imagine

[30] For a nice discussion, see Gibbons (2006).
[31] For a reliabilist understanding of 'prima facie justification,' see Senor (1996).

another case which differs from the good case only in that the reliability of the test that the doctor performs (and whose results he reliably reports), though high, is not quite high enough for knowledge. (In the case I am envisaging, you are unaware of this and the doctor does not tell you; and we will suppose further that it is not well known in the medical community that the reliability of this test, though good, falls below the threshold needed for a knowledgeable conclusion on the presence of strep, and so the doctor's failure to report this feature is not out of any epistemic irresponsibility on his part.) In this case, I submit, it is clear that even if the doctor's testimony is true and your monitoring processes are both conditionally and Terminal Phase G-reliable, this does not render you any more knowledgeable than the doctor himself. Insofar as this case is one in which there are no Gettier considerations, defeaters, or failures of local reliability, we get the result I presented in Chapter 4: G-reliability in the processes 'internal to' the hearer does not suffice to render a true, unGETTIERED belief knowledge. This strikes at the very heart of the individualistic orientation behind the objection from hallucination.

On a related note, there is another, more programmatic reason for the justification-reliabilist to reject the 'equally justified' verdict that generates Schmitt's objection. Throughout our discussion (starting in Chapter 4 and continuing in this chapter) we have been noting that reliabilist views of doxastic justification get much of their motivation from the way they honor the link between truth and justification. Belief aims at truth, and particular beliefs are justified to the extent that are formed (and sustained) in such a way that they are likely to be true. Any justification-reliabilist who feels this sort of pull should be perplexed by the 'equally well-justified' verdict in the doppelgänger sequences in Schmitt's quote. For, in effect, this verdict endorses the idea that, although a speaker's belief failed miserably in *its* relation to truth (having been formed and/or sustained in an unreliable way), so long as she expresses that belief in such a way as to have this unreliability in her testimony escape the notice of a well-functioning hearer's careful scrutiny, the hearer's belief based on her unreliable testimony is itself reliable enough to count as justified. In this way it would seem that any justification-reliabilist who (with Schmitt) endorses the 'equally well-justified' verdict is committed to a deeply implausible argument for the conclusion that testimony can generate justification. It may well be that testimony *can* generate justification (see, e.g., Goldberg 2007a and 2007b); but no reliabilist should think that this conclusion can be reached by appeal to a case in which an epistemically responsible hearer consumes what she fails to realize is unreliable testimony.

One final point can be made against the 'equally justified' verdict at the heart of Schmitt's objection. (This point is directed to Process Reliabilists in particular: they should be leery of the 'equally justified' verdict.) As noted, Schmitt's objection contends that the doppelgänger-hearers in his series should be treated in like fashion, justification-wise. Perhaps Schmitt will regard this contention as intuitive. But the justification-reliabilists should be careful in endorsing this contention: at least some of what appears to support the verdict to treat the doppelgänger cases in like fashion, justification-wise, is a kind of consideration that, in other cases, fails to move justification-reliabilists in the least. For consider what might be used to support the 'equally justified' contention. One thing that might be used to support this verdict is the claim that two hearers who are *equally epistemically responsible* in their consumption of testimony are equally well-justified. But it would seem curiously not in keeping with justification-reliabilism to be so moved by considerations of epistemic responsibility here, when data regarding epistemic responsibility are not what reliabilist theories of justification were designed to capture.[32] Perhaps the 'equally justified' contention is thought to be supported by the idea that how things currently strike each of the subjects is precisely the same, and they do the very same things with these inputs. But this consideration should not move the justification-reliabilist; after all,

---

[32] This is not to say, of course, that reliabilist theories of justification ignore issues of epistemic responsibility (the charge in, e.g., Bonjour's case of the reliable clairvoyant).

it would be easy to describe a doppelgänger sequence involving memory, where each of the subjects has the same apparent memory, but where only the first in the series is actually remembering a belief that was reliably acquired. No Process Reliabilist would feel any temptation to endorse an 'equally justified' verdict for each of the cases in this series, despite the fact that how things currently strike each of the subjects is precisely the same, and they do the very same things with these inputs. In short, it would seem that the 'equally justified' contention is not in keeping with the commitments of a reliabilist epistemology.

7

I conclude that none of the six objections I have considered is damaging to the extendedness hypothesis. My more general conclusion is that it remains reasonable to think that our epistemic reliance on others really does have the epistemic significance ascribed to it in Chapter 4. At this point I want to move on from the paradigmatic instance of this sort of reliance, seen in testimony cases, to another sort of belief that manifests our epistemic reliance on others.

6

If That Were True I Would Have Heard about it by Now

The theme of this book is our epistemic reliance on others—the sort of reliance we exhibit when we depend on others for our knowledge of the world. My claim has been that this reliance has some far-reaching implications for epistemology in general, and for Process Reliabilism in particular. So far, I have been pursuing these implications by focusing on the paradigmatic sort of epistemic reliance, which is seen in testimony cases. In this chapter, I shift my focus from testimony to one other sort of case in which we rely on others for our knowledge of the world.

In this chapter, I examine the case of beliefs that are formed through epistemic reliance on what I will be calling the *coverage-reliability* of one's community. A paradigm example of this sort of reliance is seen in cases in which, reflecting on whether p, one comes to believe that ~p on the grounds that if p were true one would have heard about it by now.[1] I argue that a proper reliabilist assessment of the formation and/or sustainment of the beliefs in question must attend to various cognitive dispositions of one or more of the members of the subject's community. My proposal for doing so will be twofold. First, I will construe "coverage-supported" beliefs as a species of inferentially acquired beliefs, where the inference is from a premise asserting the subject's

[1] I thank Frank Döring for suggesting to me (in conversation) the importance of this sort of belief.

expectation of relevant coverage. Second, I will argue that the premise-belief manifesting the subject's expectation of relevant coverage should be assessed in terms of prevailing social practices and institutions. These practices and institutions, I will argue, are part of the "background conditions" on the formation of the "coverage-supported" beliefs themselves. It is in terms of these conditions that we calibrate the reliability of the beliefs which manifest one's expectations for coverage, and deviations from these conditions constitute a potential knowledge-undermining element of luck.

I

I begin with some cases, to fix ideas.

> WMD Over lunch, you and a friend are having a discussion about overseas ventures by the US military during the administration of George W. Bush. She raises the question whether weapons of mass destruction (WMDs) were ever found in Iraq. You think for a moment and respond that, no, they were not. (You reason that if such weapons had been found, you would have heard about it by now.)

> FOREIGN POLICY As his mind is wandering, it occurs to Smith—out of the blue—to wonder whether the Prime Minister announced a new major change in foreign policy last week. Believing that if the Prime Minister had done so he (Smith) would have heard about it by now, Smith forms the belief that the Prime Minister did not announce a new major foreign policy change last week.

> HOLLYWOOD Listening to the locals discuss the goings-on of various Hollywood celebrities, McSorley overhears a juicy tidbit regarding Toothy Thompson, a particularly famous celebrity who is nearly universally regarded (including by McSorley) as a person of high integrity. According to the speaker, Toothy has actually led the life of a degenerate who has barely escaped legal

prosecution on various occasions. Given Toothy's reputation and the media's voracious appetite for Hollywood scandal, McSorley rejects the testimony: she thinks to herself that if any of this were true, she would have heard about it by now (from some more familiar source).

The phenomenon illustrated in these cases is rather common. In them, the fact that a subject has never come across a piece of testimony to the effect that p is used as support for her belief in [$\sim p$]. This support can take the form of (further) support for believing something she believed all along (WMD); it can take the form of support for the formation of a belief she did not previously have (FOREIGN POLICY); or it can take the form of support for rejecting some piece of presently observed testimony opposing a belief she presently has (HOLLYWOOD). I do not claim that these options are exhaustive.

I believe that cases of this sort are of great epistemological interest. They make clear that our dependence on others for what we know and justifiably believe outstrips our reliance on their testimony. What is more, they are quite common.[2] In this respect the following remarks of John McDowell are apt:

Consider someone who keeps himself reasonably well up-to-date on events of note; suppose he listens to a reliable radio news broadcast at six o'clock every evening. Can we credit such a person at three o'clock in the afternoon on some date late in the life of, say, Winston Churchill, with knowledge that Churchill is alive? . . . Intuitively, the answer is 'Yes.' *Something like that is the position we are all in with respect to masses of what we take ourselves to know*, concerning reasonably durable but impermanent states of affairs to whose continued obtaining we have only intermittent epistemic access. If challenged, we might say something like 'If it were no longer so, I would have heard about it'; and we are quite undisturbed, at least until philosophy breaks out, by the time-lag

---

[2] A recent typical example comes from the *New York Times* sports section of August 6, 2008. Yankees' manager Joe Girardi, commenting on Joba Chamberlain, a great young pitcher who had to leave the previous game due to experiencing a sharp pain in his shoulder, "guessed" that Chamberlain still felt strong, saying "I would have heard if he didn't."

between changes in such states of affairs and our hearing about them. . . . It would be difficult to overstate how much of what ordinarily passes for knowledge would be lost to us, if our epistemology of retained knowledge did not allow that sort of knowably risky policy to issue in acceptable knowledge claims when the risks do not materialize. (McDowell 1994/1998: 422–3)

Since I am assuming a reliabilist epistemology, my discussion of these cases will proceed accordingly. My questions will be as follows. Under what conditions are beliefs of this sort reliably formed? Under what conditions do such beliefs amount to (what the reliabilist will recognize as) knowledge, or doxastically justified belief? After addressing these questions in the sections following, I will conclude by returning to the bigger picture, discussing what these sorts of case tell us our reliance on others, and about the organization of our epistemic communities.

2

The sort of belief at issue is one whose formation or sustainment involves an appeal to the conditional *If p were true I would have heard about it by now*. I will call this the *truth-to-testimony* conditional. Beliefs formed or sustained by appeal to this conditional—a belief in [~p] formed through the subject's assumption that if p were true she would have heard about it by now—I will call *coverage-supported* belief. Although I will have more to say on the matter below, for now I simply note that the relevant notion of coverage is seen in the believer's reliance on a source to be both (i) reliably apprized of the relevant facts in a certain domain and (ii) disposed to offer reliable reports regarding the obtaining of these facts (when they are believed by the source to have obtained). In what follows I will focus on newly formed coverage-supported belief (FOREIGN POLICY) rather than cases in which coverage reliance supports a previously formed belief (WMD) or rejecting a piece of currently observed testimony to the contrary (HOLLYWOOD).

What sort of facts—about one's community, and one's place in that community—would render it likely that a newly formed coverage-supported belief will be true? Assuming reliabilism about knowledge as well as justification, we can distinguish two questions here. First, under what conditions is such a belief reliably formed, and so doxastically justified? Second, under what conditions is a coverage-supported belief sufficiently reliable to count as knowledge? (Expanding on my previous terminology, I will call the former sort of reliability 'G-reliability,' and the latter sort of reliability 'K-reliability.'[3])

I begin with the question regarding knowledge. I want to argue that there are five conditions that are jointly sufficient for K-reliability in the formation of coverage-supported belief.[4] (In Section 2.2 I will move on to consider how to think of G-reliability in connection with coverage-supported belief.)

The first condition which is part of a set of jointly sufficient conditions on K-reliably formed coverage-supported belief I call the *source-existence* condition. This condition requires that there be some subgroup of members of the hearer's community—we will call this group "the source"—who are disposed to report about the relevant sort of matters. This subgroup might be one that is traditionally recognized by virtually everyone in the community (the traditional print and TV media, for example). Or the subgroup in question might be one to which the subject herself bears some special, personal connection (a group of her friends, say, whose members are particularly interested in, and disposed to publicize to the others what they have learned about, some subject matter). I do not assume that these exhaust the possibilities.

---

[3] G-reliability is global reliability; and it would be natural for a reliabilist to think that K-reliability involves both local and global reliability.

[4] I think that they are individually necessary as well, but I will not be arguing for this in each case.

In addition to the source-existence condition, a second condition is what I will call the *reliable-coverage* condition.[5] This condition requires that the relied-upon source must be reliable in uncovering and subsequently publicizing truths about the domain in which the subject is exhibiting coverage-reliance. Let D be a domain of interest to subject H, let p be any proposition in D regarding whose truth H might take an interest, and let a be some source on whom H could rely on matters pertaining to D. Then we can characterize the relevant notion as follows:

CR a is *coverage-reliable* in $D =_{\text{def}}$

a (i) will (investigate and) reliably determine whether p, (ii) will be reliable in reporting the outcome of that investigation, and (iii) will satisfy both of the previous two conditions in a timely fashion (more on which below).

With this as our basic notion, we can then go on to define other, related, notions. For example, in many cases a subject does not rely on any *particular* source, but instead relies on there being *some source or other* who would publicize the relevant information. We can capture this as the notion of Generic Coverage-Reliance, as follows:

GCR   There is generic coverage-reliability in D relative to H $=_{\text{def}}$

There is some source or other in H's community that is coverage-reliable in D.

And I am confident that there will be other notions in the vicinity worth capturing. (I leave this for future work.)

As it is formulated, CR captures what we might call a *non-attuned* sort of coverage-reliance, one in which the subject H coverage-relies on a source, a, who may or may not know that H is so

---

[5] It is something very near this condition that the *New York Times* claims to satisfy, in its claim to publish "*All* of the News that's Fit to Print."

relying, and who (even if a knows that H is so relying) may or may not know H's specific informational needs and expectations. But there can be other cases with a source that is attuned to the scope and informational needs and expectations of its audience; and such a source will be one that can explicitly aim to render itself coverage-reliable relative to that audience. I offer the following as capturing this notion of "Attuned" Coverage-Reliance:

> ACR a exhibits *attuned* coverage-reliability in D relative to H
> $=_{def}$
> (I) a has knowledge of both the scope of the audience φ that relies on it for (some of) their informational needs, and the information-relevant expectations that members of φ have with respect to a itself; (II) H is in φ; and (III) for any proposition p in D, if it is reasonable for a to suppose, *both* that (a) members of φ would be interested in the truth-value of p, *and* that (b) members of φ are likely to rely on a for the information whether p, then a (i) will (investigate and) reliably determine whether p, (ii) will be reliable in reporting the outcome of that investigation, and (iii) will satisfy both of the previous two conditions in a timely fashion.

What is more, we might distinguish the attuned coverage-reliability captured by ACR with a sort of coverage-reliability where the scope and informational expectations of the relevant audience are *common knowledge*, had both by members of the audience and by the source itself (and where both sides know this of the other side, etc.). The difference between *common-knowledge coverage reliability* (as we might call it) and the sort of case captured by ACR is that in the common-knowledge case the fact of attunement is known to both sides, not just to the source.

Both CR and ACR include a condition, (iii), that requires the relevant discoveries and reports must be made in a 'timely fashion.' It is perhaps slightly misleading to speak of "timeliness." What condition (iii) requires is this: a (the relied-upon source) must be such that, at the time t at which a is being relied upon by H, it is true that, were there some relevant discovery to be made, a would have made the relevant discovery by t, and would have reported on the matter. I speak of 'timeliness' if only to suggest that there must be some sort of coordination between the time-related expectations of H, on the one hand, and the abilities of a to make any relevant discoveries, on the other. For this reason we might speak, not of timeliness, but of the requirement that there be an interval of time sufficient for the discovery (were one to be made) of any relevant facts. For this reason I will call condition (iii) the *sufficient interval* condition.

We can all agree, I suspect, that if a subject forms a coverage-supported belief at a point in time prior to the relied-upon source having completed its investigation, then the subject does not count as knowing, even if her belief is true. The explanation is that the sufficient interval condition was not satisfied. More complicated is the issue regarding how to determine what counts as a "sufficient interval" for the completion of a competent inquiry. By what point must a source have reported on any discovery, were there one to be made, so that her reports count as having been made in a "timely" fashion? This is a very complicated matter; here I can only offer some rather plaid generalizations. While timeliness depends to a great extent on hearer expectations, these expectations must be grounded in facts regarding how long it would standardly take the relied-upon sources to find out about, investigate, and then report on any newsworthy development. With this in mind, I submit that the "timeliness" requirement imposed by the sufficient interval condition should be relativized to the sort of news at issue, to the capacities of the sources on which one is relying for coverage, and to social customs.

Timeliness ought to be relativized to the sort of news at issue. For one thing, the requirements of timeliness will reflect the probability that changes of the sort in question occur in the interval of time since one last heard a relevant report. So, for example, imagine McDowell's subject above only listened to the radio weekly. Even so, if he is within one of the intervals between the weekly radio reports he gets on political matters, my own impression is that such a subject would still be in a position to know that the Prime Minister is still alive (given that (s)he still is); and this impression becomes overwhelming if we assume that news of the Prime Minister's death would have quickly made its way to the subject one way or another (even if not at first by radio). In other cases, more regular updating is needed, as when one aims to have knowledge (or even merely true beliefs) about the local weather forecast for the weather three weeks hence: even if one knew ten days ago, on the 1st of the month, what the weather report was for the 20th of the month, once ten days has gone by there is no impression that one continues to know, on the 10th, what the weather report is for the 20th of the month: weather reports change with great frequency. Similarly, some types of news—the outcome of major national elections, the assassination of political leaders, the start of major wars, the outcome of the widely followed championship game, scandals or deaths involving the very famous,[6] and so forth—can be expected to be announced immediately, following the relevant events. For these types of news, timeliness requires more or less immediate reporting. For other types of news, by contrast, timeliness merely requires that there be periodic reports (where the time between periods is a function not only of how quickly regular developments arise but also how often hearers expect to be updated on such matters). It is also worth noting that some types of news take longer to investigate, and this will have an effect on the requirements of timeliness. Even for those best situated to investigate such matters, corruption in government can take a very long time to investigate properly; reports on such matters can be timely even if they are issues several years after the alleged corruption took place.

[6] The death of Michael Jackson on June 25, 2009, is a case in point. He was pronounced dead by doctors at UCLA Medical Center at 2.26 p.m. (LA time), and *less than twenty minutes later* TMZ.com, an LA-based celebrity news website, posted a report of Jackson's death. Interestingly, attempts to post the news on Wikipedia soon thereafter overwhelmed that site. See "Michael Jackson's Death Roils Wikipedia," posted June 25, 2009, on cnet news: <http://news.cnet.com/8301-1023$_3$-10273277-93.html> (accessed November 4, 2009).

In addition, timeliness must be relativized to the capacity of the source(s) on which one is relying for coverage. *The Wall Street Journal* has the capacity to investigate and report daily on the major goings-on that affect world business interests (or at least those goings-on that take place in the major businesses operating in the major business centers of the world); whereas the local paper does not (it probably gets its business news from the *Journal* itself or the *AP* newswire). One might expect that the sports section of the local newspaper can get to the bottom of the alleged spat between McBeefy and Coach rather quickly; but your child, who follows the team avidly every Sunday but who does not read the sports pages, cannot be expected to do so.

In relativizing the "sufficient interval" condition to the capacity of the relevant sources, we may have to attend to various highly contingent aspects of the situation. The following 'absent reporter' case illustrates. Smith relies for his local news on his town's weekly paper *The Community Times*. Since Smith is largely bedridden, he is especially dependent on this paper for his news. Wondering whether there have been any important developments in the past two weeks in the local government's attempts to balance the budget, Smith comes to believe that there haven't been any, since if there had been he would have read it in the paper by now (as he has scoured the papers he has received in the interim). Smith knows that the local paper is highly reliable, and that the reporter who covers such news, Wonky, is an excellent reporter. (Smith knows both that Wonky regularly investigates all the relevant news regarding the local scene, and that his reports are quite reliable.) Unbeknownst to Smith, however, Wonky has been out of town for the past month, and the newspaper did not hire anyone to replace him. (The plan was that Wonky would write about all goings-on in his absence as soon as he returned.) Suppose that it's true that there have been no important developments in the past two weeks in the local government's attempts to balance the budget. Does Smith's belief to this effect amount to knowledge? Insofar as relevant developments were likely in that interim, the clear verdict is that Smith's true belief does not amount to knowledge. The explanation for this, I submit, is that there has been something wrong with the coverage Smith has been receiving over this interval. Since conditions (i) and (ii) of the coverage-reliability condition are satisfied, I submit that the proper explanation is that condition (iii) is not satisfied. Reliable coverage involves timely coverage, and whether coverage is timely in the relevant sense may depend on various contingencies (such as whether there is a substitute for a certain key reporter when that reporter goes on vacation).

Finally, timeliness must be relativized to social customs. Major foreign policy changes are typically announced in standard ways; we might reasonably expect that when these standard ways have not been used then no such policy has been announced. By contrast, there is no standardized way to announce many of the other changes in which we might take an interest.

So far, I have proposed three conditions—the *source-existence* condition, the *coverage-reliability* condition, and the *sufficient-interval* condition (part of the coverage-reliability condition)—which I am proposing as part of a set of jointly sufficient conditions on K-reliability in the process by which a coverage-supported belief is formed. Each of these three conditions are conditions on the subject's community. I turn now to the final two conditions, which are conditions on the coverage-relying subject, H, herself. First, there is what we might call the *silence condition*: this condition requires that, in point of fact, H has not encountered any relevant report to date. Second, and relatedly, there is what I will call the *receptivity condition*, requiring H to be such that she *would* come across whatever relevant reports were offered by the source(s) on whom she was relying, were one to be made. To be sure, the subject can satisfy the receptivity condition without having to receive the relevant reports directly from the source itself: it may be that there is a more extensive chain of communication linking her to the source. So long as the communication chain is itself both sufficiently reliable (preserving whatever relevant content there was in the original report(s)), sufficiently complete (passing on all of the relevant reports), and sufficiently well-publicized (reaching at least some of the places where the subject is likely to encounter the transmitted message), the subject then would have come across the reports from the source(s) on which she is relying, and so satisfies the receptivity condition.

2.2

My claim so far is that these five conditions—the source-existence, reliable-coverage, sufficient-interval, silence, and receptivity conditions—are jointly sufficient for K-reliability in the acquisition of a newly formed coverage-supported belief. At the same time, it would seem that the satisfaction of these conditions is not required for the subject to acquire a *doxastically justified* coverage-supported belief. To illustrate: in the 'absent reporter' case above, it is arguable that Smith's belief is doxastically justified, even though it falls short of knowledge. Other cases involving justified coverage-supported belief that fail to amount to knowledge would be easy to describe. Perhaps a subject is regularly informed by a source but (unbeknownst to the subject) just happens to be out of the source's reporting range on the day when a report would have been made (and our subject would have had no other way to get the report in question); perhaps sources that are highly reliable in discovering the relevant facts happen to miss a crucial fact (this happens only rarely); and so forth. In these cases it is arguable that the whole process (involving the hearer's coverage-reliance on the source) was G-reliable, despite not being K-reliable. If so, then these would be cases of doxastically justified coverage-supported belief that fail to amount to knowledge.

How then should we think of the conditions on the acquisition of G-reliable (doxastically justified) coverage-supported belief? An initial strategy would be to try to formulate weaker versions of each of the source's, reliable-coverage, sufficient-interval, receptivity, and silence conditions, where the weaker versions are satisfied so long as conditions make it *likely* (though they need not ensure) that each of the five conditions on K-reliable coverage-supported belief are satisfied. I say that this is an *initial* strategy for framing the conditions on G-reliability in the formation of a coverage-supported belief. Before we can embrace this strategy, however, we must confront what I regard as a challenge—in fact, the central challenge—facing any reliabilist account of the doxastic justification of coverage-supported belief.

The challenge can be presented in the form of a loose dilemma regarding the nature of the belief-forming process involved in coverage-supported belief, as follows. On the one hand, there are reasons to think that coverage-supported belief should be understood in terms of the extendedness hypothesis introduced in previous chapters. For one thing, the subject who forms a coverage-supported belief is manifestly exhibiting epistemic reliance on her peers, and, in Chapter 4, I argued that epistemic reliance on one's peers extends the belief-forming process involved. And, in addition, it seems plain that the cognitive processing that takes place in the mind/brain of the coverage-relying subject herself *is not what does the justifying work* for her coverage-supported belief: the lion's share of that work is done by those on whom the subject is relying for coverage, as it is their work that renders the subject's coverage-supported belief likely to be true. On the other hand, there are reasons to think that coverage-supported belief should *not* be understood in terms of the extendedness hypothesis. Not only would this proposal make the process of coverage-supported belief one that involves cognitive processing in a widely distributed network of individuals (something that can give us pause even if we accept the idea of extendedness in testimony cases). More importantly, the sort of epistemic reliance exhibited in cases of coverage-supported belief would appear to be different from that in testimony cases, in ways that bear on the question of the nature of the belief-forming process in play.

In light of this looming dilemma, let us return to the initial strategy presented above, on which G-reliability in the formation of coverage-supported belief is taken to be a matter of the high

likelihood that the five conditions from Section 2.1 are satisfied.
If this strategy is to be vindicated, the proposal that results must
accommodate the strength of the reasons on both sides of the issue
of extended processing. To this end, let us develop these reasons a
bit further, and see whether the initial strategy can accommodate
the various insights on both sides.

I begin with the reasons for thinking that coverage-supported
belief should be understood in terms of the extendedness proposal
introduced in previous chapters.

One such reason emerges from a comparison between testimonial belief and coverage-supported belief. Starting with testimonial
belief-formation, consider that part of the process that takes place
in the hearer, the consumer of testimony. This process will include
all relevant cognitive processing that takes place in her mind/brain
as she comprehends the testimony she has observed, monitors it
for trustworthiness, and moves to accept it (or not, as the case may
be). If Process Individualism is true, then this exhausts the process
of testimonial belief-fixation. But in Chapters 1–5 I argued that
the process that takes place 'in' the hearer is not what does the
lion's share of the cognitive work that renders the belief likely to
be true. Take a case where Franklin, reading the morning paper,
comes to believe that the President is in Honolulu today, through
trusting a report to this effect. As he forms this belief, Franklin is
currently thousands of miles from Honolulu (in fact he has never
been there), and he has never in his life seen the President in
person. How can it be that Franklin's belief that the President is
in Honolulu today is likely to be true? (I think that all of us, but
especially Orthodox Reliablists, are less impressed with this than
we ought to be.) It will be replied that the reliability of Franklin's
belief reflects the reliability of the processes through which he
comprehends and assesses the testimony from the morning paper.
But I think that this answer is ideologically driven: rather than
manifesting any insight about the nature of the process that renders
Franklin's belief reliable, it reflects nothing so much as a strong
prior commitment to Process Individualism. This answer is also

curious in another respect. Suppose that *the reporter's* belief that the President is in Honolulu today was acquired at first hand. If we were to ask the Process Reliabilist what renders *this* (the reporter's) belief reliable, the answer would surely cite the reliability of cognitive processing in the reporter's own mind/brain. Given that Franklin himself is relying on this reliability, it is curious that this part of the story simply drops out of the answer to the question how *Franklin's* belief achieves its reliability.[7] A better answer to our question—by which I mean a more insightful and complete answer—would be that, while processes internal to Franklin are relevant to the reliability of his belief, what does the lion's share of the work here is cognitive processing in the mind/brain of the reporter herself (together with the technologies that enable her to reliably disseminate what she has learned first hand). The extendedness proposal captures this insight, in that it regards the cognitive processing in the reporter's mind/brain to be part of the very process through which Franklin forms his testimonial belief.

Moving on to coverage-supported belief, consider now that part of the process that takes place in the subject, the one who is relying on her community for reliable coverage. Once again, this process will include all relevant cognitive processing that takes place in her mind/brain, as she forms her belief through endorsing the truth-to-testimony conditional. Given Process Individualism, this exhausts the process of coverage-supported belief-fixation. But, once again, it is natural to think that the process that takes place 'in' the hearer is not what does the lion's share of the cognitive work that renders a subject's coverage-supported belief likely to be true. To illustrate, take Franklin again. Having just noted that he has not heard from his brother Matt in the three days since Matt was supposed to have moved his whole family to Melbourne, Australia, a worry

---

[7] Lackey (2007b) makes a point very much in the spirit of this one as part of her criticism of the view that knowledge is *true belief for which the subject deserves credit*. Her point there is that we don't deserve the lion's share of the credit for (at least some) testimonial knowledge, since the lion's share of the credit belongs to the subject's informant.

flashes through Franklin's mind: maybe their plane crashed. (Yes, Franklin has these worries occasionally.) Fortunately, reason takes over immediately, and Franklin quickly reassures himself that their plane did not crash, since if it had he would have heard about it by now. Now Franklin is currently hundreds to thousands of miles from any point along the trajectory of the plane that was to have taken Matt's family to Australia; and he is thousands of miles from Australia itself (in fact he's never been there). How can it be that Franklin's belief, that his brother's family arrived safely in Melbourne, is likely to be true? Here the impression is overwhelming that *reliability in this belief is not any single individual's cognitive achievement.*

Indeed, this impression is even stronger in connection with coverage-supported belief than it is with testimonial belief. Nor should this come as a surprise; it has to do with the nature of what we might call the 'individualistic input' in the two cases—the input into the mind/brain of the subject whose belief is under assessment. In the case of testimony, that input is a perceptual experience as of an assertion that p (or something like this). In such an experience it appears to the subject as if she is receiving some linguistic signal; and the individualistic cognitive processing involved is that of recovering the force and content of the (apparent) speech act, and assessing its credibility, in order to reach a determination whether to accept the content in question. In the case of coverage-reliance, by contrast, the individualistic 'input' is nothing other than an acknowledged absence of any memory impression of having been told that ~p. By anyone's lights this should seem to be a much more meager basis for believing that p, than the basis one has when (it appears that) one has been told that p straight-out. It is for this reason that dependence on social factors for the reliability of coverage-supported belief can seem more substantial than it is in the case of testimonial belief.

This impression can lead us to suppose that, as in the testimony case, so too in the coverage-reliance case, we ought to capture the subject's epistemic reliance on her peers by postulating that the processing involved extends to include processing in the mind/brains of all of those individuals on whom the subject is relying for coverage. We might think to describe coverage-supported belief as involving reliance on a kind of "extended" or "distributed" memory,[8] where the relied-upon system itself is a massively distributed one that involves cognitive processing in the mind/brains of all of the individuals that contribute to the source's coverage-reliability, and where the output of this source is silence.[9]

Unfortunately, there would also appear to be some reasons for *resisting* the proposal to regard coverage-supported belief as involving an interpersonally extended belief-forming process. Although these reasons may not be decisive, they are sufficient to warrant interest in alternative ways of modeling coverage-supported belief.

A first reason for resisting the proposal to regard coverage-supported belief as involving an interpersonally extended belief-forming process has to do with the causal relevance of the processing that takes place in others' minds in these cases. Return to the case of Franklin's belief that his brother's family arrived safely in Melbourne. He is epistemically relying on various people for coverage: most saliently, airline and government officials as well as news reporters. (There might be others as well.) It is hard to see how processing going on in the mind/brains of all of these people is *causally relevant* to the formation of Franklin's coverage-supported belief. In this respect coverage-supported belief appears to be unlike testimonial belief. In the case of testimonial belief, the causal relevance of processes in the mind/brains of one's peers is underwritten by the causal transaction that takes place in the

---

[8] When I speak of 'extended memory' here, a point made in Chapter 5 should be borne in mind: this has no direct bearing on the cognitive-psychological taxonomy of memory processes. The point is rather that, insofar as we are interested in a reliabilist assessment of the coverage-supported belief, we need to assess, e.g., the coverage-reliability of the subject's source(s).

[9] I thank Alan Millar, John Burgess, and an anonymous referee from Oxford University Press for this suggestion.

source's *offering* and the hearer's *reception* of the testimony itself. Since coverage-supported belief does not involve any positive speech contribution from one's peers, its formation involves no such transaction. So even if some of what we might call the 'connecting counterfactuals' (for which see Chapter 5, Section 3) still hold true—for example: had one encountered testimony that p from one of the relied-upon sources, one would not currently form the belief that $\sim$p—it still seems strained to regard the processes of belief-fixation here as intersubjectively extended. There would appear to be no continuous causal sequence here through which to trace the coverage-supported belief back to cognitive processing taking place in the mind/brains of members of one's community.

One might respond to this worry about causal relevance by noting that silence itself (as well as other sorts of absences) can be causally relevant in the production of a given effect.[10] Here is not the place for an extended discussion of the causal relevance of absences. Instead, I offer the following, which I hope will be uncontroversial: even if silence (absence of testimony) can be causally relevant to belief-formation, there remain important differences between the causal relevance of testimony and the causal relevance of silence.

To see this, return to our question about the attainment of reliability in Franklin's testimonial belief that the President is in Honolulu today. There I noted that, unless we are assuming Process Individualism, it is natural to think that the proper way to characterize this attainment will appeal to cognitive processing in the mind/brain of his informant, since it is this processing that does the lion's share of the work in rendering Franklin's testimonial belief reliable. There is a general point to be made here about reliability in testimonial belief: the fact that a testimony-consuming subject's reliance is on a piece of information that

---

[10] For this point, I thank John Burgess, as well as an anonymous referee from Oxford University Press.

comes from a *particular* source motivates the idea that we must cite the relevant cognitive processing in that source's mind/brain, if we are to account for the reliability of testimonial belief itself. The case of coverage-supported belief stands in stark contrast. In a good many cases there will be no *single person* on whose reliability the subject is relying for coverage. What is more, even in those cases on which the subject is relying on a single person for coverage-reliability, his reliance on such a source for coverage does not amount to relying on the reliability with which any *particular* piece of information was produced by the source, since by hypothesis the relied-upon source has been silent. In this respect we might say that the coverage-relying subject's reliance on others does not involve a reliance on any *determinate stretch of cognitive operations* in another's mind/brain. On the contrary, it would seem more accurate to describe our coverage-relying subject in this way: he is depending on his whole situation to be such that, were there relevant information, for example, regarding a plane crash (Franklin's case), this information would have made its way to him by now. For this reason, and unlike in the testimony case, coverage reliance might be understood to be reliance on certain *general features* of one's social circumstances. The appeal to particular features of another's cognitive processing, as part of the cognitive processing involved in the subject's coverage-supported belief, appears decidedly unmotivated.

On the basis of the foregoing, I submit that the sort of epistemic reliance in play in coverage-supported belief is importantly different from that involved in testimonial belief, in ways bearing on the relevant processes involved. In Chapter 4, I glossed the sort of epistemic reliance involved in testimony cases as follows (here I call this 'primary' epistemic reliance, to set it off from the sort I want to introduce in connection with coverage-supported belief):

ER_{Pr} In forming or sustaining her belief that p, a given subject S exhibits *primary* epistemic reliance on (the reliability of) some cognitive process π (where π itself may be a component in a more encompassing cognitive process) iff (i) S's belief that p was formed and/or sustained through some belief-forming process π^*, (ii) π produced output r, whose content is that q (not necessarily distinct from p), and (iii) the reliability of the belief S formed or sustained through π^* depends on the reliability with which π produced r.

In cases of coverage-supported belief, by contrast, there is no particular (mental or linguistic) output on which one is relying, and so neither (ii) nor (iii) holds. We might formulate the more 'diffuse' sort of epistemic reliance involved here as follows:

ER$_D$ In forming or sustaining her belief that p, a given subject S exhibits *diffuse* epistemic reliance on (the reliability of) some cognitive process π (where π itself may be a component in a more encompassing cognitive process) iff (a) S's belief that p was formed and/or sustained through some belief-forming process π^*, and (b) the reliability of the belief formed or sustained through π^* depends on the reliability of the operations of π.

This sort of reliance involves reliance on the reliability of (some of) another person's (or other people's) cognitive processes, but not on any particular output produced by any of those processes.

I have just highlighted what I regard as an important difference between the sort of epistemic reliance involved in coverage-supported belief and that involved in testimonial belief: the former involves a more "diffuse" sort of epistemic reliance than the "primary" epistemic reliance I introduced (in connection with testimonial belief) in Chapter 4. I do not claim that this difference, by itself, warrants a repudiation of the extendedness model for coverage-supported belief. But I do think that this difference is important enough that it warrants our taking an interest in alternative accounts of coverage-supported belief. No doubt, any adequate account of the process by which coverage-supported beliefs are formed must satisfy other *desiderata*. Two such *desiderata* are salient. First, an account of the process of coverage-supported belief-formation must make clear that (and how) the subject herself is epistemically relying on her source(s) for relevant coverage. (An account that fails to satisfy this *desideratum* fails to treat coverage-supported belief as a case of diffuse epistemic reliance.) But, second, an account of coverage-supported belief-formation must make clear precisely how a subject's sources are to be credited with the lion's share of the cognitive work that goes into rendering her coverage-supported belief reliable. (An account that fails to satisfy this *desideratum* will leave it mysterious how coverage-supported belief depends for its reliability on the coverage-reliability of one's sources.)

My contention is this: given the recently noted difference in the kind of epistemic reliance in play, we have some reasons to favor an account of the process of coverage-supported belief that does not endorse the "extendedness" model. In the section following I aim to provide just such an account.

3

In thinking about the process by which coverage-supported beliefs are formed, let us return to our initial strategy for thinking about G-reliability in these cases. The idea, presented at the outset of Section 2.2, was that the G-reliability of coverage-supported belief is a matter of the obtaining of conditions (both social and individual) that *make it likely* (though they need not ensure) that each of the five conditions on K-reliable coverage-supported belief are satisfied. In line with this, we might say that a subject's coverage-supported belief that p is formed through a G-reliable process if and only if it is formed in such a way as to manifest the subject's sensitivity to features indicating the likelihood that these conditions are satisfied. The challenge presently before us is to develop this idea so as to meet the two *desiderata* above. I propose to meet this challenge by regarding coverage-supported belief as a species of inferential belief, where one of the premises involved is none other than (something like) the truth-to-testimony conditional itself.

Consider first the proposal to regard coverage-supported belief as a type of *inferential* belief. The relevant inference would be from the subject's currently formed belief that she has no memory of having been informed that ~p, together with her belief in the relevant instance of truth-to-testimony conditional, to the conclusion that p.[11] (This inference need not be explicit or conscious; her reliance on it might be tacit.) Such a proposal has several virtues. First, it avoids all of the objections that can be made against the proposal to treat coverage-supported belief as employing an intersubjectively extended belief-forming process. (The process of drawing an inference itself is not an intersubjectively extended one.) In addition, the inferential proposal makes clear the role of the truth-to-testimony conditional in coverage-supported belief: this conditional serves as a premise in the inference through which the coverage-supported belief is arrived at. Third, the inferential proposal represents the epistemic goodness of coverage-supported belief—e.g., its G-reliability and K-reliability—as reflecting the epistemic goodness of the inference itself, together with the epistemic goodness of the premises of the inference. Since inferentially acquired belief is belief acquired through a belief-dependent process, we get a further happy result: the reliability of a subject's coverage-supported belief will be seen to depend on the reliability of the subject's belief in the relevant instance of the truth-to-testimony conditional.

I call this last result happy, since it is here that we can see the role that social factors play in the doxastic justification of coverage-supported belief. In particular, the doxastic justification of coverage-supported belief will depend on the doxastic justification of the subject's belief in the relevant truth-to-testimony conditional; and this, in turn, will depend on whether the subject is sensitive to the conditions under which she has relevant reliable coverage. Suppose she expects coverage on matters where coverage is unlikely. In that case her belief in the truth-to-testimony conditional will be false; and if she formed it under conditions in

---

[11] For some very interesting, if somewhat dated, empirical work on the sort of inferences that might be in play here, see Collins et al. (1975); Collins (1978); and Gentner and Collins (1981).

which she was oblivious to the reigning social practices and institutions, her belief in this conditional will have been G-unreliably formed as well.[12] Since such a belief is a premise in the inference through which the coverage-supported belief is formed, the resulting coverage-supported belief will be G-unreliable as well. This result is happy, since that is precisely what one would want in a case in which a coverage-supported belief is formed under conditions in which the subject herself is not sensitive to the prevailing relevant social institutions and practices.

The inferential account of coverage-supported belief has a fourth virtue: it accounts for another important difference between the epistemology of testimonial belief and that of coverage-supported belief. Silence and testimony function differently, epistemically speaking.[13] This difference between the epistemic roles of testimony and silence is related to the asymmetry between having positive evidence for p, and *lacking* any evidence *against* p. In the case in which one has positive evidence for a claim, one's evidence supports one's claim, which (understood in Process Reliabilist terms) might be cashed out as follows: the process involved in forming the belief that p through evidence e (where e is evidence for p) is G-reliable.[14] But in the case in which one has no negative evidence against a claim, one's belief in the claim is not thereby epistemically supported. That is, it is *not* in general the case that the process involved in forming the belief that p, through a lack of evidence that ∼p, is G-reliable. After all, one might lack evidence for all sorts of reasons: one might not have looked hard enough, or in the right places, or at all, etc. It would thus appear that the reliability of belief in p, formed on the basis of a lack of evidence

---

[12] What is the process through which one forms a belief in a truth-to-testimony conditional? This is a special case of a more general question: what is the process through which one forms beliefs in subjunctive conditionals? For one characterization of this process, see Williamson (2007: Chapter 5). For my part I will assume that there is some reliabilist story to tell here, but, as I don't know what that story is, and as it would take me far afield anyway, I will not pursue such matters further.

[13] See Goldberg (forthcoming b).

[14] I don't pretend for a moment that this is an adequate description of the process. Let it be a stand-in for whatever process is used in a case of forming beliefs on evidence.

to the contrary, requires more than the mere lack of evidence. It is plausible to suppose that there is an implicit sort of inference that goes on here: one *infers* that p from the claims (first) that there is no evidence to the contrary, and (second) that had it been the case that ~p one would have likely encountered such evidence (that is, evidence for [~p]). Since coverage-supported belief that p is belief grounded in a lack of testimony that ~p, we might then expect that this sort of belief depends on the corresponding sort of inference. This is precisely what the inferential account predicts.

Let us turn, then, to the two *desiderata* mentioned at the end of Section 2.2. Does the present proposal make clear that (and how) the coverage-relying subject is exhibiting epistemic reliance on her peers? And does it make clear that (and how) the vast majority of the cognitive work that ensures the reliability of coverage-supported belief is in the cognitive (including social) dispositions of those on whom the subject is relying for coverage? More generally, does it honor the insight that the reliability of coverage-supported belief is not the cognitive achievement of any *single* individual?

To address these questions, we would do well to examine that process by which the expectations of the coverage-relying individual are calibrated so as to be brought in line with the prevailing social practices and institutions in her community. After all, it is in such a process that an individual learns when, where, and for what sorts of thing she can rely on relevant coverage in her community. By focusing on this process we might think to find out how an individual 'locks onto' those social features that underwrite the reliability of her coverage-supported beliefs. And in so doing we might hope to shed light on both the *individualistic* aspect of the achievement involved in reliable coverage-supported belief—the process by which the subject herself discerns when she is likely to have the relevant coverage—as well as the *social* aspect of that achievement—the relevant social practices and institutions that ensure relevant coverage.

Let us begin with those practices and institutions themselves. I submit that these should be seen as constituting the all-important background conditions on the formation of coverage-supported belief. In this connection we do well to highlight the following comment from Hilary Kornblith. Speaking of the epistemic relevance of the social environment within which our belief-forming processes operate, he writes:

Just as we wish to know whether our natural inferential tendencies are likely to give us an accurate or a distorted picture of the world, we also need to know whether our social institutions and practices are helping to inform us or to misinform us. And just as we need to examine our perceptual and inferential equipment against the background of the natural environment in which they operate, we also need to investigate these mechanisms against the background of the social environment in which they operate. Such investigations are straightforward extensions of the naturalistic project in epistemology.   (Kornblith 1994: 97)

Following Kornblith's suggestion, I propose that the various social practices and institutions that are relied upon in coverage-supported belief form part of "the social environment" in which coverage-supported beliefs are formed. The idea is this. We live in a world with a dizzying variety of information sources available to us. What is more, many of us structure our environments in such a way that we have easy access to the reports of a select subset of these sources. The more traditional among us read the daily paper (hard copy), watch the evening news, or—even more old school!—listen to the news on the radio. The more technologically savvy among us follow certain Twitter streams, receive News Alerts via email or other web-based technologies such as Google Reader, read the daily paper online, follow certain blogs, and so forth. And all of us rely, sometimes explicitly, sometimes implicitly, on less "official" sources for news: friends, neighbors, and so forth. The sorts of news-generating and -publicizing practices and institutions that are prevalent in one's community constitute a core part of one's "social" environment. To a large extent, epistemic subjects are at the mercy of such an environment: a subject who lives in a community with few or no channels for the communication of news, or where such channels as exist are highly unreliable in their reports, will be a subject who is seriously epistemically impoverished. In the former case, she will miss out on lots of truths, some of which may be of great interest to her; in the latter case, she will run an increased risk of acquiring false beliefs. My current point, however, is that in such a news-diminished community, the epistemic significance of silence will be affected as well. After all, the silence of one's sources in a community whose sources rarely report anything interesting may not tell us very much; whereas the silence of one's otherwise coverage-reliable sources can tell one a great deal.

It is in this spirit that I claim that the news-generating and -disseminating practices and institutions in a community constitute the background against which we assess her coverage-supported beliefs for reliability. The take-home point of the proposal is that a reliabilist assessment of coverage-supported belief can't just examine the belief-forming process that takes place within the mind/brain of the coverage-relying subject herself; such an assessment must also assess the various social institutions and practices that form the process(es) by which news is generated and disseminated in her community. Two different coverage-relying subjects, as alike skin-in as any two distinct individuals can be, might nevertheless differ in the G-reliability of their respective coverage-supported beliefs, as one subject lives in a community in which these institutions and practices provide her with highly reliable coverage on the issue at hand, whereas the other lives in a community where the coverage is less highly reliable (and where there are more issues of interest to her that are not covered). Whatever difference there is in the G-reliability of their respective beliefs supervenes on more than what is going on in their respective heads: it also supervenes on the social practices and institutions that surround them.

Let us turn now from the social to the individualistic aspect of the achievement in successful coverage-supported belief. While the social institutions and practices I have been discussing constitute the background conditions on a subject's coverage-supported belief, it is the subject's sensitivity to the existence and nature of these institutions and practices, and her sense of what they portend in terms of the coverage that she is receiving, that determine the G-reliability of her coverage-supported beliefs. More specifically, a subject who is sensitive in this way, and whose expectations of coverage are well calibrated to her surrounding community, will have reliable beliefs regarding whether she is likely to have coverage on a given topic. Any particular beliefs she has in the truth-to-testimony conditional in a given case will likely be true.

In this respect it is noteworthy that ordinary subjects typically do form coverage-supported beliefs only under conditions in which background conditions are propitious—suggesting that ordinary subjects are indeed calibrated to the prevailing social institutions and practices. Thus it is no surprise to learn that, while a good many subjects form coverage-supported beliefs regarding major news issues, or regarding topics where one is aware of a group interested in disseminating relevant information, subjects don't typically form coverage-supported beliefs on topics regarding which no one could reasonably expect coverage—the size of average fingernail clippings in the eastern United States, for example. You probably believe (or are disposed to believe) that it is not the case that a new major world war has been initiated in the last forty-eight hours, on the grounds that something that newsworthy would have been reported if it had; but you probably don't believe (are not disposed to believe) that in the last forty-eight hours there have been no minor skirmishes between the county governments of Pulaski and Massac Counties, Illinois (two counties that border one another in the southernmost part of my home state). Jones believes that her conceited and garrulous colleague X has not won a major research prize (if he had everyone would have heard about it by now); but she has no belief, and no disposition to believe, that her quiet and unassuming colleague Y has not won a major research prize (as she realizes that it would be just like the humble Y to hide such a fact from others). These examples—and many others like them could be offered—appear to support the idea that our dispositions to form coverage-supported belief do tend more or less to vary with the presence of the conditions that make it likely that these beliefs will be true. No doubt, this is because we are socialized to appreciate when we are likely to be relevantly supported, and when not. This is so much grist for my mill.

What, then, does this tell us about the G-reliability of coverage-supported belief? Take a subject who is sensitive to the prevailing social conditions (and their effects on relevant coverage). Such a subject, I said, will have a reliable belief in the relevant truth-to-testimony conditional: she will believe, reliably, that if $\sim p$ were true she would have heard about it by now. Suppose too that she hasn't heard about it by now, and that her belief to this effect was reliably formed. In that case, her coverage-supported belief in p, inferred from her belief in the relevant conditional and her belief that she hasn't heard anything to the contrary, would then be G-reliably formed. For, in that case, her coverage-supported belief was acquired through a conditionally reliable inference involving reliably formed beliefs as premises. Such is the way to understand G-reliability in the formation of coverage-supported belief.

No doubt, there is great variation in social practices and institutions worldwide, and even between local communities there can be relevant differences. What is more, social conditions are not as stable and long-lasting as, for example, the environmental invariances that constitute the background conditions for our perceptual systems. But these facts are no objection to the proposal to regard the relevant social conditions as background conditions on coverage-supported belief. For one thing, social variation and social change themselves are normal features of our environment and our world. For another, it is a normal part of socialization within a community that one becomes sensitive to prevailing social arrangements, and apprized of important social changes. Included in this socialization process is the process of learning what counts around here as newsworthy, what sorts of news one can expect (and where and when one can expect this news), and so forth.[15] Acknowledging all of this merely forces us to acknowledge that the background conditions that obtain in any given case depend on the time in question and the community in play.

This acknowledgment is not without implications. Once we acknowledge the fact of social change and recognize variation in social practices and institutions themselves, we would predict that complicated issues could arise when we assess the coverage-relying beliefs of subjects who move between communities. But in this respect our predictions appear to be borne out. Imagine a subject who grew up in a heavily news-intensive community where access to news of all sorts was pervasive, who then goes on to move into an informationally arid community where access to the news is much more limited (and must be sought out). If early in her time in the new community our subject forms a coverage-supported belief appropriate to her original community, is her belief doxastically justified? If we think not, this might be because we think the issue of doxastic justification turns on how well she has calibrated her coverage-related expectations to her *present* community: since she has not yet calibrated herself to her new community, and so is relying on coverage that in fact she is not likely to get there, we might regard her coverage-supported belief as not justified. On the other hand, we might be inclined to say that in this case her belief is justified, but fails to amount to knowledge: we would say this if we think that there remain reasons to assess the G-reliability of her current coverage-relying belief relative to what is normal conditions for her *original* community. I don't want to decide this matter here; my present point is merely that the present account predicts that there will be complications in cases involving subjects who travel between communities, and this prediction is borne

---

[15] Indeed, so far as I can tell, the epistemological issues surrounding the notion of *newsworthiness* have received no attention whatsoever from epistemologists (as opposed to scholars in journalism schools). I regard this as a lacuna in the epistemology literature. I hope to address this at some future time.

out (our intuitions about the proper verdict in these cases run in various different directions).

I see parallels here with the situation that arises when content anti-individualists assess the meanings and mental contents of a subject who travels between communities with different linguistic practices—so-called 'world-switching' cases.[16] If this parallel between these two types of world-switching cases is a good one, we would anticipate the epistemic significance of some of the emerging technologies (BlackBerries and iPhones, Twitter and Facebook, News Alerts, and Google Reader): they enable subjects to remain apprized of relevant information at any time and at any place, making it harder for any technologically savvy individual to be the victim of a relevant sort of 'world-switching' regimen.[17] (What are the effects of these technologies, if any, on the *semantics* of world-switching?) But even for subjects without these technologies the point remains: the facts (one) that over time there is a great deal of change in the social world, and (two) that even at a time there is wide variation in social practices and institutions, do not undermine the proposal to regard social conditions as part of the 'background conditions' for the formation of coverage-supported belief.

Does the present proposal acknowledge that the reliability of coverage-supported belief is not any single individual's cognitive achievement? It does: to regard the relevant social practices and institutions as background conditions is precisely to highlight that role.

In sum: the challenge facing any reliabilist account of the G-reliability of coverage-supported belief is to acknowledge the

[16] See, e.g., Burge (1988 and 1996); Ludlow (1995); Brown (2004); and Goldberg (2007c and 2007d) for a discussion of some of these latter issues.

[17] A nice example from *The Chicago Tribune* of March 25, 2009: a rider of Metra, the local high-speed suburban train to Chicago, has arranged to have information regarding any current train delays delivered to him in real time via Twitter (whereas previously he had to go online to find this information, to Metra's website). The result is that as long as he has his hand-held unit (and as long as Metra reliably and quickly updates the postings of delays), he is in a position to form G-reliable coverage-supported beliefs regarding delays on the Metra line wherever he is: the lack of relevant tweets can be the basis for a G-reliable belief that there are no relevant delays.

various considerations that appear to be relevant—both those that emphasize the subject's epistemic reliance on her social peers (for relevant coverage), and those that suggest that this epistemic reliance does not favor treating the process of coverage-supported belief-formation as an interpersonally extended one. I have tried to honor all of these considerations by treating coverage-supported belief as a species of inference-based belief, and by regarding the various social conditions relevant to the truth of the truth-to-testimony conditional as part of the 'background conditions' for coverage-supported belief. While this proposal involves treating coverage-supported belief in a way that does not parallel my earlier treatment of testimonial belief, this otherwise-unhappy lack of symmetry in my treatment is warranted (I have argued) by the different sort of epistemic reliance that is in play in the two cases.

4

I turn, finally, to the big question: how does the phenomenon of coverage-supported belief bear on the book's central theme of our epistemic reliance on others? It is a second instance of my contention that reliabilist epistemic assessment must take stock of ineliminably social factors. On the proposal I have offered here, these factors in question enter, not as part of the belief-forming process itself, but as part of the 'background conditions' on the process. What this suggests is that there are cases in which the reliability of what everyone can agree is an 'individualistic' belief-forming process nevertheless depends on aspects of the prevailing social environment.

7

Reliabilism as Social Epistemology

The thesis of this book has been that our epistemic reliance on others poses a challenge to various individualistic assumptions in epistemology. Pursuing this thesis from within the Process Reliabilist framework, I have been arguing that ineliminably social factors affect assessments of reliability. In effect, we need to 'socialize reliability,' and in so doing to recognize that reliabilist epistemology is ineliminably a social epistemology. In this chapter, I suggest that the sort of 'social epistemology' that I envisage can be seen as the unfinished agenda of Goldman's epistemological project since *Knowledge in a Social World* (1999). The connection between his earlier reliabilist approach to epistemology with his more recent veritistic social epistemology is made explicit.

I

In the previous six chapters I have argued that there are ineliminably social factors in reliabilist assessments of belief. The paradigm illustration of this was in testimonial belief, discussed in Chapters 1–5. However, our epistemic reliance on our peers is a phenomenon that outstrips testimony proper. In Chapter 6, I illustrated this in connection with coverage-supported belief, manifested in cases in which one forms a belief in p on the grounds that if ∼p were true one would have heard about it by now. In all of these cases, the ineliminability of the social dimension is illustrated in doppelgänger cases—cases involving twins that are type-identical from the skin-in, and thus identical in the proximal causal histories of their beliefs, yet who differ in the reliability of their respective belief-forming processes, owing to features of their social environment.

Although I have been challenging certain doctrines standardly associated with Process Reliabilism—in particular Process Individualism, and with it the position that I have labeled 'Orthodox Reliabilism'—the arguments I have been presenting throughout this book have otherwise been squarely within the tradition of reliabilist epistemology. Part of what I have wanted to suggest is that Process Reliabilists have a good reason to be interested in social practices and institutions, since some of these affect the reliability of our processes of belief-formation—either directly, as (in testimony cases) when the social factors themselves constitute part of the very belief-forming process itself, or indirectly as (in cases of coverage-supported belief) when social practices and institutions constitute part of the "background conditions" on belief-formation. At the same time, my argument on behalf of the relevance of social considerations to (reliabialist) epistemic assessment has been quite conservative: no assumptions have been made beyond those that every Process Reliabilist would, or at any rate should, endorse.

This last point is important. Given the radical nature of some of what goes on under the rubric 'social epistemology'[1] it is useful to see that there is a 'conservative' case to be made for the epistemic relevance of the social—a case that assumes nothing more than any

---

[1] Consider the radical nature of assertions such as the following: that it is the community, rather than the individual, that is the proper subject of knowledge ascriptions; that knowledge (alternatively: epistemic justification) is a matter of occupying a certain social status, and should not be understood as requiring objective (sometimes described as 'correspondence') truth; that truth itself is (all particular truths are) 'socially constructed'; and so forth. My argument for the epistemic relevance of the social requires none of these claims.

Process Reliabilist should feel comfortable endorsing.[2] In presenting such a case, I have been defending a position that conforms to the rubric that Kitcher introduced under the label 'minimal social epistemology,' according to which (and here I quote Kitcher):

(1) Individuals are the primary subjects of knowledge. To ascribe knowledge to a community is to make an assertion about the epistemic states of members of the community.

(2) X knows that p if and only if (a) X believes that p and (b) p and (c) X's belief that p was formed by a reliable process.

(3) The reliability of the process that produces X's belief that p depends on the properties and actions of agents other than X. (Kitcher 1994: 113)

One might think of the foregoing arguments of Chapters 1–6 as a sustained argument for (3) in Kitcher's rubric.[3]

In this final chapter, I want to suggest that the sort of position on offer can be seen as part of the unfinished agenda of Goldman's *Knowledge in a Social World*. Goldman's agenda in that book was to make clear the relevance of the social to epistemological inquiry. In so doing he endorsed a thoroughgoing veritistic approach to epistemic assessment—one that focused on the effects on the truth-value of the beliefs produced by various social processes. Such a framework shares much with the reliabilist framework: both veritism and reliabilism are interested in the history by which belief is produced, and in the truth-ratio of a process's output. Nevertheless the two perspectives are not identical,[4] and it is worth asking what might connect them.[5] We might thus say that it is part

---

[2] I borrow this use of 'conservative' in connection with my conception of social epistemology from Kornblith (1994).

[3] See also Goldman (2004), whose 'group knowledge' conception of social epistemology is very much in the spirit of the sort of social epistemology that emerges out of the arguments of this book.

[4] See Schmitt (2000). It is worth noting that Schmitt suggests that the veritistic approach Goldman favors in his later work may be in some tension with his justification-reliabilism; see Schmitt (2000: 273–7).

[5] In this respect it is worth noting that reliabilism is discussed in only five pages in Goldman (1999).

of the unfinished agenda of *Knowledge in a Social World* to determine the relevance of social considerations to epistemic assessments *beyond those pertaining to the production of (merely) true belief*. The point might be put as follows: although Goldman himself has never lost sight of the individual as the locus of epistemological assessment (see, e.g., Goldman 2004), his recent work has emphasized the social processes themselves, with less attention to traditional questions of epistemic justification and knowledge.[6] This book has aimed to reconnect social considerations with assessments of individual cognizers.

2

One question that is worth asking in this respect is whether we *ought* to continue to regard the individual as the (or at least a) locus of knowledge ascriptions, given the pervasive influence of the social on individual cognition. The literature on testimony is instructive here. Although most epistemologists who contribute to this literature take for granted that the subject of knowledge is the individual hearer (the consumer of testimony), others have argued that, so pervasive is the role of social considerations in the communication of belief and knowledge, we would do better to regard the community itself as the locus of belief and/or of epistemic assessment.[7] The most radical versions of these claims strike me as having been successfully rebutted by others;[8] I have nothing new to add here. Instead, I want to focus on the issue regarding what motive there could be, having noted the pervasive role of social factors in the acquisition, sustainment, and transmission of knowledge, to continue to regard the individual as the (or

---

[6] In one sense Goldman's veritism is all about knowledge; but he is explicit that he is interested in knowledge in the minimal sense of 'true belief.' This is not the conception of knowledge most epistemologists are interested in (Goldman himself is under no illusions about this).

[7] Versions of this view can be found in Welbourne (1986); Hardwig (1991); and Kutsch (2002).

[8] See, e.g., Kitcher (1994); Kornblith (1994); Longino (1994); and Goldman (2001: Chapter 1).

at least a) proper locus of epistemic assessment. My core claim is that in doing so we are assessing individual subjects' *management* of their epistemic reliance on their peers, and that (under certain circumstances that would appear to be prevalent) there remains a clear epistemic point to doing so.

The claim I want to make on this score can be appreciated in connection with testimonial belief. Imagine a community in which all speakers are hyper-reliable: there is no insincerity, and no one speaks without competence on any subject matter. Imagine further that members of that community rarely if ever leave the community, and rarely if ever allow outsiders to enter the community. Under these circumstances, there is little need for individuals within the community to monitor the say-so of others for trustworthiness. It is not obvious that a policy of simple credulity here would be a vice. That is, given a hearer whose life is such that she will only rarely encounter the testimony of a non-community member (if she encounters such testimony at all), a policy of accepting whatever she is told is one that will lead to a great preponderance of truth over falsity. (This is so, of course, even if she herself is ignorant of the social practices that make this policy so truth-conducive.) So long as we hold fixed the fact that she rarely (if ever) encounters the testimony of a non-community member, there is some case to be made for thinking that her testimonial beliefs are justified (despite having been formed through uncritical credulity).[9]

Now, to take the other extreme, imagine a community in which speakers typically make assertions with no regard whatsoever for getting things right. (If you think that the practice of assertion would not survive in such a community, imagine the practice to have degenerated as far as it can, consistent with its continued existence.) In this situation a policy of not taking anyone's word for anything without substantial evidence in favor of the credibility

---

[9] See Goldberg (2008), where I discuss this point in connection with testimonial beliefs of cognitively immature children.

of the say-so is obviously not a bad one. On the contrary, given a hearer whose life is such that she will only rarely encounter the testimony of a non-community member (if she encounters such testimony at all), the proposed rejectionist policy appears to make good epistemic sense.

These two 'extremes' illustrate an obvious, though perhaps under-appreciated, point: even given that one aims to believe all and only reliable testimony, the strength of the demand to "manage" one's reactions to incoming testimony can vary, as a function of prevailing social conditions. Under certain conditions one can adopt a policy of simple (uncritical) acceptance, and yet still do quite well in one's efforts to accept all and only reliable testimony; and under certain other conditions one can adopt a rejectionist policy, and yet still do quite well in one's efforts to accept all and only reliable testimony. This shows that the need for the hearer to take a more 'critical' approach to testimony arises only given that certain conditions (uniformly high- or low-quality testimony in a relatively insular community) are not prevalent.

Of course, the conditions that would warrant the policy of uncritical acceptance are not prevalent. (The same goes for the conditions that would warrant the rejectionist policy.) Quite the contrary: the quality of the testimonies we encounter varies con- siderably. We recognize that the motives of other speakers are not always honest, and that even those who are honest and upright sometimes speak on matters beyond their competence. As a result, the category of "another person's say-so" covers a range of cas- es; in this sort of context there is a clear motive for denigrating the policy of uncritical credulity. Such a verdict is supported by reliabilist considerations, as anyone following a policy of uncritical credulity in the actual world will acquire a good many false beliefs (and will leave oneself open to manipulation by others). And if we complicate matters by having a disvalue associated with lost opportunities for acquiring knowledge, then a similar thing can be said in the other case: anyone following a more rejectionist policy—one that requires a good deal of positive evidence in favor of the credibility of a piece of testimony before it sanctions acceptance of that testimony—will have the effect that subjects will fail to take advantage of a relatively easy way to acquire interesting and important knowledge in a great many cases. Thus the need to 'manage' one's response to testimony arises given conditions in which one is likely to encounter testimonies of varying epistemic quality. These conditions hold for most or all of us and for most or all of our lives.

Still, we might wonder why epistemology should focus here, on the individual subject's management of belief-fixation in reaction to testimony, rather than on the social processes that make the whole testimonial process as reliable as it is. The brief answer is that, even if the process of testimonial belief-formation is an interpersonally extended one, this is an appropriate place to introduce a normative epistemic assessment.

To begin, let it be granted that epistemological assessment should not be calibrated by reference to the epistemically autonomous agent. Such an 'ideal' of epistemic autonomy is not to be had. Process Reliabilists themselves should be sympathetic to this point. From the very start Process Reliabilism has held that it is a belief's (causal) pedigree, rather than the reflectively accessible reasons the subject can offer on its behalf, that determines its degree of doxastic justification.[10] But the relevant features of a belief's causal history need not be, and in a great many cases are not, discernible by even searching introspection on the part of the subject in question. The result is that the features that determine doxastic justification need not be, and in a great many cases are not, introspectively accessible. Insofar as the autonomous knower is one who can certify from the armchair all that she knows and justifiably believes, this ideal is not in keeping with Process (or Historical) Reliabilism's core commitment to the epistemic relevance of a belief's causal

---

[10] See Goldman (1979). Of course, a belief's causal history may involve a course of conscious reasoning, in which case the subject's reasons will be epistemically relevant; the point is that this is a special case of a more general phenomenon.

pedigree. For the reliabilist, doxastic justification is not a matter of closer and closer approximations to that ideal.

Whence the focus, then, on the individual's role in the process of belief-fixation? This question is all the more compelling given the thesis for which I argued in Chapters 1–5, to the effect that the belief-forming process in cases of testimonial belief-fixation is intersubjectively extended.

In addressing this question, we ought to bear in mind that one of the core aims of epistemology is to assess how well individual subjects conduct their attempts to acquire (interesting) true beliefs and avoid false ones. Nothing that I have argued in this book undermines this as a legitimate aim for epistemology. To see this, let epistemological theory acknowledge the pervasiveness of the phenomenon whereby human subjects exhibit epistemic reliance on our peers: each of us depends on others for a good deal of what we know and warrantedly believe (through testimony), and for relevant reliable coverage on matters of importance to us. (No doubt there are other instances of our epistemic reliance on others.) Let us grant as well that, from a reliabilist perspective, it is often the case that whether a given belief was reliably formed and sustained "depends on the properties and actions" of other agents (to borrow Kitcher's formulation). Our question is whether these facts undermine the motivation for the epistemic practice of assessing an individual's management of (her role in) the processes of belief-formation and -sustainment. I submit that they do not.

For one thing, it seems clear that, from the perspective of an interest in reliability, the individual retains an important role in belief-formation and sustainment. Return to the testimony case. Given that we live in a world in which the reliability of the testimonies we confront varies a good deal, the individual herself must play an important 'filtering' role in her attempt to accept any and only reliable testimony (see Chapter 5, Section 1). Even though it is true that there can be cases (described above) in which close conformity to this aim is achieved without any special sensitivity on the part of the would-be consumer of testimony, this fact does nothing to undermine the claim that, in real-life cases, such sensitivity (to signs of testimonial credibility) is required. Similarly, while it is true that social practices and institutions can affect the ease with which the task of discriminating credible testimonies is performed—one thinks here of the institutionalization and certification of expertise, publication through a process of peer review, and so forth—even so, the fact is that we live in a society where information is all around us, and where the channels through which it flows are many, and often not in control of anyone or any agency whose aim is to ensure credibility. This underscores the need for individuals to have an effective 'filter.' By the same token, there is a point to assessing how effective an individual's 'filter' is. It is precisely this that we are assessing when we assess how reliable a hearer is in distinguishing reliable from unreliable testimony.

My claim here is not restricted to testimony cases; analogous points can be made in connection to coverage-based belief. In the case of coverage-supported belief, it is all-important that there be a sort of 'calibration' between what the subject herself takes to be newsworthy (such that if it were true she would like to hear about it), and what the sources on which she is relying take to be newsworthy (such that if they discover it to be true they will report on it).[11] In the absence of some sort of calibration, two distinct problems can arise. In one, the individual subject takes herself to have coverage on some issue, and so forms a coverage-supported belief on the basis of not hearing otherwise, when in fact she enjoys no such coverage—in which case her belief will not be appropriately sensitive to the facts, and (depending perhaps on how widespread this phenomenon is) might not count as G-reliably formed. In the other, the individual subject takes herself not to have coverage on some issue, and so refrains from forming a coverage-supported belief despite not hearing anything regarding an issue of great importance to her, when in fact she does enjoy such coverage—in which case she will fail to take advantage of

---

[11] I develop this theme a bit more in Goldberg (forthcoming a).

a route she has for acquiring a G-reliable belief on a matter of some importance to her. Given the variety of news sources and the variety of channels of information, epistemologists do well to assess how sensitive individual agents are to the sorts of reliable coverage which they in fact enjoy.

A second reason, in defense of the claim that the pervasiveness of our epistemic reliance on others does not undermine the point of assessing an individual's management of (her role in) the processes of belief-formation, has to do with what I would call 'process decomposition.' Return once again to the extendedness hypothesis, the claim that the belief-forming process in testimonial belief-fixation is intersubjectively extended. This is a fancy way of saying that the process involves processing going on in more than one subject. But it is obvious that this process can be decomposed: very roughly speaking (and at a none-too-fine level of description), standard cases include the processes involved in the source speaker's formation, sustainment, and linguistic expression of the belief; but in addition they also include the processes involved in the hearer's comprehension of the source's speech, in the hearer's formation of the testimonial belief (which include the hearer's assessment of the credibility of the source's speech, so comprehended), and in the hearer's sustainment of the belief. No doubt, things are not quite as neatly categorized as all of this. There is reason to think that some sort of credibility assessment is involved in the process by which the hearer comprehends the source speech: interpretations that render the speech act more credible are typically favored over ones that render the speech act less credible.[12] But even if the slicing into component parts is not as easy as this sort of categorization suggests, the point remains that there are components to the process. And of these there is a very natural cut to be made at the boundaries of agents. This cut is 'natural' both in that it reflects the biologically

---

[12] This is a special case of a point that, e.g., Relevance Theorists have long emphasized, that comprehension is guided by a process of relevance-maximization (or perhaps relevance-satisficing). See Sperber and Wilson (1986). Nor need one be a Relevance Theorist to accept the point in the text; other theorists have made similar sorts of points.

grounded distinction between organisms, and in that the reliabilist epistemologist has a clear motive to assess the components in question. (The motive in question reflects the reliabilist's need to assess both the reliability of the testimony, and the conditional and Terminal Phase Reliability of the "on-board" part of the process that takes place in the hearer. See Chapter 5, Section 1.) To be sure, some might think that this 'cut' is so natural that it undermines my case for thinking that the belief-forming process in testimonial belief-fixation is intersubjectively extended; but there are ample reasons, of the sort I gave in the early chapters of this book, for endorsing the extendedness hypothesis, and the present considerations do nothing to undermine any of those reasons.

There is yet a third, more ideological, reason for thinking that the pervasiveness of our epistemic reliance on others does not undermine the rationale behind epistemic assessment of individual agents: the claim that the individual agent is the subject of epistemic properties (such as knowledge and justified belief) is an important truth in epistemology, and there is no reason to think that the pervasiveness of our epistemic reliance on others undermines this.

That the individual agent is an epistemic subject—a subject to which ascriptions of knowledge and justified belief are intelligible—is an important truth. There is ample evidence attesting to this truth. Most epistemic statuses (whether knowledge, justified belief, or rational belief) are ascribed to individual agents. It is true that we sometimes speak of what a community (or an organization, or a team, or a collection of individuals) knows, and there is a healthy debate regarding whether this sort of talk is reducible to talk about what individual subjects within the community (or organization or . . .) know. But, even if such reduction is not possible, this would not touch the claim that the vast majority of knowledge (and other epistemic) ascriptions are ascriptions to individual agents. And it would take a good deal of argument to show that these ascriptions should not be understood at face value. To be sure, the fact that our epistemic dependence on our peers is as pervasive as it is suggests that we are not fully autonomous epistemic agents; but this is a point that reliabilists accept on independent grounds anyway.[13] It is hard to see how this should threaten the very idea of individual agents as epistemic subjects.

3

The foregoing section aimed to establish that the pervasiveness of our epistemic reliance on others does not undermine the claim that the individual agent is a proper subject of epistemic assessment. Even so we might wonder what, if anything, would be lost if, instead of focusing on the assessment of individual agents, we focused instead on the reliability and/or what Goldman calls the 'veritistic value' of social processes themselves.

Consider in this light any sophisticated system whose outputs depend on the coordination of various interconnected parts of the system as these interact with one another. Suppose that we are interested in assessing the outputs of the system during a given time interval. Clearly, any assessment that focused exclusively on features of particular parts of the system would be missing a great deal of interest. We might say that a focus on individual components of the system will obscure the interrelations between these components; and since these interrelations affect the system's outputs, our proposed 'individual components' focus will not capture all that there is to be known about the functioning of the system. I suspect that something similar is true when one looks at the 'system' composed of the individuals in a knowledge community. (In this respect we might hope that the emerging theory of networks[14] might help to shed light on features of

---

[13] Indeed, this point has been granted even by those who favor a more individualistic, internalistic approach to epistemology in general, and to the epistemology of testimony in particular. See Fricker (2006a).

[14] A groundbreaking recent paper in this area, which helped to turn so-called "network theory" into a more formal (sub)discipline in its own right, is Watts and Strogatz (1998). Of course, social scientists have known about various interesting properties of social networks for some time: the famous 'six degrees of separation' result of social psychologist Stanley Milgram comes to mind. (See also Milgram (1967) for a nice overview.)

knowledge communities, conceived as a special case of a social network.[15]) But at the same time there will remain a clear point to assessing individual components of the system. Such assessment is important not only to get a more complete picture of the system, but also, in the course of troubleshooting, to identify those components that are causing problems, and those that are not. This is as true in a non-intentional system (such as a car's engine) as it is in an intentional one (such as a knowledge community).

It is important to be clear about the ways in which an assessment of individual epistemic agents can serve the twin purposes of (i) helping to provide a correct and complete characterization of a knowledge community, and (ii) helping to assess, and so to put us in a position to try to improve, the knowledge community. Just as it would be helpful to know which one(s) among us, if any, are unreliable testifiers, so too it would be helpful to know which one(s) among us, if any, are overly trusting in our reception of testimony. These facts will help to fill in the details of the sort of knowledge community we have, and will help as well in our attempts to improve our community (at least by identifying those whose epistemic behavior needs attention). Similar things can be seen regarding the roles individuals play in rendering a community coverage-reliable (in relation to a given individual).

It is here that the veritistically minded epistemologist can see the utility of reliabilist assessments of individual cognizers' belief-forming and -sustaining processes. Such assessments need not be seen as competing with veritistic assessments of social processes; rather the former can be seen as complementary. It is true that, on the account I have been offering, an individual's own contribution to the reliability of her testimonial belief-forming processes is not determinative. Even so an assessment of the individual's own contribution to the reliability of her testimonial belief-forming processes can be something useful to know from the perspective of a veritistic social epistemology: those whose filters are effective cut

---

[15] I hope to return to this in some future work.

down on the transmission of false or unreliable testimonies, and this has a clear relevance to a veritistic social epistemology.

What, then, should be said of the relationship between a reliabilist epistemology focusing on individual epistemic agents, on the one hand, and a social epistemology focusing on the veritistic value of social processes, on the other? Veritistic social epistemology gives us a snapshot of the "veritistic value" of various social processes of belief-formation, and so gives us a characterization of epistemically relevant features of a given community. These features are of interest insofar as we are interested in the epistemic success(es) and failure(s) of the community itself, and (more generally) in its role in fostering true belief and avoiding error among members of the community itself. But a complete picture of the epistemological scene requires that we attend to features of individual knowers as well.

The following loose parallel suggests itself. Characterizing the community in which a street is located is important to knowing a good deal about the characteristics of that street. (In crass terms: streets located in high crime areas will tend to be less valuable real estate than surrounding streets not in such areas; those located in areas with access to quality public transportation will tend to be more valuable real estate than similar streets without such access; and so forth.) This said, there remains a clear motive to learn about the various features of particular real estate properties that make up the community. For that we need to descend from the heights of the community, to assess the individual properties at issue. Matters are similar for epistemic communities. Individuals who live in communities whose relevant social processes have high veritistic scores will tend to be better off, epistemically, than those who don't. (From an epistemological point of view, it is better to be born into a community of skeptical scientists than into a community of dogmatic believers.) At the same time, we also have interests that should lead us to descend from the heights of veritistic social epistemology, to a reliabilist assessment of individual epistemic agents. Such assessment gives us finer resolution than that inherent in veritistic social epistemology. For some interests, this finer resolution is needed. For others, it may just get in the way and obscure trends that we would see at a more social level of description. It is in this sense that reliabilist epistemology, with its focus on individual epistemic agents, can supplement veritistic social epistemology, with its focus on social belief-forming processes. The result is a more complete, rounded-out picture of our world, as seen from an epistemic point of view.

Bibliography

Adams, F. and Aizawa, K. 2001. "The Bounds of Cognition." *Philosophical Psychology* 14/1: 43–64.

—— 2005. "Defending Non-derived Content." *Philosophical Psychology* 18/6: 661–9.

—— Forthcoming (a). "Why the Mind is Still in the Head," in P. Robbins and M. Aydede (eds), *Cambridge Handbook of Situated Cognition* (Cambridge: Cambridge University Press).

—— Forthcoming (b). "Challenges to Active Externalism," in P. Robbins and Murat Aydede (eds), *Cambridge Handbook on Situated Cognition* (Cambridge: Cambridge University Press).

—— Forthcoming (c). "Defending the Bounds of Cognition," in Richard Menary (ed.), *The Extended Mind* (Aldershot, Hants: Ashgate).

Adler, J. 1996. "Transmitting Knowledge." *Noûs* 30/1: 99–111.

—— 2009. NDPR review, 1/20/2009, of *Anti-Individualism: Mind and Language, Knowledge and Justification*. Available at: <http://ndpr.nd. edu/review.cfm?id=15087>.

Alston, W. 1994. "Belief-forming Practices and the Social," in F. Schmitt (ed.), *Socializing Epistemology* (Lanham, MD: Rowman & Littlefield), pp. 29–52.

—— 1995/2000. "How to Think about Reliability." *Philosophical Topics* 23/1: 1–29 (Reprinted in Sosa and Kim (2000)).

Audi, R. 1986/2003. "Belief, Reason and Inference," in R. Audi (ed.), *The Structure of Justification* (Cambridge: Cambridge University Press).

—— 1997. "The Place of Testimony in the Fabric of Knowledge and Justification." *American Philosophical Quarterly* 34/4: 405–22.

Banaji, M. and Baskhar, R. 1999. "Implicit Stereotypes and Memory: The Bounded Rationality of Social Beliefs," in D. Schacter and E. Scarry (eds), *Memory, Brain, and Belief* (Cambridge, MA: Harvard University Press), pp. 137–75.

Becker, K. 2006. "Reliability and Safety." *Metaphilosophy* 37/5: 691–704.

—— 2007. *Epistemology Modalized* (London: Routledge).

Beebe, J. 2004. "The Generality Problem, Statistical Relevance, and the Tri-level Hypothesis." *Noûs* 38/1: 177–95.

Bergmann, M. 2006. *Justification without Awareness* (Oxford: Oxford University Press).

Bezuidenhout, A. 1998. "Is Verbal Communication a Purely Preservative Process?" *Philosophical Review* 107: 261–88.

Bonjour, L. 1980. "Externalist Theories of Empirical Knowledge." *Midwest Studies in Philosophy* 5: 53–73.

—— 1985. *The Structure of Empirical Knowledge* (Cambridge, MA: Harvard University Press).

Brown, J. 2004. *Anti-individualism and Knowledge* (Cambridge, MA: MIT Press).

Burge, T. 1986. "Individualism and Psychology." *Philosophical Review* 95: 3–45.

—— 1988. "Individualism and Self-Knowledge." *Journal of Philosophy* 85: 649–63.

—— 1993. "Content Preservation." *Philosophical Review* 102/4: 457–88.

—— 1996. "Memory and Self-knowledge," in Martin and Ludlow (eds), *Externalism and Self-knowledge* (Palo Alto, CA: CSLI Press).

—— 2003. "Perceptual Entitlement." *Philosophy and Phenomenological Research* 67/3: 503–48.

Cassam, Q. 2007. *The Possibility of Knowledge* (Oxford: Oxford University Press).

Chalmers, D. and Clark, A. 1998. "The Extended Mind." *Analysis* 58: 7–19.

Clark, A. 2001. "Reasons, Robots and the Extended Mind." *Mind and Language* 16/2: 121–45.

—— 2003. *Natural-born Cyborgs: Minds, Technologies and the Future of Human Intelligence* (Oxford: Oxford University Press).

—— 2005. "Intrinsic Content, Active Memory, and the Extended Mind." *Analysis* 65: 1–11, 285.

—— 2006. "Memento's Revenge: The Extended Mind, Extended," in Richard Menary (ed.), *Objections and Replies to the Extended Mind* (Aldershot, Hants: Ashgate).

—— 2007. "Curing Cognitive Hiccups: A Defense of the Extended Mind." *Journal of Philosophy* 104: 4.

Coady, C. 1992. *Testimony: A Philosophical Study* (Oxford: Oxford University Press).

Cohen, S. 1984. "Justification and Truth." *Philosophical Studies* 46: 279–95.

Cohen, S. 1984. 2002. "Basic Knowledge and the Problem of Easy Knowledge." *Philosophy and Phenomenological Research* 65: 309–29.

Collins, A. 1978. "Fragments of a Theory of Human Plausible Reasoning," in D. Waltz (ed.), *Proceedings of Conference on Theoretical Issues in Natural Language Processing 2* (Champaign-Urbana: University of Illinois), pp. 194–201; reprinted in G. Shafer and J. Pearl (eds) (1990), *Readings in Uncertain Reasoning* (San Mateo, CA: Morgan Kaufmann), pp. 629–36.

——Warnock, E. H., Aiello, N., and Miller, M. L. 1975. "Reasoning from Incomplete Knowledge," in D. Bobrow and A. Collins (eds), *Representation and Understanding* (New York: Academic Press), pp. 383–415.

Comesaña, J. 2006. "A Well-Founded Solution to the Generality Problem." *Philosophical Studies* 129: 27–47.

Conee, E. and Feldman, R. 1998. "The Generality Problem for Reliabilism." *Philosophical Studies* 89: 1–29.

——2004. *Evidentialism: Essays in Epistemology* (Oxford: Oxford University Press).

Corcz, K. 2006. "The Basing Relation." *Stanford Encylopedia of Philosophy.* Available at: <http://plato.stanford.edu/entries/basing-epistemic/>; cited September 15, 2008.

Cosmides, L. 1989. "The Logic of Social Exchange: Has Natural Selection Shaped How Humans Reason? Studies with the Wason Selection Task." *Cognition* 31/3: 187–276.

——and Tooby, J. 1989. "Evolutionary Psychology and the Generation of Culture, Part II, A Case Study: A Computational Theory of Social Exchange." *Ethnology and Sociobiology* 10: 51–97.

——1992. "Cognitive Adaptations for Social Exchange," in J. Barkow, L. Cosmides, and J. Tooby (eds), *The Adapted Mind: Evolutionary Psychology and the Generation of Culture* (New York: Oxford University Press), pp. 163–228.

Cox, S. and Goldman, A. 1994. "Accuracy in Journalism: An Economic Approach," in F. Schmitt, ed., *Socializing Epistemology* (Lanham, MD: Rowman & Littlefield), pp. 189–216.

Curran, T. Schacter, D., Johnson, M., and Spinks, R. 2001. "Brain Potentials Reflect Behavioral Differences in True and False Recognition." *Journal of Cognitive Neuroscience* 13/2: 201–16.

Dartnall, T. 2005. "Does the World Leak into the Mind? Active Externalism, 'Internalism,' and Epistemology." *Cognitive Science* 29: 135–43.

Devine, P. 1989. "Stereotypes and Prejudices: Their Automatic and Controlled Components." *Journal of Personality and Social Psychology* 56: 5–18.

Douven, I. 2006. "Assertion, Knowledge, and Rational Credibility." *Philosophical Review* 115: 449–85.

Evans, G. 1973. "The Causal Theory of Names." *Proceedings of the Aristotelian Society* 47: 187–225.

Feldman, R. 1985. "Reliability and Justification." *Monist* 68: 159–74.

—— and Conee, E. 2002. "Typing Problems." *Philosophy and Phenomenological Research* 65/1: 98–105.

Fennell, C. T. and Waxman, S. R. 2006. "Infants of 14 Months Use Phonetic Detail in Novel Words Embedded in Naming Phrases," in D. Bamman, T. Magnitskaia, and C. Zaller (eds), *Proceedings of the 30th Boston University Conference on Language Development* (Somerville, MA: Cascadilla Press), pp. 178–89.

—————— and Weisleder, A. 2007. "With Referential Cues, Infants Successfully Use Phonetic Detail in Word Learning." *Proceedings of the 31st Boston University Conference on Language Development* (Somerville, MA: Cascadilla Press).

Fiss, O. 1987. "Why the State?" *Harvard Law Review* 100: 781–94.

—— 1991. "State Activism and State Censorship." *Yale Law Journal* 100: 2087–106.

Foley, R. 2001. *Intellectual Trust in Oneself and Others* (Cambridge: Cambridge University Press).

Fricker, E. 1987. "The Epistemology of Testimony." *Proceedings of the Aristotelian Society*, Supplemental Vol. 61: 57–83.

—— 1994. "Against Gullibility," in B. K. Matilal and A. Chakrabarti (eds), *Knowing from Words* (Amsterdam: Kluwer Academic Publishers), pp. 125–61.

—— 2006a. "Testimony and Epistemic Autonomy," in J. Lackey and E. Sosa (eds), *The Epistemology of Testimony* (Oxford: Oxford University Press), pp. 225–52.

—— 2006b. "Varieties of Anti-reductionism about Testimony—a Reply to Goldberg and Henderson." *Philosophy and Phenomenological Research* 72/3: 618–28.

Friedman, R. 1987. "Route Analysis of Credibility and Heresay." *Yale Law Journal* 96: 667–742.

Fromkin, V. et al. 2000. *Linguistics: An Introduction to Linguistic Theory* (Oxford: Blackwell).

Fulkerson, A. L., and Waxman, S. R. 2007. "Words (But Not Tones) Facilitate Object Categorization: Evidence From 6- and 12-Month-Olds." *Cognition* 105/1: 218–28.

Gendler, T. and Hawthorne, J. 2005. "The Real Guide to Fake Barns: A Catalogue of Gifts for Your Epistemic Enemies." *Philosophical Studies* 124: 331–52.

Gentner, D. and Collins, A. 1981. "Inference from Lack of Knowledge." *Memory and Cognition* 9: 434–43.

Geoff, L., and Roediger, H. 1998. "Imagination Inflation for Action Events: Repeated Imaginings Lead to Illusory Recollections." *Memory and Cognition* 26: 20–33.

Gibbons, J. 2006. "Access Externalism." *Mind* 115: 19–39, 457.

Gilbert, D. T., Krull, D. S., and Malone, S. 1990. "Understanding the Unbelievable: Some Problems in the Rejection of False Information." *Journal of Personality and Social Psychology* 59: 601–13.

—— 1991. "How Mental Systems Believe." *American Psychologist* 46: 107–19.

—— 1992. "Assent of Man: Mental Representation and the Control of Belief," in D. M. Wegner and J. Pennebaker, eds, *The Handbook of Mental Control* (New York: Prentice-Hall).

—— Tafarodi, R. W., and Malone, S. 1993. "You Can't Not Believe Everything You Read." *Journal of Personality and Social Psychology* 65: 221–33.

Goldberg, S. 2005. "Testimonial Knowledge from Unsafe Testimony." *Analysis* 65/4 (October): 302–11.

—— 2006a: "Reductionism and the Distinctiveness of Testimonial Knowledge," in J. Lackey and E. Sosa (eds), *The Epistemology of Testimony* (Oxford: Oxford University Press), pp. 127–44.

—— 2006b. "Testimony as Evidence." *Philosophica* 78: 29–52.

—— 2007a. *Anti-individualism: Mind and Language, Knowledge and Justification* (Cambridge: Cambridge University Press).

—— 2007b. "How Lucky Can You Get?" *Synthese* 158: 315–27.

—— 2007c. "Semantic Externalism and Epistemic Illusions," in S. Goldberg (ed.) *Internalism and Externalism in Semantics and Epistemology* (Oxford: Oxford University Press, 2007), pp. 235–52.

—— 2007d. "Anti-individualism, Content Preservation, and Discursive Justification." *Noûs* 41/2: 178–203.

—— 2008. "Testimonial Knowledge in Early Childhood, Revisited." *Philosophy and Phenomenological Research* 76/1: 1–36.

—— Forthcoming a. "If That Were True I Would Have Heard about it by Now," in A. Goldman and D. Whitcomb (eds) *The Oxford Handbook of Social Epistemology* (Oxford: Oxford University Press).

—— Forthcoming b. "The Epistemology of Silence," in A. Haddock, A. Millar, and D. H. Pritchard (eds) *Social Epistemology* (Oxford: Oxford University Press).

Goldberg, S. and Henderson, D. 2006. "Monitoring and Anti-reductionism in the Epistemology of Testimony." *Philosophy and Phenomenological Research* 72: 3, 576–93.

Goldman, A. 1976. "Discrimination and Perceptual Knowledge," reprinted in Goldman (1992).

—— 1979/2000. "What is Justified Belief?," in G. Pappas (ed.), *Justification and Knowledge* (Dordrecht: D. Reidel), pp. 1–23; reprinted in Sosa and Kim (2000).

—— 1986 *Epistemology and Cognition* (Cambridge, MA: Harvard University Press).

—— 1988. "Strong and Weak Justification." *Philosophical Perspectives* 2: Epistemology: 51–69.

—— 1992. *Liasons: Philosophy Meets the Cognitive and Social Sciences* (Cambridge, MA: MIT Press).

—— 1999. *Knowledge in a Social World* (Oxford: Oxford University Press).

—— 2001. "Experts: Which Ones Should You Trust?" *Philosophy and Phenomenological Research* 63/1: 85–110; reprinted in Goldman (2002).

—— 2002. *Pathways to Knowledge: Public and Private* (Oxford: Oxford University Press).

—— 2004. "Group Knowledge vs. Group Rationality: Two Approaches to Social Epistemology." *Episteme* 1: 11–22.

Graham, P. 1997. "What is Testimony?" *The Philosophical Quarterly* 47: 187, 227–32.

—— 2000a. "Conveying Information." *Synthese* 123/3: 365–92.

—— 2000b. "Transferring Knowledge." *Noûs* 34: 131–52.

Greco, J. 2007. "Discrimination and Testimonial Knowledge." *Episteme* 4/3: 335–51.

Greco, J. 2010. *Achieving Knowledge* (Cambridge: Cambridge University Press).

Hardwig, J. 1991. "The Role of Trust in Knowledge." *Journal of Philosophy* 88/12: 693–708.

Harman, G. 1973. *Thought* (Princeton, NJ: Princeton University Press).

Heller, M. 1995. "A Simple Solution to the Problem of Generality." *Noûs* 29/4: 501–15.

Henderson, D. and Horgan, T. 2001. "Practicing Safe Epistemology." *Philosophical Studies* 102: 227–58.

—— 2006. "Transglobal Reliabilism." *Croatian Journal of Philosophy* 6: 171–95.

—— 2007. "The Ins and Outs of Transglobal Reliabilism," in S. Goldberg (ed.), *Internalism and Externalism in Semantics and Epistemology* (Oxford: Oxford University Press), pp. 100–30.

Hinchman, T. 2005. "Telling as Inviting to Trust." *Philosophy and Phenomenological Research* 70/3: 562–87.

Horgan, T. and Tienson, M. 2002. "The Intentionality of Phenomenology and the Phenomenology of Intentionality," in D. Chalmers (ed.), *Philosophy of Mind: Classical and Contemporary Readings* (Oxford: Oxford University Press).

Horgan, T., Tiensen, M. and Graham, G. 2004. "Phenomenal Intentionality and the Brain in a Vat," in R. Schantz (ed.), *The Externalist Challenge: New Studies on Cognition and Intentionality* (Berlin: Walter de Gruyter).

Hubel, D. 1995. *Eye, Brain, Vision* (New York: W. H. Freeman).

Hurley, S. 1998. "Vehicles, Contents, Conceptual Structure and Externalism." *Analysis* 58/1: 1–6.

Kitcher, P. 1990. "The Division of Cognitive Labor." *The Journal of Philosophy* 87/1: 5–22.

—— 1994. "Contrasting Conceptions of Social Epistemology," in F. Schmitt (ed.), *Socializing Epistemology* (Maryland: Rowman and Littlefield), pp. 111–34.

Kornblith, H. 1989. "Introspection and Misdirection." *Australasian Journal of Philosophy* 67: 410–22.

—— 1994. "A Conservative Approach to Social Epistemology," in F. Schmitt (ed.), *Socializing Epistemology* (Maryland: Rowman and Littlefield), pp. 93–110.

Korscz, K. 2002. "The Epistemic Basing Relation." *Stanford Encyclopedia of Philosophy*. Available at: <http://plato.stanford.edu/entries/basing-epistemic/>; accessed September 6, 2009.

Koutstaal, W., Schacter, D., Galluccio, L., and Stofer, K. 1999. "Reducing Gist-based False Recognition in Older Adults: Encoding and Retrieval Manipulations." *Psychology and Aging* 14: 220–37.

Kutsch, M. 2002. *Knowledge by Agreement: The Programme of Communitarian Epistemology* (Oxford: Oxford University Press).

Kvanvig, J., ed. 1996. *Warrant in Contemporary Epistemology: Essays in Honor of Plantinga's Theory of Knowledge* (Lanham, MD: Rowman & Littlefield).

——Forthcoming. "Assertion, Knowledge, and Lotteries," in Duncan Pritchard and Patrick Greenough (eds), *Williamson and His Critics* (Oxford: Oxford University Press).

Kvart, I. 2006. "A Probabilistic Theory of Knowledge." *Philosophy and Phenomenological Research* 72/1: 1–43.

Lackey, J. 1999. "Testimonial Knowledge and Transmission." *The Philosophical Quarterly* 49: 197, 471–90.

——2003. "A Minimal Expression of Non-Reductionism in the Epistemology of Testimony." *Noûs* 37: 706–23.

——2005. "Memory as a Generative Epistemic Source." *Philosophy and Phenomenological Research* 70: 636–58.

——2007a. "Norms of Assertion." *Noûs* 41: 594–626.

——2007b. "Why We Don't Deserve Credit for Everything We Know." *Synthese* 158: 345–61.

——2008. *Knowing from Words* (Oxford: Oxford University Press).

Lehrer, K. 1990. *Theory of Knowledge* (Boulder, CO: Westview).

——1997. *Self-trust* (Oxford: Oxford University Press).

Lepplin, J. 2007. "In Defense of Reliabilism." *Philosophical Studies* 134: 31–42.

Loftus, E., Feldman, J. and Dashiell, R. 1995. "The Reality of Illusory Memories," in D. Schacter (ed.), *Memory Distortion: How Mind, Brains, and Societies Reconstruct the Past* (Cambridge, MA: Harvard University Press), pp. 47–68.

Longino, H. 1994. "The Fate of Knowledge in Social Theories of Science," in F. Schmitt (ed.), *Socializing Epistemology* (Lanham, MD: Rowman & Littlefield), pp. 135–58.

Ludlow, P. 1995. "Externalism, Self-Knowledge, and the Prevalence of Slow Switching." *Analysis* 55/1: 45–9.

Lyons, J. 2008. *Perception and Basic Beliefs: Zombies, Modules, and the Problem of the External World* (Oxford: Oxford University Press).

McClelland, J. 1995. "Constructive Memory and Memory Distortions: A Parallel-distributed Processing Approach," in D. Schachter (ed.), *Memory Distortion: How Mind, Brains, and Societies Reconstruct the Past* (Cambridge, MA: Harvard University Press), pp. 69–90.

McDowell, J. 1994/1998. "Knowledge by Hearsay." Reprinted in J. McDowell, *Meaning, Knowledge, and Reality* (Cambridge, MA: Harvard University Press).

McGinn, C. 1984. "The Concept of Knowledge." *Midwest Studies in Philosophy* 9: 529–54.

Mather, M., Henkel, L., and Johnson, M. 1997. "Evaluating Characteristics of False Memories: Remember/Know Judgments and Memory Characteristics Questionnaire Compared." *Memory and Cognition* 25: 826–37.

Menary, R. 2005. "Attacking the Bounds of Cognition." *Philosophical Psychology* 19/3: 329–44.

Milgram, S. 1967. "The Small-World Problem." *Psychology Today* 1: 60–7.

Mill, J. S. 1859/1978. *On Liberty* (Indianapolis, IN: Hackett Publishers).

Millikan, R. 1984. *Language, Thought, and Other Biological Categories* (Cambridge, MA: MIT Press).

—— 2000. *On Clear and Confused Ideas: An Essay about Substance Concepts* (Cambridge: Cambridge University Press).

Moran, R. 2006. "Getting Told and Being Believed," in J. Lackey and E. Sosa (eds), *The Epistemology of Testimony* (Oxford: Oxford University Press), pp. 272–306.

Moser, P. 1989. *Knowledge and Evidence* (Cambridge: Cambridge University Press).

Nozick, R. 1981. *Philosophical Explanations* (Cambridge, MA: Harvard University Press).

Owens, D. 2006. "Testimony and Assertion." *Philosophical Studies* 130: 105–29.

Peacocke, C. 2004. "Explaining Perceptual Entitlement," in R. Schantz (ed.), *The Externalist Challenge* (Berlin: Walter de Gruyter), pp. 441–80.

Plantinga, A. 1993. *Warrant and Proper Function* (Oxford: Oxford University Press).

Pritchard, D. 2005. *Epistemic Luck* (Oxford: Oxford University Press).

Recanati, F. 2002. "Does Linguistic Communication Rest on Inference?" *Mind and Language* 17/1 & 2: 105–26.

Reed, B. 2000. "Accidental Truth and Accidental Justification." *Philosophical Quarterly* 50: 57–67, 198.

Reinitz, M., Morrisey, J., and Demb, J. 1994. "The Role of Attention in Face Encoding." *Journal of Experimental Psychology: Learning, Memory, and Cognition* 20: 161–8.

Robbins, P. and Aydede, M., eds. Forthcoming. *Cambridge Handbook on Situated Cognition* (Cambridge: Cambridge University Press).

Ruben, S., Van Petten, C., Gisky, E., and Newberg, W. 1999. "Memory Conjunction Errors in Younger and Older Adults: Event-related Potential and Neuropsychological Data." *Cognitive Neuropsychology* 16: 459–88.

Rupert, R. 2004. "Challenges to the Hypothesis of Extended Cognition." *Journal of Philosophy* 101/8: 389–428.

Schacter, D., Israel, L., and Racine, C. 1999. "Suppressing False Recognition: The Distinctiveness Heuristic." *Journal of Memory and Language* 40: 1–24.

Schmitt, F. 1994. "Socializing Epistemology: An Introduction through Two Sample Issues," in F. Schmitt (ed.), *Socializing Epistemology* (Lanham, MD: Rowman & Littlefield), pp. 1–28.

—— 1999. "Social Epistemology," in J. Greco and E. Sosa (eds), *The Blackwell Guide to Epistemology* (Oxford: Blackwell), pp. 354–82.

—— 2000. "Veritistic Value." *Social Epistemology* 14/4: 259–80.

—— 2006. "Testimonial Justification and Transindividual Reasons," in J. Lackey and E. Sosa (eds), *The Epistemology of Testimony* (Oxford: Oxford University Press), pp. 193–224.

Senor, T. 1996. "The Prima/Ultima Facie Justification Distinction in Epistemology." *Philosophy and Phemenological Research* 56/3: 551–66.

Shepard, R. 1987. "Evolution of a Mesh between Principles of the Mind and Regularities of the World," in J. Dupre (ed.), *The Latest on the Best* (Cambridge, MA: MIT Press), pp. 251–76.

Shepard, R. 1992. "The Perceptual Organization of Colors: An Adaptation to Regularities of the Terrestrial World?," in J. Barlow,

L. Cosmides, and J. Tooby (eds), *Adapted Mind* (New York: Oxford University Press).

Sosa, E. 1994. "Testimony and Coherence," in B. K. Matilal and A. Chakrabarti (eds), *Knowing from Words* (Amsterdam: Kluwer Academic Publishers), pp. 59–67.

—— 1996. "Postscript to 'Proper Functionalism and Virtue Epistemology'," in J. L. Kvanvig (ed.), *Warrant in Contemporary Epistemology* (Lanham, MD: Rowman & Littlefield), pp. 271–81.

—— 2000. "Skepticism and Contextualism." *Philosophical Issues* 10: 1–18.

—— and Kim, J., eds. 2000. *Epistemology: An Anthology* (Oxford: Blackwell).

—— 2007. *A Virtue Epistemology* (Oxford: Oxford University Press).

Sperber, D. and Wilson, D. 1986. *Relevance: Communication and Cognition* (Oxford: Blackwell).

Sterelny, K. 2004. "Externalism, Epistemic Artefacts and the Extended Mind," in Richard Schantz (ed.), *The Externalist Challenge* (Berlin: Walter De Gruyter).

Sunstein, C. 1992. "Free Speech Now." *University of Chicago Law Review* 59: 255–316.

—— 1993. *Democracy and the Problem of Free Speech* (New York: Macmillan).

Swain, M. 1979. "Justification and the Basis of Belief," in G. Pappas (ed.), *Justification and Knowledge* (Dordrecht, Holland: D. Reidel).

—— 1981. *Reasons and Knowledge* (Ithaca, NY: Cornell University Press).

—— 1985. "Justification, Reasons and Reliability." *Synthese* 64/1: 69–92.

Watts, D. and Strogatz, S. 1998. "Collective Dynamics of 'Small-World' Networks." *Nature* 393: 440–2.

Welbourne, M. 1986. *The Community of Knowledge* (Aberdeen: Aberdeen University Press).

Wiggs, C. and Martin, A. 1998. "Properties and Mechanisms of Perceptual Priming." *Current Opinion in Neurobiology* 8: 227–33.

Williamson, T. 2000. *Knowledge and Its Limits* (Oxford: Oxford University Press).

—— 2007. *The Philosophy of Philosophy* (Oxford: Blackwell).

Wilson, R. 1994. "Wide Computationalism." *Mind* 103: 351–72, 411.

Wunderlich, M. 2003. "Vector Reliability: A New Approach to Epistemic Justification." *Synthese* 136: 237–62.

—— Unpublished manuscript: "Avoiding the Generality Problem for Process Reliabilism."

Zeki, S. 1993. *A Vision of the Brain* (Oxford: Blackwell Scientific).

Index